WHAT PRICE THE POOR?

Rethinking Classical Sociology

Series Editor: David Chalcraft, University of Derby

This series is designed to capture, reflect and promote the major changes that are occurring in the burgeoning field of classical sociology. The series publishes monographs, texts and reference volumes that critically engage with the established figures in classical sociology as well as encouraging examination of thinkers and texts from within the ever-widening canon of classical sociology. Engagement derives from theoretical and substantive advances within sociology and involves critical dialogue between contemporary and classical positions. The series reflects new interests and concerns including feminist perspectives, linguistic and cultural turns, the history of the discipline, the biographical and cultural milieux of texts, authors and interpreters, and the interfaces between the sociological imagination and other discourses including science, anthropology, history, theology and literature.

The series offers fresh readings and insights that will ensure the continued relevance of the classical sociological imagination in contemporary work and maintain the highest standards of scholarship and enquiry in this developing area of research.

Also in the series:

Defending the Durkheimian Tradition
Jonathan S. Fish
ISBN 0 7546 4138 4

What Price the Poor?
William Booth, Karl Marx and the London Residuum

ANN M. WOODALL
London Guildhall University, UK

ASHGATE

Published by
Ashgate Publishing Limited
Gower House
Croft Road
Aldershot
Hants GU11 3HR
England

Ashgate Publishing Company
Suite 420
101 Cherry Street
Burlington, VT 05401-4405
USA

Ashgate website: http://www.ashgate.com

British Library Cataloguing in Publication Data
Woodall, Ann M.
    What price the poor? : William Booth, Karl Marx and the
    London residuum. - (Rethinking classical sociology)
    1.Booth, William, 1829-1912 2.Marx, Karl, 1818-1883
    3.Salvation Army - History 4.Unemployed - England - London
    - Social conditions – 19th century 5.Poverty - England -
    London - History - 19th century 6.Unemployment - Social
    aspects - England - London 7.London (England) - Social
    conditions - 19th century
    I.Title
    287.9'6'092

Library of Congress Control Number: 2005923704

ISBN-10: 0 7546 4203 8

HC
258
.L6
W66
2005

Printed in Great Britain by Antony Rowe Ltd., Chippenham, Wiltshire

Contents

List of Tables

Acknowledgements

This book is the outcome of a personal obsession and the input and encouragement of many people over fifteen years. I am grateful to all who played a part in the project.

My thanks are due to my supervisors at what was then London Guildhall University during the preparation of my Ph.D. thesis: William Dixon, Peter Mandler, Dave Wilson and the late Michael Cowen.

I also owe a special debt to Sheila Hornsby for typing my early notes, to Adrian Wood for suggesting that I approach Ashgate about the possibility of publishing, and to Norman Murdoch for his support.

Laurence Hay, Gordon Taylor and John and Heather Coutts were all painstaking in their efforts to render the manuscript readable and accurate.

Lastly, this book is dedicated to my parents, Doris and Syd Woodall. They introduced me to The Salvation Army and gave me the confidence to follow my dreams.

Series Editor's Preface

One reason often given for passing over the classical tradition in sociology is that there are, 'limitations at source', as Giddens once wrote. This is only partly accurate. Recent work in classical sociology which interrogates the tradition from emerging concerns with issues to do with death and dying, racism, auto/biography, culture, travel, ethics and commitment, children and private life and so on, leads one to draw a different inference: namely, that the ignorance and dismissal of the classical tradition is due more to the limitations of contemporary readers who presume to know the answers to questions without researching, and presume to know what classical authors wrote without actually reading their writings and engaging with an eye on their context and on ours. Of course, the blame for some of these limited views is to be lain at the feet of the history and teaching of sociology itself which has served to create an image of classical sociology as arcane or needlessly abstract or as being too firmly rooted in its own context rather than being richly connected to a human experience that often transcends boundaries of time and place. It is this very connection with lived human experience across the life-course that provides a strong motivation for consciously and energetically rethinking classical sociology.

Within this rethinking of classical sociology it is necessary to critically consider how social policy and practice, the practical application of sociological values and insights, became divorced in the history and teaching of the discipline from what we might call, classical sociological theory. Given this differentiation we are unable to see the dialogues and continuities between classical thinkers themselves, and leads us to elevate certain writings at the expense of others within any one classical sociological oeuvre, thus only gaining a partial view of their sociological projects. For example, Herbert Spencer's evolutionary sociology needs to be read alongside his own impassioned attempts to resist growing militarism at the end of the Victorian era; Max Weber's studies of rural life in the Eastern German Empire and the impact of agrarian capitalism and nationalist policies on the German and Polish peasantries is as central to understanding his sociology as the unravelling of his conception vocabulary in *Economy and Society*. We need to critically consider classical substantive studies alongside classical conceptual, historical and theoretical legacies, and explain how substance, method and theory became separated from each other in the demarcation of classical sociology and constituted what we were meant to learn from it.

It is also important in our re-thinking classical sociology to critically consider the history of the tradition and reception of these texts from the past. Recent developments in social and cultural studies have led to the realisation that the classical canon is a highly selective listing, not only of the works of classical sociologists that are not contested within the canon, but also of a range of many other fascinating and significant examples of writing from voices frequently left unheard or consciously ignored. For example, the works of William Dubois and of Charlotte Perkins Gilman readily come to mind as creative sociological thinkers whose work deserves to be much better known. So, it is time to re-consider the texts of a Weber, Marx, Durkheim, Simmel or Parsons that have been overlooked, just as it is time to reconsider those whose status within the history of sociology has yet to be fully established for a number of reasons, not of all which are traceable to limitations in the originals. William Booth's *Darkest England* is one such text that needs to be considered, alongside such other substantive classics, however normatively driven, such as Riis' *How the Other Half Lives*, Mayhew's *London Labour and the London Poor*, Jack London's *The Abyss*, and more social survey influenced studies produced by Charles Booth and Joseph Rowntree. These studies, and many others that are not remembered today of course formed part of the intellectual context for classical sociology as well as being important studies in their own right that we should not ignore.

I am delighted that Ann Woodall's volume is part of our series, since it directly addresses a number of the themes mentioned briefly above, and moreover, investigates two significant social thinkers from the late 19th century- Karl Marx and William Booth- who have never been considered side by side before. The sociological concerns of William Booth, given his character and normative commitments, took a radically different direction from those of Marx, and yet they both share a passionate value commitment and were responding, as Woodall demonstrates, to similar social conditions. Marx is often presented in the history of sociology as perhaps one of the few social thinkers who not only wanted to accurately describe the social world, but also to seek to change it. When such a social conscience is married with an evangelical religious spirit, as it was with William Booth, it is striking to realise that it is the latter that directly, if albeit at times dictatorially, immediately effected social change through the practical implementation of his version of the social gospel.

Ann Woodall's study is particularly apposite to our series' concern with posing the question: What was the relationship between ways of thinking, writing and doing that we identify as sociological today, and ways of thinking, writing and acting that seemingly appertain to different pursuits and disciplines, such as literary and biological imaginations, and, especially pertinent to this study, theological approaches to ethics, society and social change? Woodall provides us with some answers to such questions through a concentration on the biography, contexts, theories and practical activities of two important figures from the time when sociology had yet to be fully institutionalised and in a climate in which theological and religious world views interacted, and often clashed with, sociological perspectives and socialist commitments. Classical sociologists sought to 'live out' their sociology, making public and private decisions in the light of their studies, hence suggesting that biography is indeed one of the tools to be utilised in rethinking classical sociology: we not only need to bring the text back in to consideration but the person who wrote those texts too. For some of these classical practitioners, the right career choice was not to enter institutionalised sociology but to remain as reformers, writers, journalists and so on.

In this fascinating book, Ann Woodall investigates and compares the work and thought of William Booth and Karl Marx, who both arrived in London in 1849. She draws comparisons between their responses to the intractability of the poverty of the 'submerged tenth' of London's population and argues that Booth's pioneering work in establishing the Salvation Army and the development of Marx's economic theory began in their interactions with the London residuum. Each recognised that much of the suffering was caused by the workings of laissez-faire capitalism and that its total solution required a challenge to the existing economic system.

What Price the Poor? raises important questions about the relationship between theological discourse and the sociological imagination and it firmly places the development of theoretical and practical social analysis and application within the context of social history. It will appeal to all with interests in classical sociology and the history of social activism.

I hope you will enjoy this volume and the others that will follow in our series, and be inspired to join us in our attempts to rethink classical sociology in such a fashion that historical considerations and contemporary concerns are given their due weight, so we can truly appreciate the continuing relevance of classical sociology and classical social and moral thought to our own thinking and practice.

Professor David J. Chalcraft

To my Parents

Chapter 1

Introduction

William Booth and Karl Marx both arrived in London in the second half of 1849. Marx had visited London before but from 1849 it was to be his base. Booth's arrival in London in 1849 was his first visit to the city. It became his base from 1865.

Karl Marx was born in 1818. By the time he arrived in London in August 1849, he was a married man with a family – and a reputation as a political activist which had caused his departure from several countries. He was also a polemicist: one year earlier he had collaborated with Friedrich Engels to produce *The Communist Manifesto*. Once in London, he had little opportunity for further activism, but his research and writings were to have an immense influence on world history. Yet the British authorities – unlike their continental counterparts – did not think that he posed any serious threat.

William Booth arrived in London a few weeks later, aged just 21. Finding work initially in the pawnbroking business, he soon became involved in full time evangelism. After some time as a Methodist minister, he became an itinerant evangelist. Seeing the East End as his 'destiny', he stayed there in 1865 to lead what was first called the 'Christian Revival Union'. As this organisation grew in numbers and expanded the area of its work, it became successively the East London Christian Mission, the Christian Mission and eventually The Salvation Army.

Through their arrival in London both Marx and Booth were to be exposed to the impact of the industrial revolution on the working population of London. There they would also see those who were outside the industrial advance and were either unemployed or rarely employed. They were the underclass and were referred to by some of the social commentators of the day as the 'residuum', a word that spoke of society's view of them as the 'left-overs'. William Booth would refer to this same group as the submerged tenth, while Marx categorised them as relative surplus population. Within this group Marx made a further division between the reserve army of labour, who could well enter the workforce at certain points in the economic cycle, and the 'lumpenproletariat' who were either unemployable or permanently unemployed.

The similarity of the facts of industrial life that Booth and Marx observed can be drawn from the example of the matchmakers. In Volume I of *Capital* Marx wrote about conditions in the matchmaking industry:

> The manufacture of matches dates from 1833, from the discovery of the method of applying phosphorus to the match itself. Since 1845 this branch of industry has developed rapidly in England, and has spread out from the thickly populated parts of

London ... The manufacture of matches, on account of its unhealthiness and unpleasantness, has such a bad reputation that only the most miserable part of the working class, half-starved widows and so forth, deliver up their children to it ... With a working day ranging from 12 to 14 or 15 hours, night labour, irregular meal-times, and meals mostly taken in the workrooms themselves, pestilent with phosphorus, Dante would have found the worst horrors in his Inferno surpassed in this industry.[1]

Booth wrote *In Darkest England and the Way Out* in 1890 and included in his proposals:

[W]e propose at once to commence manufacturing match boxes, for which we shall aim at giving nearly treble the amount at present paid to the poor starving creatures engaged in this work.[2]

The back cover of the 1970 reprint of *Darkest England* showed an illustration of the 'Lights in Darkest England' matches. These 'Salvation Army' matches were first produced in 1891 with the aim of both increasing the wages of the workers and eliminating phosphorus from the process:

For making these safety matches William Booth paid his workers 4d. a gross, instead of the usual 2½d., thus helping to stamp out necrosis ('phossy jaw') caused by phosphorus matches and enabling 'a woman to earn a decent wage'.[3]

The three quotations above underline the differences in approach between Marx and Booth, with Marx eruditely detailing the conditions of the makers of matches as part of his total attack on capitalism and Booth rushing to produce a practical solution to a specific problem. Marx was seeking a macro-solution and Booth a micro-solution. Yet the quotations also show that Marx and Booth were absorbing comparable events and information into their thought and action. Exposure to the London residuum of the mid-nineteenth century constituted a key element in the intellectual development of both men.

The link between Booth and Marx is not simply that they were in London at the same time and were both interested in and affected by the unemployed population there. There was a certain homomorphism in the way that the London residuum impacted upon them.

Friedrich Engels wrote in *Dialectics of Nature* about the law of the transformation of quantity into quality, and vice versa. It was a concept he had already defended in *Anti-Dühring*:

This is precisely the Hegelian nodal line of measure relations, in which, at certain definite nodal points, the purely quantitative increase or decrease gives rise to a

---

1 Marx, 1886, p. 356.
2 Booth, 1970, p 110. The book will be referred to as *Darkest England*. The scheme that grew out of the plan of the book and was accounted for in the Darkest England Trust will be referred to as the Darkest England Scheme.
3 Booth, 1970, back cover.

qualitative leap: for example, in the case of heated or cooled water, where boiling-point and freezing-point are the nodes at which - under normal pressure - the leap to a new state of aggregation takes place, and where consequently quantity is transformed into quality.[4]

Marx used the concept himself in *Capital* when he wrote, 'not every sum of money, or of value, is at pleasure transformable into capital. To effect this transformation, in fact, a certain minimum of money or of exchange-value must be presupposed in the hands of the individual possessor of money or commodities.'[5]

The 'nodal points' in quantity that had a qualitative impact and influenced Marx's thought were the size of the residuum in London and in particular the size of the reserve army of labour. The quantitative features of the East End that influenced Booth's were the size of the residuum and the length of time the existence of the submerged tenth remained unchallenged. In addition he had been marked by the level of poverty he saw around him during his boyhood in Nottingham and, in later life, his work was to be affected by the size to which the Salvation Army grew.

The nodal points will form the focus of the following chapters. The next chapter, *The Pawnbroker's Apprentice,* examines the level of urban poverty in the decades prior to 1850, looking at the evidence, including the writings of influential thinkers of that time, and arguing that the urban poverty that arose in the aftermath of the industrial revolution was such that people like the stockingers of Nottingham lived lives that were qualitatively different from those of the poor of previous generations. It was in the face of such poverty that William Booth served his apprenticeship to a Nottingham pawnbroker and the person he would become was forged in the interaction between this poverty, its political impact and evangelical Christianity.

The Reverend William focuses on Booth's life between 1850 and 1870 and the development of his thought and work. This period included Booth's critical decision to base his future work in Whitechapel. The size and density of the London residuum was crucial to this decision and the chapter examines the living conditions of the people of Whitechapel, their work, poverty and lifestyles and the impact these had on Booth. The first interactions between Booth and the London residuum took place in these two decades and of pivotal importance to the discussion of Booth's development is the way in which he was drawn back to the poor, to those whose lifestyles resembled those of the stockingers who had haunted him in Nottingham and how, in order to succeed, he had to relearn in London the lessons of his early days.

The Revolutionary Philosopher focuses on Karl Marx's treatment of the underclass in his writings, with the emphasis on the changes that can be traced to the influence of what he learnt after 1849 about the London residuum, including its size. In particular Marx's developing understanding of the relative size and importance of the reserve army of labour and the lumpenproletariat within the

---

4 Engels, *Anti-Dühring*, in Marx/Engels, *Collected Works,* Vol. XXV, pp. 42-3.
5 Marx & Engels, 1987, p. 115.

relative surplus population is scrutinised through the differences noted between his writings about the underclass of London and that of Paris.

The Philosopher as a Prophet? moves the examination of Marx's writings into the sphere his 'vision' of the resolution to the problem of the poverty caused by the advance of capitalism. Because for Marx there is no individual redemption except through a 'redemption' of society, the focus of the chapter is on the function of the reserve army of labour in creating the conditions for that redemption, the overthrow of capitalism, and also on the new society that would emerge.

The Making of a General looks at the development of Booth and his organisation from 1870 to 1890, the date of the publication of *In Darkest England and the Way Out,* outlining the proposal for his social scheme. The chapter focuses on the major part played by the long-term poverty in the East End of London in bringing about the decision to launch such a scheme. The seeming permanence of poverty played a parallel role to that of the size of the residuum in 1865 in drawing Booth back to a focus on the poor. Booth is shown within the context of a widely growing public interest in the problems of the East End.

Because Booth was involved in high profile social issues he cannot be judged solely within the religious sphere and needs to be assessed in relation to others who were commenting on and tackling similar problems. *The Making of a General's Mind* examines the writings of two economists whom Booth claimed as influences. These were Robert Flint and W. H. Mallock. Their influence on what Booth wrote can be traced but it also becomes clear the Booth never belonged to one school of thought but 'cherry-picked' those ideas that were able to be used to further the goals he had set himself.

The General in Command considers the results of the Darkest England Scheme in terms of meeting its own goals and in its effect on the Salvation Army; for example, was its incomplete implementation eventually negative or positive for the organisation? The chapter also examines the impact of the increasing size of the Salvation Army on its work and ethos, and on Booth himself.

Fifty Years On, the concluding chapter, looks at Booth's social scheme in terms of its impact on the two elements of Marx's surplus population, the lumpenproletariat and the reserve army of labour. It also assesses the work of the Salvation Army under the three categories of Marx's criticism of religion. In addition an assessment is made of the role played by the London residuum in the development of the thought of Booth and Marx.

The real link, then, between the two men, Marx and Booth, is the impact of the size (and, to a lesser extent, the permanence) of the residuum. The outcome for both men was to broaden their conception of the lowest level of the poor, the lumpenproletariat, to see them as victims of a capitalist system that needed to be changed. For Marx the new element was to see the different layers in what he had previously simply termed pauperism and to understand that many of those layers were necessary to capital and all were a result of the capitalist impulse. For Booth the new element was to see the solution to the needs of the poor as calling for a challenge to the system that created a residuum and not simply a challenge to individual members of the residuum.

The truth of Engels' theory of the dialectics of numbers is implicit in the play

Major Barbara, which is centred on George Bernard Shaw's view of the Salvation Army. Andrew Undershaft, whom Shaw described as the hero of the play, is an arms manufacturer and the father of Major Barbara. At one point in the play Undershaft offers to contribute twopence to the work of the Salvation Army, to receive the reply from his daughter, 'You can't buy your salvation here for twopence: you must work it out.' [6] However as the play progresses Undershaft's offer of a donation of five thousand pounds is gladly accepted by Barbara's leaders causing another character to exclaim, 'Wot prawce selvytion nah?' [7]

Can a parallel be drawn between the result of a difference in size of a donation and the impact on William Booth and Karl Marx of the size of the London poor? That is the question discussed in this book.

---

6 Shaw, 2000, p. 99.
7 Shaw, 2000, p. 107.

Chapter 2

The Pawnbroker's Apprentice

Introduction

William Booth arrived in London for the first time towards the end of 1849. London was pivotal in the development of Booth's thought and work, but many of his beliefs and ideas had already been formed, or at least seeded, by his experiences as a pawnbroker's apprentice in Nottingham. Crucial in the early crystallisation of Booth's ideas was the profound and chronic poverty he faced daily across the pawnbroker's counter. Such poverty was a new phenomenon in England, resulting from industrialisation and the resultant urbanisation of a large proportion of the rural poor.

To live in urban poverty in the mid-nineteenth century was a qualitatively different experience from that of the poor in previous centuries, with a new degree of suffering. This was particularly true for the stockingers of Nottingham as they progressively lost their livelihood in competition with industrial capitalism.

In old age William Booth said that the poverty he saw in Nottingham when he was young still haunted him. Poverty affected Booth personally, in the suffering of his own family. More indirectly he was influenced by the part that poverty played in the growth and strength of Chartism in Nottingham, a movement that appealed strongly to Booth in his youth.

It was also in Nottingham that Booth imbibed the main influences that shaped his Christian faith: Methodism and American evangelicalism. The huge impact that the London residuum had on Booth was conditioned by the person he had already become through the interaction in his youth of poverty and evangelical Methodism.

Industrialisation and Urbanisation

In England, the period prior to 1850 was a time of intense change in the way of life of the nation, a change that had sufficient impact for it to be termed an industrial revolution. The main technical innovations of Britain's industrial revolution had been made by 1850. From 1815 to 1850 prices and wages generally fell, with production increasing and the technical changes already made being introduced to more and more industries. Between 1830 and 1860, the production of pig-iron rose from 29 to 132 kilograms per person while the comparative figures for Continental Europe were 4 and 10. In the same period the consumption of raw cotton rose from 4.7 to 15.1 kilograms per person, with the comparable figures for Continental Europe at 0.3 and 1.1. By 1860 the production of iron in the United Kingdom corresponded to 53 per cent of world and 58 per cent of European production, although the British population was 2 per cent and 10 per cent of world and European populations. These figures give some idea of the scale of industrialisation in the United Kingdom, which had the highest Gross National Product per head in the world until being overtaken by the United States in about 1880.[1]

The first two decades of the railways were the 1830s and 1840s, during which the requirements for coal and iron almost trebled, largely due to the amounts needed for laying new track. The expansion of the railways was pushed by the amounts available for investment from middle-class businessmen and investors who were savers, rather than spenders, of the profits they were starting to make. This in turn led to investment in the capital goods essential to push forward industrialisation.[2] The rates of growth of industrial production for the UK were high during the nineteenth century, especially from the 1820s to the 1850s when the percentage increases per decade were 38.6, 47.2, 37.4 and 39.3 respectively.[3]

Changes in economic structures caused by the rapid industrialisation led to corresponding stresses on traditional social structures. There was a move from rural to urban living, a greater variation in living standards and an increase in class tensions. The historian Eric Hobsbawm has described the position of the poor as industrialisation reached each new area or type of work, as finding themselves 'in the path of bourgeois society, and no longer effectively sheltered in still inaccessible regions of traditional society.'[4] He argued that at such a point the poor had three choices: to submit, to seek to climb out of poverty into the bourgeoisie themselves, or to rebel. Any of the three choices, even seeming submission, held within it the seeds of possible social conflict.[5]

Nottingham was a centre of stocking making. There were something in the condition of the stockingers and handloom weavers in the 1830s and 1840s that caused social observers of the time and historians since to see them as epitomising the suffering caused to those who had no positive part to play in the advance of industrialisation. William Booth grew up imbibing the reality of their distress and discontent.

The stockingers' plight did worsen with industrialisation but it was not only from competition with factory production. In the eighteenth century many of the stockingers had owned their hand knitting frames but by the 1830s the majority of frames were hired. With the hiring of frames there had grown up a number of middlemen who took part of what had previously been the income of the stockingers. Not only did these middlemen take rent from the stockingers but they divided the work. There was a labour surplus in the industry so that the middleman could divide the work he had negotiated with the hosiers between as many stockingers as he had frames to let, regardless of whether each would thereby have

---

1 Crouzet, 1982, pp. 4-5.
2 Hobsbawm, 1995(a), p. 81.
3 Hobsbawm, 1990, p. 68 footnote.
4 Hobsbawm, 1995(a), p. 245.
5 Hobsbawm, 1995 (a) p. 245.

a full week's work. The stockinger would still have to pay a full week's rent and, where the frame was in the master's shop, rather than his own home, a standing charge as well:

> Thus it was not uncommon in 1844 for 3s in charges to be deducted from weekly earnings of 10s; and there were cases where those who had had work for only two or three days in the week found that they had worked for nothing else than the frame rent.[6]

There were further charges on the stockingers that were created by the middleman from his position of strength. In comparison the stockingers were simply desperate for some of the work available. The middleman sometimes charged a commission for any work 'given out'. Any changes to the frame to cope with a change in style, for example, were to be paid for by the stockinger and he could also be docked a sum of money for an alleged fault in his work. The stockingers could not dispute these charges without the risk of losing future chances to work.

From the above it is clear that even before a steam-powered factory system developed, the independence of the labourer was being eroded and his relationship to his work deformed, but when he moved into a factory it was vastly more so. For a labourer in a factory his relationship became simply that of the sale of his labour for cash: 'To describe the changed relations of men with men, the removal of spiritual and social obligations and their replacement by economic and financial ones, [Carlyle] coined the phrase "cash-nexus".' [7]

Karl Marx made a similar argument in the Communist Manifesto, written in 1848:

> The bourgeoisie, wherever it has got the upper hand, has put an end to all feudal, patriarchal, idyllic relationships. It has pitilessly torn asunder the motley feudal ties that bound man to his 'natural superiors,' and has left remaining no other nexus between man and man than naked self-interest, than callous 'cash payment'.[8]

Once the cash relation was established then, in an even more intrusive way in factories than for the stockingers, discipline and power could be imposed by means of cash fines. This was the dehumanization that Kolakowski stated Marx was combating in his work.[9] There was a list of cash fines in force in a spinning mill near Manchester in 1823 that included a fine of 1 shilling for whistling at work. [10]

Such a grotesque attempt at enforcing discipline was in one way a result of the insecurity of the owners and masters themselves, many of whom had only recently left the ranks of the working classes and, with little theoretical knowledge, believed that they only made their profit in the last hour's labour of every working

---

6 Harrison, 1988, p. 44.
7 Heffer, 1995, p. 194.
8 Quoted in Smelser, 1973, p. 75.
9 Kolakowski, 1989, p. 222.
10 Hopkins, 1992, p. 12.

day. The resultant exploitation of the factory workers and the outworkers was to create a different kind of poverty from that known in the past. In addition to the impact of factory work per se the quantitative drop in income led to a qualitative change in lifestyle for it involved a loss of humanity in the total derogation of human rights. Even some of the ancient rural rights were being superseded, small rights whose abrogation, like the fines imposed by the factory owners, could be pivotal to the quality of life of those they affected:

> Those petty rights of the villagers, such as gleaning, access to fuel, and the tethering of stock in the lanes or in the stubble, which are irrelevant to the historian of economic growth, might be of critical importance to the subsistence of the poor.[11]

With industrialisation came urbanisation. Not only did the population in the towns increase because the total population of Great Britain increased but the percentage of the population who lived in an urban setting also increased, rising from 40 per cent in 1821 to 54 per cent in 1851.[12]

The move from country to town was due partly to the push from the country because of a surplus rural population, relative to work available, and partly to the pull of the town, the increase in factory jobs, the improved wages for many of the skilled and semi-skilled jobs, increased independence for young people away from families, the simple lure of 'city lights' and adventure and even anonymity for those who required it. As the cities grew, people began to realise that the speed and manner of their growth had created new social phenomena and tensions that caused an increasing fascination with cities in both social reports and novels. Such a move from country to town was one of the prerequisites of continuing industrialisation and increased capacity.[13]

The size of London drew attention to its problems but the effect of urbanisation was felt not only there. One important factor in the social shifts in Great Britain was the experience of so many people moving from a rural into an urban setting, 'where the essential properties of larger systems of social relations are grossly concentrated and intensified.'[14]

> [S]ocial relationships ... of the country are more typically few, narrow, family-based, personal and enduring; those of the town more numerous, extra-familial, impersonal and casual ... [S]econdary contacts predominate in the city, primary contacts in the country.[15]

Louis Wirth argued that urbanisation is not simply a matter of the number of people who live in cities rather than in rural areas:

---

11 Thompson, 1991, p. 239.
12 Morris & Rodger, 1993, p. 3.
13 Hobsbawm, 1995(a), p. 187.
14 P. Abrams quoted in Morris & Rodger, 1993, p. 12.
15 Waller, 1991, pp. 12-3.

The influences which cities exert upon the social life of man are greater than the ratio of the urban population would indicate; for the city is not only increasingly the dwelling-place and the workshop of modern man, but it is the initiating and controlling centre of economic, political and cultural life.[16]

Industrialisation and urbanisation created unrest and insecurity for many of those who lived through the first half of the nineteenth century. It created both more wealth and more poverty. There was a greater range and diversity of both and a bigger gulf between the two, what Gertrude Himmelfarb described as the break-up of the continuum from poverty to wealth, with the 'ragged classes' now becoming a separate entity, viewed with fear by the rest of the poor and as a challenge by reformers.[17]

Hobsbawm described the social changes as more fundamental than simply increased or decreased wealth. At the point that the Industrial Revolution impacted on people's lives: 'it destroyed their old ways of living and left them free to discover or make for themselves new ones, if they could or knew how. But it rarely told them how to set about it.'[18]

Poverty

There is no universally accepted measure of the degree of poverty in England in the first half of the nineteenth century. There is much difficulty in achieving a definite gauge of the quality of life. Nevertheless there is ample evidence of the impact that the particular suffering of certain groups had on specific individuals, such as William Booth. In the introduction to his social scheme in 1890 he referred back to the poverty he had seen in Nottingham half a century before:

> When but a mere child the degradation and helpless misery of the poor Stockingers of my native town, wandering gaunt and hunger-stricken through the streets droning out their melancholy ditties, crowding the Union or toiling like galley slaves on relief work for a bare subsistence, kindled in my heart yearnings to help the poor which have continued to this day and which have had a powerful influence on my whole life.[19]

Thomas Carlyle was another who was shocked by the poverty he saw, firstly in London in1824. He wrote to his brother of 'children puddling in the gutters, ragged, wild and careless.'[20] In 1832 he was still offended by the poverty around him and what in later works he would call the 'condition of England' question. He wrote an essay in 1832 in which he presaged William Booth's cab-horse charter (see p. 160) by almost sixty years: 'Mournful enough that a white European Man

---

16 Wirth, 1964, pp. 60-61.
17 Himmelfarb, 1984, p. 398.
18 Hobsbawm, 1990, p. 80.
19 Booth, 1970, preface.
20 Quoted in Heffer, 1995, p. 76.

must pray wistfully for what the horse he drives is sure of, - That the strain of his whole faculties may not fail to earn him food and lodging.'[21]

Hobsbawm has argued that the very fact of there being so much discussion of increasing poverty in the 1830s and 1840s is significant, as in times of obvious prosperity there is little discussion of poverty.[22] In addition the 'massive discontent of the labouring poor, which broke out time and again, in vast movements of radicalism, revolutionary trade unionism, Chartism, in riots and attempted armed risings' is difficult to dismiss as people being mistaken about their true situation, for 'such discontent as was endemic in Britain in these decades cannot exist without hopelessness and hunger'.[23]

Quantitative calculations of living standards in the 1830s and 1840s suggest this period was generally a time of depression for the majority of the population. Phyllis Deane and W. A. Cole, in their historical study of British economic growth, have produced tables of money wages which show that, for the 100 years from 1805 to 1906, money wages were lowest during the period 1835 to 1850. Concentrating on the production of cotton, they further estimated that the percentage of wage costs in the gross value added in production decreased over the same time scale: from 44 per cent in 1821 to 35 per cent in 1835, to less than one third in the 1840s before beginning to rise again,[24] suggesting not just that some labourers were suffering absolute poverty but that they were all receiving a reduced share of the value of production.

The arguments for improvements in wages over the same period point to increases in production, output and the Gross National Product. However such wealth was not evenly distributed across the population. As Arnold Toynbee explained: 'The effects of the Industrial Revolution prove that free competition may produce wealth without producing well-being.'[25] One problem was the lack of security and stability. Technological changes could mean sudden increases in wages followed by lack of work. The household budgets of many workers did not allow for any time out of work. S. R. Bosanquet investigated the budgets of London families in 1841 and found that a skilled workman could earn 30s a week and live comfortably.[26]

However 30s per week was a high wage for that time. An ordinary labourer would earn nearer 15s per week. This was the limit for a family with three children to exist, according to Bosanquet. Existing in this instance did not involve buying milk, or vegetables other than potatoes. The total amount of food consumed per family member was also less for the family of an ordinary labourer than for the family of a skilled labourer. Furthermore, a reduction in wages led to a switch from meat to bread and potatoes in a family's diet. A survey in Manchester in 1841 showed the changing percentages spent on meat and bread according to the income

---

21 Quoted in Heffer, 1995, p. 130.
22 Hobsbawm, 1979, p. 106.
23 Hobsbawm, 1990, p. 73.
24 Deane and Cole, 1980, pp. 23, 189.
25 Toynbee, 1969, p. 93.
26 Burnett, 1968, p. 67.

per family member. Where the income was 7s 1½d per family member the
percentages spent on bread and meat were equal at 17.5. Where the income per
family member was only 2s 3d those percentages were 32.8 and 9.4 respectively.[27]

The level of need also varied with the point reached in the family cycle, that
is the proportion of earning units to family members. The proportion was generally
highest just after marriage when both husband and wife were working, falling
when the children arrived, until the elder children commenced work, and then
falling again as the parents reached old age and the children left home.[28]

Such levels of income and expenditure still exceeded those of the stockingers
and weavers that Booth saw in Nottingham at the same time. While it may well
have been possible for families to survive on such a budget, J. F. C. Harrison has
argued that it is probably no exaggeration to say that the majority of ordinary
labouring families went hungry at some point during the 1830s and 1840s. During
this period a large number of labouring men found themselves in a position where
they could not work. Now referred to as unemployed, they were regarded at the
time as surplus or redundant labour and these unemployed were 'so numerous and
so constant that they have to be classified not as an exception but as a separate,
though changing and fluctuating, category of the labouring poor.'[29]

Much was made at the time, and has been made since, of the way in which
the poor spent their money; want was often seen by the middle and upper classes as
improvidence. Emphasis was laid on the way the poor lived on credit, lost money
by constantly pawning and redeeming their goods and bought frequent small
amounts of food. Amartya Sen has drawn on illustrations from other eras to show
that such attitudes to the victims of poverty are often displayed by those with the
economic and political power:

> The conviction of cultural superiority merges well with the asymmetry of political
> power. Winston Churchill's famous remark that the Bengal famine of 1943, which
> was the last famine in British India (and also the last famine in India altogether), was
> caused by the tendency of the natives to breed 'like rabbits' belongs to this general
> tradition of blaming the colonial subject ... Charles Edward Trevelyan, the head of the
> Treasury during the Irish famines, who saw not much wrong with British economic
> policy in Ireland (of which he was in charge), pointed to Irish habits as part of the
> explanation of the famines. Chief among the habitual failures was the tendency of the
> Irish poor to eat only potatoes, which made them dependent on one crop ... [T]he
> pointing of an accusing finger at the meagreness of the diet of the Irish poor well
> illustrates the tendency to blame the victim. The victim, in this view, had helped
> themselves to a disaster, despite the best efforts of the administration in London to
> prevent it.[30]

27 Burnett, 1968, pp. 69-70.
28 Wohl, 1978, p. 189.
29 Harrison, 1988, pp. 39-40.
30 Sen, 1999, pp. 174-5.

In the late 1880s Charles Booth, the social investigator, the results of whose surveys William Booth would refer to in his Darkest England proposal, emphasised that the habits of the London poor were exacerbating their poverty:

> This family live, to the greatest possible extent, from hand to mouth. Not only do they buy almost everything on credit from one shop, but if the weeks tested are a fair sample of the year, they every week put in and take out of pawn the same set of garments, on which the broker every time advances 16s., charging the, no doubt, reasonable sum of 4d for the accommodation. Fourpence a week, or 17s 4d a year, for the comfort of having a week's income in advance! On the other hand, even on credit they buy nothing till actually needed. They go to their shop as an ordinary housewife goes to her canisters: twice a day they buy tea, or three times if they make it so often; in 35 days they make 72 purchases of tea ... Of sugar there are 77 purchases at the same time.[31]

While the fact that the poor bought items in minute quantities is usually given as an argument that more money was spent than necessary, it also needs to be borne in mind that if the poor had found the means to buy in bulk they might well not have had any way of storing their purchases. In addition, Ellen Ross, whose research has done much to challenge perceptions of the role and views of the most poverty-stricken mothers of that time, has argued:

> Buying in small quantities not only was a product of limited flows of cash but also - despite the higher costs of this method per unit - could save money because it would keep the always-hungry families from eating up the next day's provisions. With perishable items like meat, it reduced the risk of spoilage.[32]

As Mrs Pember Reeves was to write at the beginning of the next century: 'If the poor were not improvident they would hardly dare to live their lives at all.'[33]

Because the poor spent so high a proportion of their income on bread, the cost of wheat became of crucial importance. W. W. Rostow, in his study of the British economy in the nineteenth century, has calculated an index of social tension based on the wheat price in any year, seeking to show the correspondence between the cost of wheat and social tension. It is an approximate calculation but it is significant that, during the 1830s and 40s, the years when the index is lowest, and therefore the risk of social tension highest, are 1837 to 1842, and 1847 to 1849, which correspond to the years of the greatest influence of Chartism.[34]

Hobsbawm made particular reference to Nottingham in 1842 when he argued for a link between poverty and the strength of Chartism: 'Twenty per cent of Nottingham... might be actually destitute. A movement like Chartism in Britain would collapse, time and again, under its political weakness. Time and again sheer hunger ... would revive it.'[35] The level of poverty, the quantitative fall in living

---

31 Booth, 1889, Vol. 1 pp. 142-3.
32 Ross, 1993, p. 52.
33 Mrs. Pember Reeves, *Round about a pound a week,* quoted in Keating, 1978, pp. 308-9.
34 Rostow, 1949, pp. 50-1, 108-125.
35 Hobsbawm, 1995 (a), p. 252.

standards, was leading to a definite shift in the quality of life. It was so bad as to move people from a passive acceptance to an active resistance.

Poverty in Nottingham

While a level of disagreement exists between historians concerning the relative differences in living standards in the second quarter of the nineteenth century, there is little disagreement about the suffering of the stockingers in Nottingham who made such an impact on Booth:

> The one clear instance of a decline in conditions can be seen when the competition of the factory with its steam driven machinery drove a hand-trade out of existence. The classic case is that of the hand-loom weavers who worked desperately long hours in the vain effort to compete with iron and steam. The frame-work knitters producing stockings in Nottingham and Leicester are another example.[36]

The stockingers are an example of what Amartya Sen called the 'irreducible absolutist core' of poverty:

> If there is starvation or hunger, then – no matter what the *relative* picture looks like – if relevant – has to take a back seat behind the possibly dominating absolutist consideration.[37]

Arnold Toynbee also used the stockingers as an example of the worst suffering under the impact of industrialisation. He used the example of Leicester but both the situation and the impact of Chartism were similar in the two cities of Nottingham and Leicester. Toynbee spoke of the stockingers in the middle of the eighteenth century as being remarkably prosperous, working ten hours a day for between three and five days a week.[38] One hundred years later Thomas Cooper, a Chartist, visited Leicester and found the stockingers working sixteen hours a day for 4s 6d a week,[39] about one third of the amount Bosanquet had estimated was necessary for a family of five to exist. Such figures underline the real suffering of the stockingers and their families and the acute poverty that Booth would have seen around him.

Rosa Luxemburg, the Marxist activist, quoted an address by the Nottingham frame-work knitters that was printed in the Edinburgh Review of 1820:

> After working from 14 to 16 hours a day, we only earn from 4s. to 7s. a week, to maintain our wives and families upon; and we farther state, that although we have substituted bread and water, or potatoes and salt, for that more wholesome food an Englishman's table used to abound with, we have repeatedly retired, after a heavy

---

36 Hopkins, 1992, p. 5.
37 Sen, 1982, p. 9.
38 Toynbee, 1969, pp. 90-1.
39 Harrison, 1988, p. 44.

day's labour, and have been under the necessity of putting our children supperless to bed, to stifle the cries of hunger. We can most solemnly declare, that for the last eighteen months we have scarcely known what it was to be free from the pangs of hunger.[40]

These stockingers, who had such an impact on Booth, were victims. E. P. Thompson, in his book, *The Making of the English Working Class*, has argued that it was in the overstocked outwork industries that the exploitive relationship anatomised by Marx in *Capital* was least modified by counteracting influences. There were always more people seeking jobs than work available and the stockinger became an 'instrument' or an entry among other items of cost.[41] So Booth was seeing at first hand the suffering of the reserve army of labour and the part its members were enacting in the advance of capitalism.

However, the stockingers were not passive in their victimisation. They were as prominent as factory hands in the radical agitation from 1817 to the end of Chartism and they met the exploitation in the knowledge of their history and traditions:

> The changing productive relations and working conditions of the Industrial Revolution were imposed, not upon raw material, but upon the free-born Englishman - and the free-born Englishman as Paine had left him or as the Methodists had moulded him. The factory hand or stockinger was also the inheritor of Bunyan, of remembered village rights, of notions of equality before the law, of craft traditions.[42]

And Booth must have absorbed some of these ideas.

The increased level of poverty was not the only negative impact from the industrialisation of England. Relative poverty between the unemployed and the employed, as well as the unskilled and the skilled, was also increased. The fact that more people were living in close proximity in cities underlined these differences and heightened the sense of social injustice.

Such differences emphasised social division. Poverty brought with it a loss of pride and a sense of alienation. Booth's work as an apprentice to a pawnbroker would have underlined, for him, the loss of pride that poverty brought. Charles Dickens, whose novels and other writings did so much to disseminate pictures of poverty and the lives of the poor, wrote of visits to pawnbrokers and the cost to self-respect: 'the transparent hypocrisy of looking at the silver forks ... the furtive, skulking slide round the corner.'[43] Dorothy Scannell, looking back on her childhood in the East End, remembered the way in which the visits to the pawnbroker seemed to be hidden and camouflaged from those outside the immediate family circle:

---

40 Quoted in Luxemburg, 1963, p. 174.
41 Thompson, 1991, pp. 222-3.
42 Thompson, 1991, p. 213.
43 Dickens, Charles, with W.H. Wills, 'My Uncle' in *Household Words* 6 December 1851 quoted in Ackroyd, 1991, p. 76.

> We were rich, for Mother wrapped Father's suit in a sheet of brown paper which was
> put away very carefully each week. A friend of mine was very envious of this sheet of
> brown paper for she had to take the clothes to be pawned in an old piece of shirt, but
> once she managed to save a penny and she bought a sheet of brown paper. This was
> her most cherished possession for the years of her childhood and each week she ironed
> this so that it always looked new, and each week she regained her pride and felt she
> could look the world in the face.[44]

Booth not only saw the poverty of others but his own family suffered a
financial reversal and was forced to live in relative poverty. Although this is
something he does not refer to in later life, he must have known the sense of
exclusion that accompanies a loss of wealth. Roy Hattersley's biography of
William Booth emphasised the uncertainty brought into Booth's childhood and
youth by the instability of the family finances:

> The family fortunes fluctuated. Sometimes a new business venture prospered.
> Sometimes it failed. The curse of William's childhood was uncertainty ... We can ...
> be certain that the family lived in constant insecurity ... William endured a strange
> upbringing even by the standards of the time. It was made all the more debilitating by
> his mother never allowing him to forget that the family hovered precariously between
> solvency and bankruptcy and that she had once known something better.[45]

Peter Ackroyd, in his biography of Charles Dickens, has assessed the impact
of a similar experience on Dickens, with the fear it created that he would be forced
from the 'genteel' class. Dickens had in his youth been forced to work in a
blacking factory and had felt degradation in working alongside 'common men and
boys'.[46] He was, in Ackroyd's phrase, 'perilously hovering between classes',
which led to an ambivalence towards the poor in later years, with a mixture of an
imaginative sympathy and a desire to emphasise his elevation above such a state:
'as if he still needed to put a distance between himself and his own similarly
wretched childhood'.[47]

Angus Wilson has written about an emphasis on gentility in Dickens' early
novels that he felt to be more acute precisely because the Dickens family only just
qualified for such a status themselves. He described Charles Dickens as being
'born on the outer edge of the world he wished to belong to.'[48] The flux in wealth
suffered by so many at this time could lead to a loss of more than financial security
and cause feelings of alienation.

Insecurity and alienation were negative consequences of the ferment of
industrialisation. However, it could be argued that such an experience enriched the
writings of Dickens and added to his appeal. Victoria Glendinning, a biographer of

---

44 Scannell, 1974, pp. 43–4.
45 Hattersley, 1999, pp. 12-17.
46 Ackroyd, 1991, p. 84.
47 Ackroyd, 1881, p. 440.
48 Wilson, 1972, p. 17.

the novelist Anthony Trollope, has made a similar assessment of Trollope as 'an outsider within the system, and that gave him his cutting edge.'[49]

Booth's experience of exclusion from the life he had earlier known could also be interpreted as having a positive result, for it became a central focus of his work that those who were alienated from society were not thereby alienated from the Christian gospel.

David Lyon, in his assessment of Marx's thought and life from a Christian perspective, has made a similar claim about the positive results of alienation for Karl Marx:

> Marx was an alienated man. Born into a family which was excluded from full social participation, unable to obtain an 'establishment' university teaching post, moved on by police from one country to another, he finally lived as a foreigner in London ... As a social critic, the personal experience of not feeling at home in the world gave him a unique vantage-point.[50]

Attitudes to Poverty

The actual level of poverty and its visibility tend to have an influence on attitudes towards the poor. The dominant ideas about the causes of poverty will in turn affect policy and actions and so impact back on the real level of poverty suffered. There were influential thinkers who had already helped to create the environment in which Booth grew up and others whose influence was being felt at that time.

Because of the impact of industrialisation, and furthered by the unrest of some of the labouring population, including the Chartist movement, poverty and its social repercussions began to have a higher claim on people's attention towards the middle of the nineteenth century. However, utilitarian ideas from the late eighteenth century were still affecting events and attitudes when Booth and Marx reached London in 1849.

The works of Thomas Malthus and Jeremy Bentham were published at the end of the eighteenth century but their influence was felt well into the nineteenth century and was particularly crucial in the Poor Law Amendment Act of 1834, which, in its turn, affected the level and manner of poverty that people suffered. Their works were also used in the ongoing argument about whether the poor were victims or responsible for their own plight. Many of the arguments at this time had a religious element in the way conclusions were reached and were often couched in religious vocabulary.

Malthus

The work for which Malthus is best known is his theory of population growth. The basis of this theory is that the growth of population, if left unchecked, rises in a

---

49 Glendinning, 1993, p. 52.
50 Lyon, 1988, p. 43.

geometric progression while the means of subsistence can only increase along an arithmetic progression. In Malthus's own words:

> A slight acquaintance with numbers will shew the immensity of the first power in comparison with the second. By that law of our nature which makes food necessary to the life of man, the effects of these two unequal powers must be kept equal. [51]

While Malthus modified some of his conclusions in later years, he maintained his belief in this central thesis. The implication of his thesis was that checks have to be made on the growth of the population in order that the population level does not exceed that level for which food is available. In his original work, Malthus stated that all checks could be resolved into vice and misery. By the time of the third publication of his *Essay*, he had found three categories of checks: moral restraint, vice and misery. In the sixth edition of his work, Malthus sanctioned emigration to the colonies by the 'surplus' workers as an escape from the impact of poverty, a solution William Booth was to propose more than fifty years later. [52]

Malthus's thesis was used in argument against Poor Relief, or even charitable giving, on the basis that the sufferings of the poor, early death and chronic illnesses, lack of food and warmth, were part of those necessary checks in the system to prevent the population growing too fast. Malthus himself seemed to argue for a harsher treatment of the poor than that provided by the laws of the early nineteenth century, seeing the system that operated prior to 1834 as not giving enough 'encouragement' to the poor to help themselves:

> The love of independence is a sentiment that surely none would wish to be erased from the breast of man, though the parish law of England, it must be confessed, is a system of all others the most calculated gradually to weaken this sentiment, and in the end may eradicate it completely. [53]

The system to which Malthus and his supporters objected was known as the Speenhamland System, whereby a supplement was paid out of parish rates to those whose earnings did not reach an agreed minimum, dependent on the price of bread and the number of children in a family. The new Poor Law of 1834, based in part on the arguments to be found in the works of Malthus, sought to introduce a principle of 'less-eligibility', making relief available to the able-bodied, only within the confines of the workhouse. It was hoped to make relief so unpalatable, both more meagre and more rigorous than the wages and work of the labouring poor, that only desperation would induce the poor to seek relief. The 1834 Poor Law was aimed at remedying what had been seen as the most serious weakness of the previous system, the 'leakage of benefits from the deserving to those who were either non-needy or undeserving'. [54]

---

51 Malthus, 1985, p. 71.
52 Desmond and Moore, 1992, p. 265.
53 Malthus, 1985, p. 91.
54 Besley et al., 1993, p. 7.

This New Poor Law has been described as 'a Malthusian bill designed to force the poor to emigrate, to work for lower wages, to live on a coarser sort of food.'[55] With its introduction Malthus became a focus for argument about the poor:

> His name was on everyone's lips, as either Satan or Saviour. His doctrine of population, progress, and pauperism was no longer academic. It was the very kernel of poor-law policy: the stuff of inflammatory oratory, popular defiance, and government propaganda.[56]

The Poor Law was class legislation in that it was enacted by one class, the middle class, in relation to the situation of another class, the working class. More than that, in Harrison's words, it blatantly 'trampled on so much that the poor held dear'.[57]

J. L. and Barbara Hammond, historians of the Chartist movement, have argued that the attitude and language of the Poor Law Commissioners had embittered the struggle by altering the public's intrinsic perception of paupers as passively suffering their fate to one that suggested that paupers had actively participated in bringing about their own poverty:

> 'What is a pauper?' asked Cobbett, and he answered, 'A very poor Man.' That is what the pauper seemed to the poor. He was a man on whom misfortune had fallen, whether it had come as sickness or unemployment, as the paralysis of old age or the pinching want of the hand-loom weaver. The logic of 1834 rested on a different conception. The pauper was as much culprit as victim. At any rate, he was so often a culprit that it was dangerous ever to treat him as a victim.[58]

Ursula Henriques has underlined, in her study of social administration at that time, that this philosophy was often diluted in practice and that there was some ambivalence in the attitudes of those administering the Poor Law which meant that it was not always implemented identically in all areas. For the aged who entered the workhouse there was a sense in which it could be viewed as a refuge and those responsible for running it would treat them accordingly and yet it needed to be seen as an incentive for the poor to save for their old age and for children to take responsibility for their parents.[59]

Unsurprisingly, Malthus raised a furore of antagonistic responses. Poverty was a very emotive subject and many of the attacks were personal. His first essay was written when he was quite young and his language was not always guarded. His biographer claims that the tone of his writing was due to his own personal unhappiness at the time.[60] Despite a changing tone in later editions it was to be the

---

55 Desmond and Moore, 1992, p. 196.
56 Desmond and Moore, 1992, p. 197.
57 Harrison, 1988, p. 89.
58 Hammond, 1930, p. 78.
59 Henriques, 1979, pp. 50–1.
60 Janes, 1979, p. 100.

infelicitous phrases from the first edition that were to be remembered and used against him in argument. For example:

> A man who is born into a world already possessed, if he cannot get subsistence from his parents on whom he has a just demand, and if the society do not want his labour, has no claim of right to the smallest portion of food, and, in fact, has no business to be where he is. At nature's mighty feast there is no vacant cover for him.[61]

Because Malthus himself used religious vocabulary, and because of the centrality of religious authority at the time, the argument raised the issue of a Christian view of and response to poverty.

There was some reaction from churchmen against the implementation of the New Poor Law, those who saw it as going against the laws of God; for example, the Reverend Joseph Rayner Stephens:

> Is it to be borne by men, whose fathers were free, and whose God has always broken the fetters of the bondsman, that they should be declared to have no right to liberty, because the wickedness of their taskmaster has made them poor, and their very babes no right to life, because Malthus has 'proved' that there is no room for them, at nature's feast. These 'Principles' of our boasted philosophy, these 'results' of our modern discoveries in political economy, these 'amendments' of God's laws in the kingdoms of nature, providence and grace are ... thoroughly detestable, truly diabolical.[62]

This was an argument that would continue through the rest of the century. On a national level, as religion and religious vocabulary occupied a smaller place, the argument shifted. For William Booth, however, the critical question would remain that of deciding the Christian response to poverty.

Jeremy Bentham

Jeremy Bentham's Utilitarian theory was often joined with the Malthusian theory of population in political decision making in the early nineteenth century. Both theories were considered 'scientific' ways of regarding social problems in that they used mathematical formulae or terminology. This was essentially pseudo-scientific in that no real effort was made to prove the accuracy of the formulae. Bentham is accepted as the founder of utilitarianism and his is a pure utilitarianism. More contemporary with Marx and Booth was J. S. Mill who, although a utilitarian, sought to modify the extreme Benthamite form.

In Bentham's theory all decisions were made according to a felicific calculus that sought to promote the greatest happiness of the greatest number. This was calculated according to measures of pain and pleasure. Each action was to be judged by the net pleasure over pain that it produced. Pleasure was measured by giving the correct weighting to its intensity, duration, certainty, propinquity,

---

61 Janes, 1979, p. 100.
62 Stephens, 1839, pp. 20-1.

fecundity and purity, with the additional factor for community decisions of the number of people affected. In a similar way the painful results, for example inconvenience and loss, were measured. Once these were added together a decision would be made on the purely quantitative grounds of which side, pain or pleasure, was the greater. By its very nature, therefore, the philosophy emphasised numbers of people and gave little weight to the suffering of one individual among many:

> Bentham ... may be seen as the father of Victorian realpolitik. The 'greatest happiness of greatest numbers' theory was based on the callous but realistic view that pleasing everyone is impossible. The secret of a stable society is to isolate and emasculate the miserable. [63]

There is some disagreement about whether Bentham seriously expected people to use this felicific calculus but it explains his philosophy with its emphasis on decisions being made solely on the basis of their effect on people's happiness and allowing no room for moral judgements concerning the intrinsic good of a course of action. It was, as Hobsbawm has argued, a singularly inappropriate tool for measuring the impact of the Industrial Revolution, which was 'not merely a process of addition and subtraction' in people's lives and situations but 'a fundamental social change.'[64]

Mill was to modify Bentham's views to some extent in seeking to argue that there were qualitative as well as quantitative judgements to be made in measuring outcomes, and also in accepting the idea of self-abnegation as a rational choice if the outcome were to be greater happiness for more people. The tensions between quantitative and qualitative issues, and individual and social good, were those that both Marx and Booth would have to grapple with, on completely different planes, during the period they were in London.

Influential Writers about Poverty

Public opinion and attitudes were wider and more varied than could be contained within the parameters of official policy. There were more voices influencing the populace than just those whose ideas were becoming incorporated into law. With the spread of magazines and newspapers, and with increased literacy, those who were able to write their ideas and have them published were having more impact. Two who had a high profile around 1850 were Charles Dickens and Thomas Carlyle. Booth's biographer stated that Booth disliked the writings of Dickens and loved the work of Carlyle, although it is not stated how early in his life he reached these conclusions.[65]

---

63 Wilson, 2002, p. 38.
64 Hobsbawm, 1990, p. 80.
65 Begbie, 1920, Vol. I, p. 378.

Dickens

No explanation is given for Booth's dislike of Dickens and the reasons for this are difficult to ascertain. There could be two reasons, either the way in which Dickens depicted poverty in London or the way in which he wrote about religion. Dickens was a popular novelist by 1850 and his books are often read as factual accounts of the life of the poor at that time. Among the middle-class readers of his own day they may also have been taken as such. However, Dickens' books were far from straightforward accounts of the actual lives of the poor and, although many working people were among his readers, his very skill at writing could have added to misunderstanding and misapprehension on the part of his readers from the higher classes.

In addition to entertaining with his novels Dickens could use satire to communicate a political view, as in the following depiction of political economy:

> Having satisfied himself, on his father's death, that his mother had a right of settlement in Coketown, this excellent young economist had asserted that right for her with such a steadfast adherence to the principle of the case, that she had been shut up in the workhouse ever since. It must be admitted that he allowed her half a pound of tea a year, which was weak in him: first, because all gifts have an inevitable tendency to pauperize the recipient, and secondly, because his only reasonable transaction in that commodity would have been to buy it for as little as he could possibly give, and sell it for as much as he could possibly get; it having been clearly ascertained by philosophers that in this comprised the whole duty of man - not a part of man's duty, but the whole.[66]

Such irony would not be lost on Booth and it might be expected that he would approve of Dickens's goal in writing in this way.

Charles Dickens was the one who drew the attention of many people to the poverty in London and, because much that he wrote about was shocking, his readers may have taken his description too literally, forgetting that he was a novelist and an entertainer as well as a social investigator. Dickens was, by his very nature as a novelist, rewriting the world to suit his narrative and imagination. Such unreality could have been a part of the reason for Booth's dislike of Dickens' writing, especially if his judgement was reached when he had experienced the reality of poverty in East London and its effects. Humphrey House concluded that Dickens created his own world that was unlike any other world there has ever been, and that within this world was a revolt against the nonconformist spirit, the Malthusian gloom and other negative influences, as Dickens saw them. He created a world of extravagance, with much overeating and brandy-drinking that the poor in his novels took to gladly.[67] Booth's own response to Malthusian gloom and his experience of what was a harsher reality may have caused his negative reaction to the writings of Dickens.

---

66 Dickens, 1985, p. 150.
67 House, 1941, pp. 224, 276.

Extreme exaggeration can be seen to be such. However, there was also within Dickens' work much that seemed to be a true account, although filtered through Dickens' imagination. For example, there is confusion over the period about which he was writing. Dickens first knew London when he was a boy and those first impressions of early nineteenth-century London formed what Ackroyd has called the landscape of his imagination. But that London retained many of the characteristics of the eighteenth-century city. By the time Dickens came to write his novels the earlier London had already changed but it still formed the backdrop for Dickens' imagination and he peopled it with events and encounters from the later period. By the combination it became, despite its roots in reality, a London that never really existed.[68]

Added to the confusion of time was the self-censorship that Dickens practised out of respect for his readers and because of the conventions of the time he omitted any details likely to cause offence. So the real horror and squalor of life in the East End was not communicated in his novels. Despite his apparently detailed descriptions of poverty no suggestion is given of the stench and the filth in which people had to live and work. House argued that the real facts of life for the prostitutes and drunks are not even hinted at.[69] The result, notwithstanding all the claims that Dickens was a social reformer, is that the depth of poverty in such areas as Saffron Hill, the setting for Oliver Twist, is idealised. It is possible that Booth's dislike of the novels of Dickens came from his sense that the true picture of the East End was being sanitised and romanticised. Nevertheless Dickens was crucial in drawing attention to the poor and he achieved this as few others did or could in 1850, in a way that would never have been equalled by a straightforward statement of facts.

House argued that it was Dickens' middle-class morality that gave his writing about the poor an unreality at times. His sense of humiliation at working with 'common' people when he was young can be sensed in some of his writing.[70] Ackroyd described middle-class London as Dickens' realm and claimed that his 'proper subject' was the agonizing over such things as manners and fashion by the middle and lower-middle classes.[71] These were not subjects that would claim Booth's attention.

Dickens criticised religion in some of his novels and this is the most likely cause of Booth's disapproval. There is little mention of Christian motivation in Dickens' work; instead much is made of a kind of natural benevolence. The most quoted example is Pickwick who is seen as the embodiment of this benevolence:

> [T]here is in the peregrinations of Pickwick that dream of idleness, that dream of ease and freedom, which accounts for its idyllic aspects. No God here. No sex. Just a

---

68 Ackroyd, 1991, p. 94.
69 House, 1941, p. 217.
70 House, 1941, p. 152.
71 Ackroyd, 1991, p. 161.

timeless world in which good feelings win through and in which Pickwick enters Eden, as it were, after ploughing through the world of discord.[72]

Such a philosophy would be anathema to Booth with his emphasis on the atonement and the need for salvation. Dickens did not believe in the doctrine of original sin and, according to House's argument, there is no mention of sin, as opposed to crime, in his novels. This is not the case for all of Dickens' work. For example, in *Hard Times*, there is the following description:

> She erected in her mind a mighty Staircase, with a dark pit of shame and ruin at the bottom; and down those stairs, from day to day and hour to hour, she saw Louisa coming.[73]

House described Dickens' philosophy as: 'Virtue is for him the natural state of man, and happiness its concomitant.'[74]

In addition, Dickens' portrayal of religion was a joyless picture. In particular, missionaries and missions were a pet hate because he saw them as a way of avoiding helping those nearby by concentrating help overseas. Ackroyd blames this attitude, in part, on Dickens' racism.[75] Dickens also suspected religion of being opposed to those things that added enjoyment to life, such as ornaments and entertainment. He strongly opposed the Sunday Trading Bill, which was an Evangelical measure.

There is only one illustration of Booth showing any appreciation of the works of Dickens and that was when he recited from *A Christmas Carol*, at an informal gathering.[76] This story contains an element of individual redemption and 'many religious motifs which give the book its particular seasonal spirit; not only the Christmas parties and dancing but also the Christmas of mercy and love which binds a community to itself.'[77] The judgement of A. N. Wilson at the beginning of the twenty-first century is:

> Many of the 'benevolent' characters in Dickens will strike some readers as clumsily drawn and manipulative of our tear-ducts ... Yet each time one reads *A Christmas Carol,* it works. The ethics of Scrooge (which are the ethics of Adam Smith and Jeremy Bentham, the ethics of the mill-owners and factory-builders who created the wealth of Victorian England) are held in check by a tremendously simplified form of Christian charity.[78]

---

72 Ackroyd, 1991, p. 209.
73 Dickens, 1985, p. 227.
74 House, 1941, p. 111.
75 Ackroyd, 1991, p. 572.
76 Smith, 1949, p. 61.
77 Ackroyd, 1991, pp. 429, 435.
78 Wilson, 200, p. 22.

Booth's two favourite novels were *Jane Eyre* by Charlotte Brontë and *Les Misérables* by Victor Hugo,[79] both of which contain a strong element of individual redemption in their theme and would seem to suggest that a part of Booth's reason for a dislike of the work of Dickens was Dickens' treatment of religious themes, in books other than *A Christmas Carol*. It may simply have been that Booth did not enjoy novels for themselves, without some element of a moral.

Carlyle

Begbie has claimed that, in contrast to his reaction to Dickens, Booth loved the writings of Thomas Carlyle, who was one of the most influential writers and thinkers in England in the 1840s. Carlyle showed great concern for material and moral conditions in England. Dickens was an admirer of Carlyle and dedicated *Hard Times* to him. Begbie wrote that Booth's favourite book by Carlyle was *The French Revolution*. He had tried to read *Frederick the Great* but failed to finish it.[80] The impact of the writings of Carlyle on the people of his time was enormous. The author Charles Kingsley has the eponymous hero in *Alton Locke* share Booth's view of *The French Revolution* in the following words:

> I know no book ... which at once so quickened and exalted my view of man and his history, as that great prose poem, the single epic of modern days, Thomas Carlyle's "French Revolution." Of the general effect which his works had on me, I shall say nothing: it was the same as they have had, thank God, on thousands of my class and of every other. But that book above all recalled me to the overwhelming and yet ennobling knowledge that there was such a thing as Duty; first taught me to see in history not the mere farce-tragedy of man's crimes and follies, but the dealings of a righteous Ruler of the universe, whose ways are in the great deep, and whom the sins and errors, as well as the virtues and discoveries of man, must obey and justify.[81]

Carlyle did not share the kind of evangelical faith that Booth espoused, although he retained from his childhood a belief in the importance of the transcendent. However Carlyle's faith, as expressed in his writings, was no longer based on the Bible but was in history. Le Quesne has pointed out that among other nineteenth-century thinkers who shared Carlyle's faith in history were Hegel and Marx but they interpreted history in different ways: to Hegel partially and to Marx wholly, history was an autonomous and self-justifying process; to Carlyle it was something more like a theatre for the workings of a providence which itself remains firmly outside history.[82]

Carlyle was greatly affected by the plight of the poor. But even in his sympathy there was a suggestion of the poor being less than fully human and it was this latter sentiment that was to become more marked in his later writings. Carlyle

---

79 Begbie, 1920, Vol. I, p. 378.
80 Begbie, 1920, Vol. I, p. 378.
81 Kingsley, 1898, pp. 262-3.
82 Le Quesne, 1993, pp. 39-40.

produced a pamphlet in 1850, called *The Present Time*, which included plans for
the regimentation of the poor. Heffer assessed the pamphlet:

> It is good satire because it makes the point of the atrociousness of the workhouses, and
> the government's failure hitherto to provide properly for the poor; but it still takes for
> granted that those poor are little better than animals and ridicules their aspirations.[83]

Carlyle sought to attack what he saw as the priggishness and smugness of
liberals and philanthropists who believed that the lower orders could be improved
and reformed. He argued that to give liberty to the classes who were 'subject'
might be desirable in theory but could have horrific effects if put into practice.[84]

Nevertheless, there are ideas within Carlyle's writings that Booth was to
follow closely in his own writings in 1890, in addition to the basis for Booth's cab-
horse charter. The closest that the writings of Carlyle approximate to Booth's
philosophy is in *Past and Present*, which has been described as:

> [A] tract for its times of compelling power, by reason of the intensity of its moral
> concern for the future of British society, and the depth and sincerity of the sympathy
> for human suffering upon which it is based.[85]

It was from this book that Booth quoted in the appendix to *Darkest England*,
the quotations he chose being mainly related to the advisability of an emigration
scheme.

Carlyle explained in *Past and Present* the impact upon him of seeing the men
outside the workhouse of St Ives in Huntingdonshire: 'They sat there ... in a kind of
torpor, especially in a silence, which was very striking ... There was something that
reminded me of Dante's Hell in all this.' Carlyle's biographer concluded that it was
this experience that sowed the seed for *Past and Present*.

Carlyle had been brought into contact with poverty on a previous occasion,
with a handloom weaver toiling under conditions similar to those of the stockingers
who had so affected Booth:

> Carlyle had heard 'a loom at work till twelve o'clock at night and ... before seven in
> the morning ... he was told there was a weaver next door - a man with a wife and six
> children - earning six shillings a week by his seventeen hours of daily work.' Carlyle
> felt that these were desperate men who, sooner or later, would launch insurrection, as
> their fellow sufferers had in France half a century earlier, since the aristocracy took no
> notice of their misery.[86]

Carlyle's pamphlet, *Model Prisons*, was a particularly ferocious attack,
written in 1850, when he discovered that the inmates of Millbank Penitentiary were

---

83 Heffer, 1995, p. 35.
84 Heffer, 1995, p. 98.
85 Le Quesne, 1993, p. 74.
86 Heffer, 1995, p. 85.

being better cared for than many of the poor outside the prison. Booth was to write forty years later:

> I sorrowfully admit that it would be Utopian in our present social arrangements to dream of attaining for every honest Englishman a gaol standard of all the necessaries of life. Some time, perhaps, we may venture to hope that every honest worker on English soil will always be as warmly clad, as healthily housed, and as regularly fed as our criminal convicts - but that is not yet.[87]

Carlyle's writings also contained an emphasis on the importance of an individual, charismatic leader. It was this element in Carlyle's writing that was seized upon by the young Thomas Huxley. Huxley's biographer claimed that reading Carlyle gave Huxley 'a sense of religion which owed nothing to a decrepit theology'. Huxley learned from Carlyle that 'new heroes were needed - Great Men with a sense of destiny.'[88]

Such a philosophy would have been likely to appeal to Booth in later life, when he too believed in the ability of one individual to effect change. '[T]he mark of the hero is that he is sent by God to do God's work; and since God is not a pluralist, there is no call for democracy.'[89]

The Chartists

Although the date of Booth's reading of both Dickens and Carlyle is to some extent speculative, the direct influence of the Chartist movement during his youth is known. The first indication of any political influence on Booth came at the time of the visit of Feargus O'Connor to Nottingham when Booth was young. Both Begbie and Ervine are agreed that Booth was influenced by O'Connor and Begbie quotes Stead as saying that he was 'a physical force Chartist of course, being a boy and therefore uncompromising.'[90]

This statement is not quite as significant as it may appear. There were two strands of policy within Chartism, the Moral Force Party led by William Lovett and the Physical Force Party led by Feargus O'Connor.[91] The Hammonds described the leaders of the Chartist movement as being sharply divided on policy and hating each other 'with that peculiar bitterness which often makes the controversies of rival reformers the most truculent controversies of all.'[92] Hobsbawm attributes the ultimate defeat of Chartism to these disagreements and to an inability to organise concerted national action.[93]

---

87 Booth , 1970, p. 19
88 Desmond, 1994, p. 7.
89 Heffer, 1995, p. 206.
90 Begbie, 1920, p. 50 and Ervine, 1934, p. 34.
91 Beer, 1984, p. 227.
92 Hammond, 1930, pp. 268-9.
93 Hobsbawm, 1995(a), p. 262.

Given that it is likely that Booth only heard O'Connor of the Chartist leaders, the statement that he was a Physical Force Chartist does not imply that, having heard and considered the two arguments, he had chosen the Physical Force Party, rather that, due to Booth's youth and O'Connor's noted skill at oratory, he was completely swept away by the power of the arguments he heard. Within the geographical divisions of Chartism, O'Connor was particularly identified with Nottingham, winning a Nottingham seat at the 1847 election to become the first and only Chartist MP.

The impetus for Chartism grew out of a number of dissatisfactions among the working class, those who were hungry, those who were angry about the deportation in 1834 of the Tolpuddle Martyrs for their membership of a union, those who opposed the New Poor Law and those who were disappointed at the lack of inclusiveness of the 1832 Reform Act. With such a variety of motives, it is hardly surprising that there were disagreements over methods and priorities.

In Nottingham and Leicester the stockingers became the backbone of the Chartist movement. They had already proved the backbone of Luddism. E. P. Thompson has described the signal for Luddism as coming first 'not from the croppers, but from the framework knitters,' who had 'a long history of both constitutional and violent defence of their conditions.'[94]

The working-class culture that Booth would find in the East End in 1865 also included a history of activism by framework-knitters: 'In 1710 there was violent rioting by framework-knitters which presaged decades of unrest and disorder in the poor urban districts such as Whitechapel and Shoreditch.'[95]

> For the whole of the eighteenth century the handloom weavers of London proved a defiant and virtually unassailable body: they might march to Parliament one day with black flags flying to petition against foreign imports and another offer oaths and pledges of loyalty; they might happily arm themselves with pistols and cutlasses, disguise themselves as sailors and in the dead of night go to the homes of blacklegs and smash looms; they might demand increased wages and form themselves into a trade association called the Bold Defiance; they might pick up guns, as they often did, and fight running battles with soldiers and magistrates hunting for cutters (loom destroyers). No government could afford to antagonize the weavers for long, only the coming of water and steam power would finally prove fatal to their aristocracy.[96]

An editorial in O'Connor's newspaper, *Northern Star*, on 23 June 1838, also addressed the weavers:

> Let the poor handloom weaver bear in mind that the unrestricted use of machinery has thrown him completely out of the market and let those who are yet fortunate enough to be at work recollect that the said handloom weavers at all times serve as a corps of

---

94 Thompson, 1991, p. 579.
95 Ackroyd, 2000, p. 393.
96 Bloom, 2003, p. 158.

reserve to be cheaply purchased by the masters and hold those at work in submission.[97]

The term, 'a corps of reserve', describes those who were to fulfil a pivotal role in the analysis of Karl Marx, where he used the terminology 'the reserve army of labour', and whose plight was to claim the attention of William Booth half a century later. At this point Booth was growing up with the plight of those who served as 'a corps of reserve' in front of his eyes. He was also being inculcated with the background of Nottingham dissent and radicalism.

Booth was more likely to be a Physical Force Chartist not only from the place of his birth but also because of his social position. Max Beer has argued in his history of British socialism that the split between the Physical and Moral Force parties was mainly along class lines and that, since the supporters of O'Connor were more militant in their language and more hostile to the middle classes, they therefore appealed more to the proletariat while the intellectual workers were more inclined to approve of moral force tactics.[98] At this time Booth was a pawnbroker's apprentice. In addition he was surrounded by stockingers who, along with handloom weavers and nailers, formed the main categories of the Physical Force Chartists, while the main categories of workers in the Moral Force section were carpenters, tailors and shoemakers.[99]

The choice between physical and moral force was described by E. P. Thompson as the dilemma of radical reformers up to this time. The implied threat in the numbers of those who they claimed supported them lost its impact eventually if there was no clear preparation for revolutionary action. This led in turn to a loss of confidence among the Chartist supporters.[100]

The rights that all parties in the Chartist movement were agitating for were contained in the six points of the People's Charter. These were:

(1) Universal Suffrage
(2) Equal Electoral Districts
(3) Abolition of Property Qualifications for Parliamentary Candidates
(4) Annual Parliaments
(5) Secret Ballots
(6) Payment of Members of Parliament.[101]

This was seen as a fight for social justice, to regain ancient rights that were granted under natural law. Beer argues that it was because the people saw themselves as fighting for the restoration of ancient rights, rather than struggling to gain new rights, that the arguments and tactics of Feargus O'Connor were bound to be more popular, because they more closely corresponded to the fundamental ideas of Chartism.[102] Had they been fighting for new rights they would have needed to rely

---

97 Stedman Jones, 1996, pp. 158-9.
98 Beer, 1984, p. 227.
99 Hopkins, 1992, p. 49.
100 Thompson, 1991, p. 176.
101 Beer, 1984, p. 220.
102 Beer, 1984, p. 227.

on intellectual backing for their claim for implementation of the six points of the Charter, but the restoration of traditional rights required above all a passionate commitment, and the stockingers of Nottingham had a history of such.

Gareth Stedman Jones has emphasised the importance of the political agenda to the Chartists.[103] Although the basis of much of the support for Chartism was born out of hunger and suffering the demands were not simply social, they were political. R. G. Gammage, the first historian of Chartism, writing as early as 1854, claimed:

> The masses look on the enfranchised classes, whom they behold reposing on their couch of opulence, with the misery of their own condition. Reasoning from effect to cause there is no marvel that they arrive at the conclusion - that their exclusion from political power is the cause of our social anomalies.[104]

William Booth, therefore, had a background in which he saw the poor claiming their political rights positively and not as recipients of middle-class charity. In his teenage years he was passionate about these rights. Despite the fact that he may not have maintained a commitment to such a political agenda, it was part of his personal history and background and must have coloured his thinking when he began his evangelical work among the poorest members of the East End. Stedman Jones described Chartism as persuading its followers to interpret their distress or discontent in the terms of its own political language and this political language was a part of Booth's youthful vocabulary.[105] He may have later eschewed politics but he was to bring some of that vocabulary into focus again when he launched his social scheme for the alleviation of poverty.

It cannot be said that Booth retained the beliefs of a Physical Force Chartist throughout his life. However, threads can be drawn from that early experience which were woven into his later life. The memory of the suffering of the poor stayed with him. Feargus O'Connor, with his oratory, was almost certainly the first person to suggest to Booth, in an inspirational and convincing way, that something could be done to redress the situation of acute poverty and the lack of rights that accompanied it.

Booth lost his belief in physical force as a solution and was to give his lasting approval to schemes of co-operation as the way to a 'pacific re-adjustment of the social and economic relations between classes in this country.'[106] He was never to become involved in pressing for parliamentary and electoral reform. His later writings were to show that he no longer considered such things a priority. It was the element of social justice in the demands of Chartism that was to remain with him all his life. He abhorred the suffering caused by poverty and injustice, which led him to fight against these evils, sometimes by seeking to help individuals and, later, by seeking to challenge the system.

---

103 Stedman Jones, 1996, p. 96.
104 Gammage (1854) quoted in Stedman Jones, 1996, p. 100.
105 Stedman Jones, 1996, p. 96.
106 Booth, 1970, p. 73.

St. John Ervine, in his rather imaginative biography, described how Booth, after hearing O'Connor, 'hurried to the pawnshop to keep his encounters with poverty and began to see himself in the part of a deliverer.'[107] There is no real evidence to support this view but there is evidence that Booth, in his teenage years, when he made his earliest efforts to help the poor of Nottingham and attempted to take some of the poorest people of the city to Church, was not only appalled by poverty and injustice on an emotional or intellectual level but also felt committed to 'doing something' about it. His conviction that the status quo was not immutable but could be challenged was certainly born of Chartism.

Chartism did not receive great support from the churches. At the time of the Chartists' greatest numerical strength only the Primitive Methodists, among the Christian denominations, were prepared to identify with their claims. For the Primitive Methodists it was difficult to understand how the social teachings of Christ did not impel his followers to help the poor in their effort to improve their lot. The other churches stood aloof from politics except when their own interests were at stake.[108] Instead they offered faith in the life to come: 'It was possible not only to imagine the "reward" of the humble but also to enjoy some revenge upon their oppressors, by imagining their torments to come.' [109]

There are two more practical legacies of Feargus O'Connor that may have had their bearing on Booth's later development. Epstein wrote about O'Connor's skill as an orator and his 'extraordinary ability to rally mass working-class support around the figure of the radical gentleman of the platform.'[110] He fired people's imaginations by comparing their lives as they were with how they could be in a just society. Booth learnt much about preaching skills and techniques from the example of American evangelists but he may also have had an earlier role-model.

The second of O'Connor's legacies was more ideological. He advocated a return to the land as a solution to the problems of urban poverty. He saw the industrialisation of the worker as in some way artificial and his ideal was a rural community peopled with small independent farmers, weavers and craftsmen. O'Connor, in putting forward his proposals, showed himself to be part of a much older and wider stream in English radical tradition: the belief in 'agrarianism'. It was not a dream of a return to a rural idyll, but part of a claim for the redistribution of wealth, by claiming the land as 'the people's farm'. The attachment to the concept of 'the land' was part of a response to the dislocation caused by industrialisation:

> Industrialization did not then replace the landlord with the capitalist as the object of radical scorn. Rather, it led to an enhanced awareness of how inequality in the ownership of land, 'the womb of wealth', reinforced inequalities in all other spheres of economic activity.[111]

---

107 Ervine, 1934, p. 34.
108 Vidler, 1990, p. 94.
109 Thompson, 1991, p. 37.
110 Epstein, 1982, pp. 2-3.
111 Chase, 1988, p. 4.

Thompson has described O'Connor's land plan as part of the 'social myth of the golden age of the village community before enclosure and before the Wars'.[112] So O'Connor spoke of the time 'when the weaver worked at his own loom , and stretched his limbs in his own field, when the laws recognized the poor man's right to an abundance of everything.'[113] In Thompson's words: ' The savage penal code, the privations, the bridewells of old England were forgotten; but the myth of the lost paternalist community became a myth in its own right.'[114]

The rationale for O'Connor's land scheme, as for many others, was that the transfer of labour from industry to agriculture, from the 'artificial' to the 'natural' economy, would undermine the basis on which low wages rested, that is the reserve army of labour would be employed on the land and, thus, would not be available to take over the work of those labourers who sought to resist and improve their conditions of employment.[115]

Chase described the schemes to introduce what he terms 'spade husbandry' as being one of the 'few objects of unanimity between the great radical figures of the day.'

> At one and the same time spade husbandry appeared capable of breaking the fetters on nature's fecundity, of absorbing so-called 'surplus' labour, and of providing a form of work which was healthful and even ennobling.[116]

It is possible that Booth thought back to O'Connor's land scheme nearly half a century later when he was writing his plans for a farm colony as part of his social programme.

O'Connor's land scheme was based on his belief in the labour theory of value which, he believed, the dominance of capital over labour in the factory system had distorted. It was, in terms of historical rights and wrongs, the most direct redress available against the power of capitalism.

> Although in the newer form of radicalism the capitalist ownership of machinery was often stressed as the reason for competition between labourers, low wages and the existence of 'a reserve corps of labour', it remained true that the usurpation of their natural rights to cultivate the soil had made them 'landless' wage slaves in the first place, and that the resumption of rights to the land would be the most effective answer to the tyranny of the mill owner.[117]

While O'Connor's scheme was never to become a reality, and the aims of Chartism were not achieved at the time, the theories, traditions and legacies of the Chartist movement were a basis for the work of Karl Marx and Friedrich Engels, as well as the co-operative and trade union movements of Great Britain, each of

---

112 Thompson, 1991, p. 254.
113 Thompson, 1991, p. 255.
114 Thompson, 1991, p. 255.
115 Chase, 1988, p. 175.
116 Chase, 1988, p. 139.
117 Stedman Jones, 1996, p. 154.

whom used and transformed them, 'according to their education and experience.' Morton and Tate have argued strongly for the continuing impact of Chartism:

> Marx and Engels, who were in England during much of this time, not only helped the Chartists with advice and information but learnt from them: the experiences of the struggle for the Charter had a big share in the formation of the doctrines of scientific socialism.[118]

Booth and Marx were both to bring an appreciation of O'Connor and of the demands of Chartism to their response to the London residuum.

John Wesley

The pawnbroker's apprentice was not only brought face to face with poverty and politics in Nottingham, he also met religion; in particular Christianity as preached by John Wesley (1703-1791). John Wesley was a leading figure in the evangelical revival of the eighteenth century that was still influencing the life of the church in the nineteenth century. He was also very influential on William Booth, who once said:

> I worshipped everything that bore the name of Methodist. To me there was one God, and John Wesley was His prophet. I had devoured the story of his life. No human composition seemed to me comparable to his writings, and to the hymns of his brother Charles; and all that was wanted in my estimation for the salvation of the world was the faithful carrying into practice the letter and spirit of his instructions.[119]

John Wesley discovered his vocation as an evangelist when he was preaching in the open air[120] and was later to defend his right to preach anywhere as having being granted in his Anglican ordination. He considered that in practising this form of preaching he followed in a long line of itinerant preachers in Church history.[121] All through his life Wesley remained a member of the Anglican Church and always expressed the hope that the Methodists would not secede from the Church of England. He saw them as a group fulfilling a specific function within the church - taking the Christian gospel to those who would not enter church buildings to hear it, and building up the faith of Christians by means of class meetings. Several commentators see Wesley's success as springing more from his ability to organise the Methodist groups by such means as these classes than from his effectiveness as a preacher, for example E. P. Thompson:

> As preachers and evangelists, Whitefield and other early field-preachers were more impressive than Wesley. But it was Wesley who was the superlatively energetic and

---

118 Morton & Tate, 1956, p. 58.
119 Quoted in Guy, 1994, p. 3.
120 Outler, 1991, pp. 14-5.
121 Outler, 1991, pp. 25-6.

skilful organizer, administrator and law-giver. He succeeded in combining in exactly
the right proportions democracy and discipline, doctrine and emotionalism.[122]

However, Wesley also made a strong contribution to theological thought. He
brought his Oxford education with its classics emphasis, together with his
knowledge of Scripture and theological history, to bear when writing the sermons
that were to provide the basis of Methodist doctrine. There were two main strands
in Wesley's doctrine - justification and sanctification, evangelical faith and the
ideal of holy living. Both of these were to be central in Salvation Army doctrine.

For some of Wesley's critics there was a tension between these two strands
However, for Wesley, this criticism was answered by his 'order of salvation', in
which the stages are:

(1) Prevenient grace - the work of the Holy Spirit in giving an awareness of sin;
(2) Repentance before justification - including the move from simply a
conviction of sin to faith in the power of God to forgive those sins;
(3) Justification and new birth. Justification is the righteousness of Christ
imputed to the believer, the forgiveness of sins by the sufficient merits of
Christ's sacrifice. New birth is righteousness imparted to the believer by the
Spirit's work of regeneration. In Wesley's theology justification and new
birth are bestowed simultaneously.
(4) Repentance after justification leading to growth and ultimately
sanctification. Wesley taught that there is a growing awareness of sin after
conversion. Though justified, an individual is still liable to sin but the
renewing work of God can transform that person. The possibility of entire
sanctification (freedom from all voluntary sin) was preached by Wesley as
attainable but he never claimed to have attained it himself.[123]

The main sources of Wesley's theology were Puritan but he differed from the
Calvinists on two main points. Firstly, the Calvinists preached the doctrine of
election and Wesley was unable to subscribe to this. The idea of an elect
predestined to be saved implied that those outside the elect had no hope of
salvation. In Wesley's view the doctrine of election negated the idea of God's love
for humanity as a Father and made him instead a tyrant: 'it made [God] invite the
weary and heavy-laden to come unto him, while knowing they could not come.'[124]

It was Wesley's supreme belief in the universality of God's love and of the
offer of salvation which gave the impetus and urgency to all his evangelical work
and that of all those who would follow his lead. Wesley's rejection of the doctrine
of election and his insistence on salvation being available for all led to him being
labelled Arminian by the Calvinists although Albert Outler, in his study of
Wesley's sermons, casts doubt on whether Wesley developed his theology directly
from reading Arminius.[125]

---

122 Thompson, 1991, p. 41.
123 Outler, 1991, p. 88.
124 Ayling, 1979, p. 174.
125 Outler, 1991, p. 45. Arminius rejected the doctrine of predestination, believing that

A connected doctrine of Calvinism, also rejected by Wesley, was that conversion once achieved was for ever. Wesley believed that good works followed faith and that if a justified person did not do the good that he should then it was still possible for him to lose the grace he had received and perish eternally. He saw in the Calvinist belief a danger of Antinomianism - that the elect believed themselves totally immune from God's wrath and thus able to break the moral laws with impunity.[126]

Unlike William Booth, John Wesley is remembered almost entirely as an evangelist and, until recently, very little attention has been paid to his social ethics. Perhaps this is partly because the organisation he founded did not 'institutionalise' his social ideas. Wesley saw himself as called specifically to preach to the poor. He wrote in his journal on Saturday 17 November, 1759, (London):

> I spent an hour agreeably and profitably with Lady G.H. and Sir C.H. It is well a few of the rich and noble are called. O that God would increase their number! But I should rejoice (were it the will of God) if it were done by the ministry of others. If I might choose, I should still (as I have done hitherto) preach the gospel to the poor.[127]

Giving to the poor was one of the good works that should follow justification and Wesley organised his Methodist societies accordingly to work for relief of poverty and to visit the sick.[128] He considered that 'ethical passivity and justifying grace are mutually exclusive.'[129] In addition to any work actually done, and Wesley's own belief in his vocation to the poor, there were in his theology and organisation two things that fundamentally affected the manner in which the poor were treated.

Firstly, because of his belief that salvation was available to all, it followed that the poor had souls for which Christ had died and this gave them great value. This meant that, in giving aid to the poor, Methodists should remember the value given to the poor by the death of Christ and treat them accordingly. Acting upon such a belief would reduce any sense of patronage in the giving of Methodists.[130]

Secondly, the Methodist classes were open to all members, whatever their rank in society. Within these classes there was equality and a sense of communal solidarity, the effect of which could lead to the breaking down of social class and wealth barriers.

There is disagreement among historians about the effect on England of the Evangelical Revival of the eighteenth century and John Wesley's Methodism in particular. Halevy virtually credits the Methodist movement with preventing a revolution:

Christ had died to redeem the sins of all, not simply to guarantee the predestined place in heaven of an 'elect' minority.
126 Ayling, 1979, p. 126.
127 Wesley, 1993, p. 172.
128 Ayling, 1979, p. 126.
129 Marquardt, 1992, p. 101.
130 Marquardt, 1992, p. 101.

> Why was it that of all the countries of Europe, England has been the most free from revolution, violent crises and sudden changes? We have sought in vain to find the explanation by an analysis of her political institutions and economic organisation.... But the elite of the working class, the hard working and capable bourgeois, had been imbued by the Evangelical movement with a spirit from which the established order had nothing to fear.[131]

K. S. Inglis, among others, challenges this assumption and claims that there were always large numbers of the working classes who never attended public worship in towns, and therefore the Evangelical movement's influence on the working classes was less than has been imputed to it.[132]

In the same way that O'Connor was the first major political influence upon him, Wesley was the first major theological influence on Booth. However there are also links between Wesley and Booth in terms of social involvement. No direct comparison can be drawn between their social work because of the revolution that had taken place in social conditions between their periods of activity. Wesley worked at a time before the polarisation of the classes in England, caused in part by the industrial revolution, and before the creation of the huge urban proletariat that was to be so influential on Booth's work.

Wesley became involved in personal charitable work when he was still a student at Oxford. Right from the start he saw acts of charity as part of the Christian life, not an optional extra. In this he was part of a tradition of helping the poor out of Christian piety but such care was aimed at individual sufferers and was carried out as much for the personal sanctification of the one who helped as for the benefit of the one in need, with the corollary that there was little chance of the causes of poverty being questioned or challenged.

Wesley did not look upon poverty as being self-incurred or as a stigma of divine punishment, in which attitude, Marquardt argues, he was well ahead of his times. According to Marquardt, Wesley helped to create the conditions and attitudes in which a serious effort to solve the problems of poverty and introduce social justice could be made.[133] Wesley saw poverty as caused more by illness, weakness or a surplus of labour rather than by the laziness of the workers. He sought to spread knowledge of these causes among those who condemned the poor, an attitude paralleled by Booth when he published the Darkest England scheme to inform people of the suffering of the poor and to explain what was too easily condemned.

Modern interpretations of the attitudes of Wesley and of Booth to the poor are very similar. Marquardt wrote of Wesley's philosophy:

> Sympathy and courtesy are owed even to the most utterly corrupt and depraved, the poor and the outcast, who should be loved for the sake of their Creator and redeemer. Their body and soul, their temporal and eternal happiness, are valued equally with others.[134]

---

131 Halevy, 1987, Vol. 1, p. 371.
132 Inglis, 1963, p. 2
133 Marquardt, 1992, pp. 30-2.
134 Marquardt, 1992, p. 33.

William Fishman has written of Booth: 'For William Booth, there was no undeserving poor: to be poor was, by definition, to be deserving.'[135]

Wesley used to preach about the needs of the poor and any money raised from such preaching would be used to buy essential foodstuffs for the needy. Wesley also introduced two further schemes: a loan fund and a system for finding jobs for the unemployed. Wesley was ahead of his time in recognising unemployment as one of the chief causes of poverty.[136] When it often proved impossible to find work he arranged work projects, such as twelve persons engaged in processing cotton in the London meetinghouse one winter.[137] In the following century, Booth included a people's bank and a labour bureau in his Darkest England scheme.

Wesley was conservative in his politics and did not seek political change in any way. Like Booth in his earlier years as a preacher, he saw the best way of improving people's material situation as being the offer of salvation. In a passage that foreshadows the reports of dramatic conversions in the early *Christian Mission Magazine*, Wesley wrote about the social changes brought about by conversion:

> The drunkard became sober and moderate; the whoremonger abstained from adultery and fornication; the unjust from oppression and wrong ... The sluggard began to work with his hands that he might eat his own bread. The miser learnt to deal his bread to the hungry and to cover the naked with a garment. [138]

Wesley's own three rules concerning the economic responsibility of the individual were: 'Gain all you can; save all you can; give all you can.'[139]

In practise the Methodists were upwardly mobile because of their diligence and thriftiness. In addition, the sense of fellowship within Methodism gave its members a sense of self-worth which 'laid the groundwork for an otherwise inconceivable social ascent'.[140] Wesley was concerned about the effect of wealth on the Methodists and explained what had happened as being due to their obeying the first two rules and forgetting the third. Marquardt wrote that it is a fundamental falsification of Methodist ethics to divide them in this way, to divorce the 'striving for economic success from ethical obligation.'

The idea of social responsibility for both Booth and Wesley grew out of their firm belief that good works would always follow true conversion, which was a behaviour-changing experience. David Guy has pointed out that for both of them there is in the accounts of their own conversions an immediate ethical result.[141] In his journal Wesley described his conversion as follows:

---

135 Fishman, 1988, p. 83.
136 Marquardt, 1992, p. 29.
137 Marquardt, 1992, p. 29.
138 Marquardt, 1992, p. 120.
139 Marquardt, 1992, p. 35.
140 Marquardt, 1992, p. 34.
141 Guy, 1994, p. 61.

> I felt my heart strangely warmed. I felt I did trust in Christ, Christ alone for my salvation; and an assurance was given me that he had taken away my sins, even mine and saved me from the law of sin and death. I began to pray with all my might for those who had in a more especial manner despitefully used me and persecuted me.[142]

Booth was to use these words to describe his conversion to Christianity:

> I remember, as if it were but yesterday, the spot in the corner of the room under the chapel, the hour, the resolution to end the matter, the rising up and rushing forth, the finding of the young fellow I had chiefly wronged, the acknowledgement of my sin, the return of the pencil case, the instant rolling away from my heart of the guilty burden, the peace that came in its place.[143]

Wesley founded a denomination for the poor, and Robert Colls, in a study of Primitive Methodism, has argued that despite being an autocrat Wesley was forced to shift his stance by the pressure of the views of all those who had joined the Methodists. There was not a one-way traffic from Wesley to his followers but by their input the organisation became more suited to the needs of the working class and thereby more 'owned' by them:

> In the heated moment of revival, and in the cold tempering of the human personality through the organisation thereafter, a reactive exchange took place. The historical result was an intermittent fusion between that which grew to be called 'Methodism', and the needs and culture of the poor.[144]

By the time Booth joined their church in Nottingham in the 1840s, the Methodists had become more middle-class and, while there was still a wide social mix with no social barriers within each Methodist society, it very often happened that there was a middle-class elite that provided most of the money and leadership.[145] That such a social shift could be perceived among the Methodists can be seen in George Eliot's novel, *Adam Bede*, written in 1859:

> I cannot pretend that Seth and Dinah were anything else than Methodists - not indeed of that modern type which reads quarterly reviews and attends in chapels with pillared porticoes; but of a very old-fashioned kind. They believed in present miracles, in instantaneous conversions, in revelations by dreams and visions; they drew lots, and sought for Divine guidance by opening the Bible at hazard, having a literal way of interpreting the Scriptures, which is not at all sanctioned by approved commentators; and it is impossible for me to represent their diction as correct, or their instruction as liberal.[146]

---

142 Wesley, 1993, p. 56.
143 Begbie, 1920, Vol. I, p. 54.
144 Colls, Robert, 'Primitive Methodists in the northern coalfields' in Olbelkevich et. al., 1987, pp. 327-8.
145 Helmstadter, R. J. 'The Nonconformist Conscience' in edited Parsons, 1988, Vol. IV, p. 77.
146 Eliot, 1994, p. 29.

Wesley had been aware during his lifetime of the tendency of the Methodist lifestyle to move people from lower to middle class and had warned of the especial dangers to the Methodist spirit of a middle-class lifestyle:

> The Methodists grow more and more self-indulgent, because they grow rich ... And it is an observation which admits of few exceptions, that nine in ten of these decreased in grace in the same proportion as they increased in wealth. Indeed, according to the natural tendency of riches, we cannot expect it to be otherwise. [147]

However, Booth saw himself as returning to the original precepts that Wesley had introduced when he began work among the poor of the eighteenth century.

Chartism and Methodism in Nottingham

Booth imbibed influences of both Chartism and Methodism that were to significantly affect the kind of person he became and the form of organisation he eventually founded. Nottingham was the ideal place for him to assimilate these two influences.

As already shown, Nottingham played a crucial role in the development of early nineteenth century radicalism and of Chartism. Thompson argued that there was a continuity of political and cultural traditions in working-class communities that was deeper and more far-reaching than a reaction to the opening of factories. 'From 1817 onwards to Chartism, the outworkers in the north and the Midlands were as prominent in every radical agitation as the factory hands.'[148] It was the diminution of work available to each individual outworker, such as the stockingers, that led to their political radicalisation.

The contemporary suffering of the stockingers in Booth's youth was allied to a communally remembered history of Luddite resistance that was in Thompson's words 'far from primitive' but showed discipline and self-restraint that indicated the existence of 'a working-class culture of greater independence and complexity than any known to the eighteenth century.'[149]

This working class culture was 'opaque' to outsiders who sought to investigate it, but Booth, working as a pawnbroker's apprentice in Nottingham, would have been a participant and it may well have helped him to understand better the complexities of that other opaque culture, in the East End of London, later in his life.

There are clear indications that Methodism within Nottingham may have been less passive than the denomination is usually portrayed. Thompson has argued that much of Methodism, with its emphasis on the after-life, was thereby counter-revolutionary in its impact, and that any emotions and energies of its members that might otherwise have been dangerous to social order were 'released in the harmless

---

147 Marquardt, 1992, p. 39.
148 Thompson, 1991, p. 211.
149 Thompson, 1991, p. 658.

form of sporadic love-feasts, watch-nights, band-meetings or revivalist campaigns.'[150]

However Nottingham was prominent in its support for two breakaway Methodist societies. Firstly there was the Methodist New Connexion, founded by Alexander Kilham in 1797, in which Booth was later to become a minister. Several members of the New Connexion were prominent Chartists, including Ben Rushton, a weaver-preacher whose preaching injected a moral fervour into the Chartist movement and whose listeners and co-workers did not support Moral Force Chartism. 'On the contrary, they served a God of Battles whom the men of the New Model Army would have understood.'[151]

Nottingham was also an important centre for the early Primitive Methodists, the only denomination openly to support the Chartists. In 1816-1817:

> [T]he Primitive Methodists broke through into the framework-knitters of Nottinghamshire, Derbyshire and Leicestershire, and the relationship between revivalism and political radicalism appears to have been especially close.[152]

In contradistinction to the usual argument for Methodism causing a counter-revolutionary attitude the impact of the Primitive Methodists among the frame-work knitters in Nottinghamshire appears to have been a synergy between religious and political belief so that:

> [T]he Methodist political rebel carried through into his radical or revolutionary activity a profound moral earnestness, a sense of righteousness and of 'calling', a 'Methodist' capacity for sustained organizational dedication and (at its best) a high degree of personal responsibility.[153]

Booth was therefore far from alone in the combination of Methodist and Chartist influences, and in Nottingham he had the opportunity to absorb the history and the contemporaneity of these two major forces in working-class culture.

Not all Nottingham Methodists, however, embraced Chartism. Many followed the route of social ascent and Booth met this increased sense of 'respectability' among the Methodists soon after his conversion, when he took into the Wesley Chapel a group of young lads from the slums and sat with them in the 'best' pews. This early adventure in evangelism was not greeted with unrestrained delight by the other members of the congregation and he was told that in future these people could only be brought in by the back door and must sit in 'obscure benches reserved particularly for the impecunious and shabby.'[154] It was the first of many occasions when he would seek to bring the 'roughs' to hear the gospel and so would offend the 'respectable'.

---

150 Thompson, 1991, p. 419, p. 405.
151 Thompson, 1991, p. 440.
152 Thompson, 1991, p. 428.
153 Thompson, 1991, p. 433.
154 Begbie, 1920, Vol. I, p. 71.

The Old Woman of Nottingham

There was another event in William Booth's life soon after his conversion to which hindsight can add extra relevance. It concerned a poor woman, well known around Nottingham, who used to beg in the streets and sleep in doorways and under hedges. The fact that she was well known makes it almost certain that Booth knew of her before his conversion. At that time Booth was greatly attracted to the Chartist cause, but that commitment had not led to any practical offer of help to the woman begging in the streets. It was only after Booth's conversion that he sought to help her. This he did by collecting money among his friends, furnishing a small cabin, installing the woman in it and supplying her with provisions.[155]

Many arguments and theories have been raised about Booth's motivation in involving the Salvation Army in social work. Two of them would seem to be refuted by this event. The first argument is that Booth's concern for the poor was a direct result of his personal experience of poverty and his attraction to Chartism and is therefore coincidental to his Christianity. This story of the old woman suggests quite the opposite, that prior to his conversion he was able to see poverty without feeling the impulse to become personally involved in its alleviation. It was his conversion that led to a sense of personal responsibility to address an individual's material need. This accords with Booth's theological stand on conversion as a life- and behaviour-changing experience with ethical consequences.

The other, more prevalent, argument is that Booth turned to social activity only to bolster his organisation's falling numbers. Put bluntly, because he was not as successful as he wanted as an evangelist he decided to add a second string to his bow. This story shows that long before Booth became a full-time minister and founded an organisation, when he had no advantage to gain in terms of numbers or 'success', he cared enough about the poor to go to considerable personal effort to meet the material need of a vagrant woman.

Conclusion

By 1849, when Booth left Nottingham to travel to London, the impact upon him of the poverty he had seen, together with that of Chartism and Methodism, had worked to create strands of thought that were to be present throughout his work. They were the elements that he was to bring to his own 'reactive exchange' with the London residuum. Important as the residuum was in the exchange, the person Booth had already become was equally important.

Booth had gained a knowledge of poverty and its effects from his own family's situation and from what he saw around him in his work at the pawnbroker's shop. He had been a victim himself as well as seeing at close hand some of the worst victims of poverty, the stockingers. Yet his experience of Nottingham Chartism led him to appreciate that the poor were not necessarily

---

155 Begbie, 1920, Vol. I, p. 60.

passive victims, and to see their suffering as something that was not inevitable but preventable. His attitude to poverty was influenced not only by these experiences but also by the teaching of Wesley, with his emphasis on the value given to each member of the underclass by the death of Jesus.

The poor boys whom Booth took to church and the needy woman he tried to help presage the two foci of his life and of the denomination he was to found. For Booth the Salvation Army became a movement that was raised up by God to offer personal and social salvation to 'the people'. For the achievement of these aims he pragmatically adopted and discarded programmes and methods at will.

Chapter 3

The Reverend William

Introduction

William Booth came to London to look for work, as once his apprenticeship was completed he was unable to find employment in Nottingham. Some years later, some autobiographical notes prepared by Booth had the one word, loneliness, under the title, 'London'. Writing in greater detail, Booth was later to emphasise the importance of the scale of population to a newcomer to London:

> The sensations of a newcomer to London from the country are always somewhat disagreeable, if he comes to work. The immensity of the city must especially strike him as he crosses it for the first time and passes through its different areas. The general turn-out into a few great thoroughfares, on Saturday nights especially, gives a sensation of enormous bulk. The manifest poverty of so many in the most populous streets must appeal to any heart...The crowding pressure and activity of so many must always oppress one not accustomed to it.[1]

Finding work as a pawnbroker in London he saw, at first hand, the lives of those who formed the underclass. He had seen the depth of poverty in Nottingham. Now he saw the size and scope of London poverty. There he met the class referred to as the 'residuum', a word that spoke of society's view of them as the 'left-over'. This group was comprised of those who were outside the industrial advance and were either unemployed or rarely employed.

> Pitted against the dominant climate of moral and material improvement...was a minority of the still unregenerate poor: those who had turned their backs on progress or been rejected by it. This group was variously referred to as 'the dangerous class', the casual poor or most characteristically, as 'the residuum'.[2]

The Size of the London Residuum

In the 1850s and 1860s, the people who made up the residuum had a political, an economic and a social significance. Their political significance lay in the need of the upper and middle classes to ensure that the residuum remained outside the scope of any electoral reform proposals:

---

1 Begbie, 1920, Vol. I, pp. 99-101.
2 Stedman Jones, 1992, p. 11.

The question was to decide where lay the point which divided the population whose enfranchisement was a negotiable issue - on the grounds of their now being capable of enlightened individualism - from the unenfranchisable 'residue' still in a condition of degradation ... There was general agreement in the ranks of the Reform league as much as in the House of Commons about excluding the unworthy 'residuum'. The problem was in drawing the line.[3]

The residuum did not have real political power, they were not well organised enough. However they were large enough in number to pose a potential threat to social stability and therefore have a political relevance.[4]

Harrison has argued that it was the fact that the unemployed were so numerous and such a relatively constant group that they had to be classified as a separate category of the poor.[5] Their separateness was emphasised by the spatial segregation of the classes in the towns and especially London.[6] A contemporary report saw the segregation as leading to a lack of knowledge of one class about the other:

Owing to the vastness of London - owing to the moral gulf which there separates the various classes of its inhabitants - its several quarters may be designated as assemblages of towns, rather than as one city; ... the rich know nothing of the poor; - the mass of misery that festers beneath the affluence of London ... is not known to (its) wealthy occupants.[7]

However Hobsbawm has argued that the rich *chose* not to see or to know the poverty and suffering around them:

The period which culminated about the middle of the century was therefore one of unexampled callousness, not merely because the poverty which surrounded middle class respectability was so shocking that the native rich learned not to see it, leaving its horrors to make their full impact only on visiting foreigners, but because the poor, like the outer barbarians, were talked of as though they were not properly human at all.[8]

There was a sense of there being too many poor to encompass within the system and part of the callousness came from a desire to let economic imperatives take their course and reduce the size of the residuum: 'There were ... too many poor for their own good, but it was to be hoped that the operations of Malthus' law would starve off enough of them to establish a viable maximum.'[9]

The desire to hide the truth of their own significance from the poor, for fear that, in knowing their own numbers, they would understand their power, was to

3 Shannon, 1976, pp. 27, 60.
4 Hobsbawm, 1991, p. 35.
5 Harrison, 1988, p. 57.
6 Morris & Rodger, 1993, p. 119.
7 Morris & Rodger, 1993, p. 120.
8 Hobsbawm, 1995(a), p. 242.
9 Hobsbawm, 1995(a), p. 242.

endure throughout the century. In the 1890s a similar fear of the size of the poor, and therefore their economic and social significance, made employers suspicious of sharing the details of their employees' finances with social investigators. One employer replied to an investigator:

> Do not those statistics tend to foster discontent among the poor, and instead of directing them to exercise the discipline, industry and thrift by which their condition might be bettered, rather suggest that while such multitudes are poor, and so few are rich, the many might plunder the rich?[10]

Harrison described the increase in the population of Britain as crucial 'in determining what sort of lives they are likely to be living.' He suggested that the number of people was one of the most determinate variables in the quality of life of its citizens which 'sets the bounds for the potentialities and limits of human achievement.'[11] If such was true of the size of a national population, it was doubly so for the numbers of people in the relatively small area of London.

Lewis Mumford, in his study of the city in history, pinpointed the size of all large cities as the crucial element that negatively affects the lives of those who dwell in them: 'It was the change of scale, the unrestricted massing of populations and industries that reproduced some of the most horrendous urban effects.'[12] However, Asa Briggs, concentrating on the Victorian city in particular, saw some positive effects in that the sheer numbers concentrated in cities drew attention to failings and abuses that had been ignored when on a smaller scale.[13] There was a submerged population in the countryside as well as the towns and cities, who suffered irregular employment and poor housing, but they were too few in number in any one place to have an impact.[14] The perception of many of the social problems changed when they affected more people and the quantity of people did change the quality of the problem. For example in respect of epidemics:

> It is true that conditions in rural villages or weaving hamlets may have been quite as bad as conditions in Preston or Leeds. But the size of the problem was certainly worse in the great towns, and the multiplication of bad conditions facilitated the spread of epidemics.[15]

The size of London was remarkable, its population twice that of Paris, its nearest rival. One of the first to write about the qualitative impact of this size was the journalist C. F. G. Masterman, who wrote in the years around the turn of the nineteenth century. Keating wrote of Masterman having the 'awareness that for democracy one of the critical factors in coming to terms with any social problem was to be the "numbers" involved.'[16]

---

10 O'Day & Englander, 1993, p. 120.
11 Harrison, 1988, p. 15.
12 Mumford, 1974, p.519.
13 Briggs, 1990, p. 71.
14 Waller, 1991, p. 199.
15 Thompson, 1991, p. 352.
16 Keating, 1978, p. 29.

Masterman wrote as if he was one of the poor of London and there are two quotations from his works that describe the impact of quantity on quality for the underclass of London:

> We had thought that a city of four millions of people was merely a collection of one hundred cities of forty thousand. We find it differing not only in degree, but in kind, producing a mammoth of gigantic and unknown possibility. Hitherto it has failed to realise its power. How long before, in a fit of ill-temper, it suddenly realises its tremendous, unconquerable might?[17]

> There is so much of us, and that quantity so continually increases. That is our misfortune that is costing us more than all our crime ... This then is the first thing to note of us, not our virtues or vices, beauty, apathy or knowledge; but our overwhelming, inconceivable number - number continually increasing, multiplying without a pause, coming not with observation, choking up the streets of the great city, and silently flowing over the dismal wastes beyond.[18]

As Masterman's words suggest, the question of size and numbers became particularly an issue in relation to the poor in the cities and the most acute case was the slums of the East End, which were to be a focus of political and social attention throughout the second half of the century and, for most people, the first thing noted was indeed the 'overwhelming, inconceivable number.'

The impression many people received of the poor in any city was also of overwhelming numbers, of an 'aggregate of masses' which by its size was viewed as something 'portentous and fearful.'[19] With this concept of 'masses', came a danger that was illuminated by a Leeds clergyman as early as the 1840s: 'Our judgements are distorted by the phrase. We unconsciously glide into a prejudice. We have gained a total without thinking of the parts.'[20] Here was the issue that would confront all those who faced the problem of poverty and its possible alleviation: the individual in the mass.

Jack London wrote of its effect on him in 1903:

> [A]s far as I could see were the solid walls of brick, the slimy pavements, and the screaming streets; and for the first time in my life the fear of the crowd smote me. It was like the fear of the sea; and the miserable multitudes, street upon street, seemed so many waves of a vast and malodorous sea, lapping about me and threatening to well up and over me.[21]

John Henry Newman also described the city as resembling a sea, because of the inability of any individual to really have an impact on its 'population of human beings, so vast that each is solitary, so various that each is independent, which, like

---

17 Masterman, *From the Abyss,* in Keating, 1978, p. 244.
18 Masterman, *From the Abyss,* in Keating, 1978, p. 244.
19 Briggs, 1990, p. 61, quoting William Cooke Taylor.
20 Quoted in Briggs, 1990, p. 62.
21 London, *People of the Abyss*, in Keating, 1978, p. 226.

the ocean, yields before and closes over every attempt made to influence and impress it.'[22]

One of the main points of contact between the residuum and the upper and middle classes was in the giving of charity but Peter Mandler, in his study of charitable giving in Victorian times, has argued that the size of the residuum had an impact even on the kind of charity that was offered. There were too many who were poor to make it feasible to offer cash and material help to everyone. Such a policy would have a negative effect on such vast numbers as could be found in the slums of a city, even if it were a viable option. Therefore the visits from charity workers to the slums became largely 'educational and hortatory'.[23]

If the numbers dwelling in slums called forth contradictory or ambiguous responses from those outside looking in, they also created contradictory responses from those who lived there, the crowds offering both liveliness and loneliness. There seemed to be abundant evidence from the numbers making their way to the city of the theory that 'the force of attraction in human groups, like that of matter, is in general proportionate to the mass.'[24]

In contradistinction, there is the fact that the increase in numbers in a community changes the nature of social relationships. Above a few hundred it becomes impossible to know each member of a community and, in a large city, each individual will know a smaller proportion of the inhabitants. His knowledge of those he does know will be more specialised and narrower. His relationships to them will often be more compartmentalised. There is not necessarily any relation between an individual's divergent social groups, rather they are tangential to each other and do not intersect in any stable fashion. Louis Wirth wrote that such a series of secondary contacts is more easily reduced to a purely cash nexus.[25]

Public Opinion of Poverty

The early 1850s were a time of confidence among the English ruling classes. Prince Albert in a speech in 1850 said:

> Nobody, however, who has paid any attention to the peculiar features of our present era, will doubt for a moment that we are living at a period of most wonderful transition, which tends rapidly to accomplish that great end, to which, indeed, all history points - the realization of the unity of mankind.[26]

At the same time Macaulay wrote in his diary: 'There is just as much chance of a revolution in England as of the falling of the moon.'[27] However Stedman Jones

---

22 Ker, 1990, p. 343.
23 Mandler, 1990, p. 13.
24 Briggs, 1990, p. 60.
25 Wirth, 1964, pp. 70-81.
26 Speech in 1850 at Mansion House Banquet, printed in Golby, 1992, p. 1.
27 Thomas Babington Macaulay's diary (1 May 1851) printed in Golby, 1992, p. 3.

argued that in the early 1850s and towards the end of the 1860s there were periods of anxiety about the conditions of the London working class. *Punch* in 1844 had underlined the paradox between attitudes to poverty in London and poverty in Africa:

> [J]ust as connoisseurs take a backward step truly to consider the beauties of a picture, so do many good folks require distance to see the miseries of human nature through an attractive medium. They have no taste for the destitution of the alley that abuts their dwelling place, but how they glow - how they kindle at the misery somewhere in Africa.[28]

Some of the distinction may have come from a continuing fear of the poor of London. Miall made a similar remark about the attitude of the churches in 1849: 'We carry our class distinctions into the house of God....We have no negro pews, for we have no prejudice against colour - but we have distinct places for the pennyless, for we have a morbid horror of poverty.'[29]

In one sense these quotations suggest that attitudes to poverty remain the same as they were earlier in the century, but there was a suggestion of change in that irony was being used to draw attention to prejudice, so that at least some were recognising the prejudice for what it was. This moved on still further forward by 1865 when Ford Madox Brown explained his painting, *Work*:

> Past the pastry-cook's tray come two married ladies. The elder and more serious of the two devotes her energies to tract distributing, and has just flung one entitled, 'The Holman's Haven, or drink for thirsty souls', to the somewhat unpromising specimen of navvy humanity descending the ladder: he scorns it but with good nature. This well intentioned lady has, perhaps, never reflected that excavators may have notions to the effect that ladies might be benefited by receiving tracts containing navvies' ideas! nor yet that excavators are skilled workmen, shrewd thinkers chiefly, and, in general, men of great experience in life, as life presents itself to them.[30]

By the late 1860s there were the signs that those who were thinking deeply about the issues of poverty, and how to tackle them, were questioning previous assumptions. Much of the dynamic and impetus for this questioning had come from the changes in religious belief that had been occurring during the same period.

Changes in Religious Belief

During Booth's early years in London, and before he began his work in the East End, there were significant changes in the religious and philosophical climate of the day. Booth began his ministry with evangelical certainties, but he worked in an

---

28 *Punch* (1844), vol. vi, p.210 quoted in Bradley, 1976, p. 79.
29 Golby, 1992, p. 33.
30 Golby, 1992, p. 115.

era when people were beginning to feel less certain of beliefs and theories that had been dominant for decades, sometimes centuries.

During the nineteenth century much that had previously been accepted as true was brought into question and new ideas about the world and morality were being discussed publicly. Chadwick described three main influences, of natural science, historical criticism and moral feeling that were causing the churches to reassess their doctrines:

> Natural sciences shattered assumptions about Genesis and about miracles. Criticism questioned whether all history in the Bible was true. Moral feeling found the love of God hard to reconcile with hellfire or scapegoat-atonement.[31]

Natural Science

Although Darwin's *The Origin of Species,* with its theory of natural selection, was not the only threat to Christian orthodoxy in the mid-nineteenth century it is probably the most well-known. Chadwick has taken the date and publication of the book, 1859, as marking a watershed, despite the growth of doubt being a continuum throughout the nineteenth century:

> Until that year [doubt] scarcely touched the national life, the assumptions of legislators, the convictions of moralists. We can study early Victorian England and its churches as though doubt was almost as rare and academic as a century before. After 1859 that is not possible.[32]

While Darwin's findings were bound to raise religious controversy and he resisted publishing them for some years from just this fear, the level of debate was raised and given a higher profile at the express initiation of T. H. Huxley.[33] In one sense it was Huxley's own character that insisted on viewing the issue as a 'war' between science and theology.[34]

To begin with, much of the opposition to Darwin came from other scientists who could not accept his thesis of natural selection. For many orthodox Christians their defensive position was that Darwin could not be correct because he contradicted the Bible. This kind of argument was to lead eventually to a split between physical science and theology, as scientists refused to be told what conclusions they could or could not reach based on the evidence of the natural world. In an important area of national life the Church, as an institution, was losing its power and influence.

Biblical Criticism

Darwin was not the only scientist with findings that contradicted established belief. Geologists in their studies of rocks and fossils were also undermining belief in the

---

31 Chadwick, 1992(a), p. 551.
32 Chadwick, 1992(a), p. 2.
33 Desmond, 1994, p. 269.
34 Desmond, 1994, p. xiii.

literal truth of the first chapters of Genesis, and orthodox Christians were reacting as if to refute one chapter of Genesis was to refute the whole Bible. But it was not only scientists who were creating this uncertainty. Biblical criticism was also playing its part. This had mainly originated in Germany and did not just question a few chapters in Genesis but sought to analyse the authorship, sources, motivation and accuracy of all biblical writings. Many of the results of such analysis were anathema to those who believed in the literal and direct divine inspiration of the Bible.[35]

The questions raised by Biblical criticism brought with them an attempt to look more closely at the life of Christ as a human biography. The new emphasis upon the humanity of Jesus was to have a far-reaching impact on the theology and social conscience of the Church. The first book to do this was one which extended Biblical criticism by investigating the sources for the four gospels and was entitled *Life of Jesus* by David Friedrich Strauss, a German theologian. The book was translated into English by George Eliot. The first similar book written in English was *Ecce Homo*, published anonymously in 1865, and later found to have been the work of J. R. Seeley.

Both natural science and biblical criticism articulated a changing background to the life of the church. They spoke of movement in what had previously been accepted by many as immutable. Neither of them were necessarily crucial issues to most of the population but they helped create or publicise a general climate that contained fewer certainties. In doing so, some of the barriers between religion and social issues were broken down; people felt able to accept some of the teachings of the church while feeling free to question others.

Those who rejected the rigidity of church doctrine were picking those elements of Christian teaching that could be interpreted in social and economic terms; the converse of what Booth would do when he picked out just those elements in social and economic theory which suited his evangelical aim.

Moral Feeling

However, much of the doubt and uncertainty was being raised within the Church rather than being caused by external criticisms. In this regard one of the most important events was the publication of *Essays and Reviews* in 1860. This was a collection of essays by six clergymen and one layman. Chadwick has condensed the main ideas contained in the book as follows:

> (1) A gap has opened between Christian doctrines and the real beliefs of educated men. It is time to seek reconciliation between Christianity and the modern man.
> (2) All truth is of God so do not be afraid of any sane investigation of the truth.
> (3) Do not tie the truth of Christianity to the maintenance of the exact truth of a detailed record of events. Parable, myth, legend, poetry all give religious truth, even if the event which the parable described did not happen.

---

35 Althloz, J.L. 'The Warfare of Conscience with Theology' in Parsons, 1988(d), p. 69.

(4) Do not prove the truth of revelation by the traditional method of citing miracles and prophecy. The truth of the revelation of God does not hang upon miracles, but the truth of miracles hangs upon the revelation of God.[36]

These continual questions, including the publication of a book by Bishop Colenso of Natal stating that the Pentateuch was unhistorical, then raised the issue of whether Church of England clergymen had the right to question orthodox Anglican beliefs and still remain clergymen. In other words, could clergymen also choose which elements in church doctrine they could accept and reject?

This all helped to increase the sense that old certainties were shifting and that along with political, social and technological changes the religious life of the nation was in a state of flux. There was a decline in orthodox religion but, at the same time, an increased emphasis on the socialising and humanising effect of religious belief and teaching.

While the old beliefs were being threatened and in some cases jettisoned it remained true that the whole question of religious beliefs and religious life remained important and central in a way that had not been true in the eighteenth century and would not be so in the twentieth. The discussions going on within the Church were still seen by those who had left it as having a crucial bearing on the wider social issues:

> The attitudes of these outsiders - who had left the church but who related to it from a stance of doubt - toward the question of belief was inevitably coloured by their perception of what the social effects of ecclesiastical developments might be.[37]

There was another element in the religious climate that gave the nineteenth century its flavour. As part of the influence of the evangelical spirit, there came into the churches a sense of striving to reach people with the gospel, and this tended to create an atmosphere of competition between some of the denominations and sects. There was already an increase in the number of sects. During the century there was an erosion of the constitutional barriers that had existed to the participation of denominations other than Anglican in public life and hence they gained a heightened confidence and profile. Gradually in an effort to reach those who were not Christian an increased aggressiveness could be seen in most denominations.[38] Even within denominations there was more than one view on matters of doctrine, liturgy and organisation. For example the Church of England had the Evangelicals, whom some accused of pulling the Church towards dissent, and the Oxford Movement, whom others accused of pulling the Church towards Roman Catholicism. Within the Methodists less than 50 years after the death of John Wesley there were the Methodist New Connexion, the Primitive Methodists and the Wesleyans.

---

36 Chadwick, 1987(b), p. 7.
37 Turner, F. M. and Von Arx, J.' Victorian Ethics of Belief: A Reconsideration' in Parsons, 1988(d), p. 210.
38 Chadwick, 1987(a), pp. 4-5.

This level of diversity led to a shift in the authority of the Church. There were fewer and fewer matters on which the churches spoke with one voice. Many would say that as long as they were agreed on fundamental doctrine that was sufficient. But once the Church no longer spoke unitedly on social matters, it tended to become marginalised in that part of national life.

Evangelicalism

While a state of flux spoke of freedom to some, it was seen as threatening by others. To those who were threatened the evangelicals, who retained the old doctrines, could be seen as a 'haven'. Despite the questions and doubts being articulated around it, the evangelical revival was successful in that more people were going to church as the century progressed. One result of this was that many Christians had the sense of being part of an upsurge in religion and the period from 1840 to 1890 was generally one of religious optimism. So much so that when statistics seemed to show that while actual figures for church attendance were increasing, the figures as a percentage of population were declining, this did not douse their optimism so much as act as a spur to greater endeavour.[39]

The term evangelicalism is one closely associated with this period and often used as one of the stereotypes of Victorian times. The word is sometimes used interchangeably with nonconformity but the evangelical revival in the mid-nineteenth century was also important in the Church of England and the importance of evangelicalism in defining the spirit of the Victorian age in many people's eyes was mostly due to the influence of evangelical Anglicans. The evangelicals were the spiritual heirs of the puritans and it was the impression they gave of sourness of spirit and opposition to amusement that called forth the most virulent criticism of them. The ideas of evangelicalism when carried to extremes and viewed from a distance can be made to look ridiculous, as this paragraph from Jeffrey Cox's book shows:

> The puritanical image was exacerbated by acrimonious debates within Nonconformity over the propriety of certain kinds of entertainment in the Chapel. The pastor of Chatsworth Road Baptist Church, Archibald Brown, continued to circulate his pamphlet called 'The Devil's Mission of Amusement', which had led to accusations in the liberal Nonconformist press that he was a kill-joy, a sour bigot, and a victim of religious melancholia. (*The Daily Telegraph* entered the debate by predicting future volumes entitled 'Is Seven Hours of Sleep Satanic?', 'The Sinfulness of a Country Walk' and 'Lawn Tennis a Short Cut to Perdition.')[40]

While their views lent themselves to parody the issues raised by evangelicalism were far too complex to be reduced in this way. Ian Bradley has entitled his book on evangelicals in the Church of England *The Call to Seriousness* and evangelicals of all denominations were very serious about their religion. Their

---

39 Chadwick, 1987(b), p. 219.
40 Cox, 1982, p. 86.

theology pointed to a personal responsibility to bring about the salvation of others and this led to activities and efforts for this end becoming extremely important and to an enhanced sense of duty. While there were critics of the achievements actually made by evangelicals and queries concerning their long-term value, there was little disagreement that evangelicals did work. Chadwick stated that even their most hostile enemies admitted that they worked, they set up charitable organisations and activities for home and abroad, increased the number of services and communions and sought to raise the standards of reverence in worship.[41]

Bradley argued that this emphasis on work and 'usefulness' sprang from a need to escape their consciences. Because of the emphasis on the depravity of man and the fear of the Day of Judgement, evangelicalism could become introspective and cause much self-examination and soul-searching. The intense activity of the evangelicals was a reaction to this.[42] G. M. Young, whose book *Portrait of an Age* is viewed by many as best capturing the spirit of the time, explained evangelicalism's power and its identification with early capitalism in the following way:

> [T]he powers of Evangelicalism as a directing force lay less in the hopes and terrors it inspired, than in its rigorous logic, 'the eternal microscope' with which it pursued its argument into the recesses of the heart, and the details of daily life, giving to every action its individual value in this life, and its infinite consequence in the next. Nor could it escape the notice of a converted man, whose calling brought him into frequent contact with the world, that the virtues of a Christian after the Evangelical model were easily exchangeable with the virtues of a successful merchant or a rising manufacturer ... To be serious, to redeem the time ... are virtues for which the reward is not laid up in heaven only ... An unguarded look, a word, a gesture, a picture, or a novel, might plant the seed of corruption in the most innocent heart, and the same word or gesture might betray a lingering affinity with the class below.[43]

The evangelicals believed that it was the responsibility of those who were saved to worry about the souls of those who were not. One by-product of this according to Inglis was a change in the view of the work and responsibilities of clergymen.[44] Charles Darwin's biographers describe how his father decided that Charles should become a Church of England parson, which is indicative of an earlier view:

> There was, however, a safety-net to stop second sons becoming wastrels: the Church of England. Dr Darwin, a confirmed freethinker, was sensible and shrewd. He had only to look around him, recall the vicarages he had visited, ponder the country parsons he had entertained at home. One did not have to be a believer to see that an aimless son with a penchant for field sports would fit in nicely. Was the Church not a haven for dullards and dawdlers, the last resort of spendthrifts? What calling but the

---

41 Chadwick, 1987(a), p. 443.
42 Bradley, 1976, pp. 23,25.
43 Young, 1986, p. 2.
44 Inglis, 1963, p. 8.

highest for those whose sense of calling was nil? And in what other profession were the risks of failure so low and the rewards so high?[45]

Other factors were at work in introducing the idea of the clergy as a profession but evangelicalism played its part. It also helped to spread the idea that members of the clergy could be 'called' to work in specific areas for reasons other than personal convenience, for example, the Anglican priests who were prepared to work in slum parishes. A related issue is raised by Chadwick when he wrote that the 'evangelicals perceived the contrast between the teeming masses of east London and the vacant empty spaces of St. Paul's.'[46]

Along with so much activity came a rigid code of duty that the evangelicals sought to apply not only to themselves but to impose on others through, for example, temperance movements and Sabbatarianism. Such efforts were partly responsible for their reputations as kill-joys but evangelicalism was not opposed to enjoyment in itself. It just found 'pleasure' a 'problem'.

There was some ambiguity in its position on entertainment and enjoyment. The increase in entertainment gradually becoming available to the public would be competition for the churches. For example, the introduction of the bicycle was seen as a real threat to attending church on a Sunday. As a result, many evangelical churches began to arrange entertainment either inside, or connected with, the church as a way of attracting people to it.[47]

Most historians of Victorian evangelicalism seem to be agreed that all this practical effort to take the gospel to the people was not matched by intellectual effort. Richard Helmstadter suggested that the emphasis laid on personal experience and feeling would necessarily lead towards practical rather than intellectual activity. In addition evangelical clergymen were being trained to preach an expository sermon that led to conversion rather than a teaching sermon to build up religious knowledge.[48] Edwards argued that one of the reasons for the apparent dearth of Victorian evangelical intellectuals is that theologically they were on the defensive against the onslaughts of Darwinism and biblical criticism.[49]

The opinions of two Victorian prime ministers show a similar view concerning the lack of intellectual content in evangelical theology. Salisbury wrote that evangelicalism:

> never made much way with the higher class of intellects. But it has stood its ground because it has always been popular with children, with women, and with half-educated men. The plumpness and almost juridical precision of its statements make it eminently suitable for minds that are too blunt for subtle distinctions, and both too ignorant and too impatient to be satisfied with half-truths.[50]

---

45 Desmond and Moore, 1992, p. 47.
46 Chadwick, 1987, p. 524.
47 Inglis, 1963, p. 79.
48 Helmstadter, R. J., 'The Nonconformist Conscience' in Parsons, 1988(d), p. 69.
49 Edwards, 1989, Vol. 3, p. 171.
50 Roberts, 1999, p. 25.

Gladstone wrote that '[t]he Evangelical movement did not ally itself with literature, art and general cultivation, but it harmonised well with the money-getting pursuits.'[51]

It was partly due to the theologically defensive attitude that much of the hold of evangelicalism began to weaken. There were still many evangelicals who continued to resist the claims concerning parts of the Bible being myth or folk-lore but, among those who had the most influence in national life and were the most vocal, there was less certainty.

There arose a questioning about some of the old beliefs about God consigning people to everlasting pain and torture. As people's sympathy for the physical suffering of the poor became more pronounced, so there was a corresponding sympathy for those who were to suffer eternal damnation.[52]

The uncertainty and questioning, in turn, pushed those who remained in the evangelical tradition into a more entrenched position. Bradley claims that after the threats to literalism became known the members of the Evangelical movement in the Church of England were more fanatical, more bigoted and more introverted.[53]

He also argues that as those outside their tradition called more and more beliefs into question and raised doubts and fears there was a measure of escapism in clinging to the moral absolutes of evangelicalism and that its rigid codes of duty and behaviour were reassuringly straightforward to people who felt threatened by the uncertainties being voiced by others.

Despite their emphasis on personal salvation there were evangelicals who worked hard for the material improvement of the poor. Among the leaders of those who actively championed the rights of the poor in the first half of the nineteenth century was Viscount Ashley, later the seventh Earl of Shaftesbury. He brought the condition of the poor to the notice of the public and thereby helped to shape public opinion. He was most noted for his work toward the Ten Hour Bill, shedding light on the long hours worked by factory workers, in particular by child labour.[54] His work on behalf of children working in factories and other causes he embraced was closely linked to his evangelical faith. By 1840 he was the leading evangelical layman in the country:

> Shaftesbury was the noblest philanthropist of the century. He promoted more good causes, and was therefore more cordially disliked, than any other politician of the Victorian age ... His stature was national; partly because working men knew that for all his aristocratic conservatism he was their friend, partly because his unbending consistency gained the rueful respect of gentlemen who saw more clearly the need to compromise, and partly because he spoke for evangelical religion in an age when evangelical religion seemed suddenly to be the most potent religious and moral force in England.[55]

---

51 Jenkins, 1995, p. 31.
52 Helmstadter, R. J. 'The Nonconformist Conscience' in Parsons, 1988(d), p. 83.
53 Bradley, 1976, p. 17.
54 Battiscombe, 1974, p. 85.
55 Chadwick, 1992(a), p. 454.

The above quotation underlines the certainty with which evangelicals held their faith and did their duty, with very little leeway for questions and compromise.

Part of Shaftesbury's motivation in his campaigns came from his evangelical faith. His biographer has described the link as follows:

> An eschatological awareness rather than a compassionate humanitarianism gave strength and urgency to Ashley's efforts on behalf of the poor, the oppressed and the outcast. The force which drove him was a compassionate concern for souls. He believed that factory children, chimney-sweeps and lunatics all had souls to be saved and that very little time remained in which to save them.[56]

There are two implications of such a view. While it is paternalistic and may lead to an attitude that is both condescending and patronising, it is not necessarily more so than viewing the poor as helpless victims of a system, and, when allied to the enthusiasm and search for usefulness that was also part of evangelicalism, was more likely to lead to some practical benefit. One certainty is that the efforts of the then Lord Ashley helped to keep the plight of the poor high on the political agenda and in the public consciousness for most of the period up to 1850.

The crucial link from evangelicalism to Booth's redemptive schema is that evangelicals believed not simply that 'factory children, chimney-sweeps and lunatics all had souls to be saved', but that *each* child, *each* chimney-sweep and *each* lunatic had a soul to save and very little time remained in which to save them.

The evangelical belief in the value of each soul, the offer of individual salvation through the Atonement, added to the urgency and, for Booth, would increase the emphasis on the micro-element in any social scheme.

Development of Booth's Theology

Finney and Caughey

Evangelicalism was prominent in the United States of America as well as Britain in the mid- nineteenth century. There were also evangelists from America who were to have an impact in Britain, and on William and Catherine Booth, at this time. The best known were Charles Finney and James Caughey. Finney's book, *Lectures on Revivals of Religion*, was part of Booth's chosen dinner-time reading when he was a teenage apprentice in Nottingham.[57] Finney was a Presbyterian, later to be described by Bramwell Booth, William's son, as a 'Presbyterian Salvationist',[58] who rejected the rigid Calvinism of the Presbyterians, including the doctrine of election. The Salvation Army in 1882 published his autobiography, of which the title page proclaimed: 'The inner and outer life of C. G. Finney, the Great Presbyterian Lawyer and Soul-Saver, who did not believe, as some foolishly

---

56 Battiscombe, 1974, p. 102.
57 Railton, 1912, p. 17.
58 Bramwell Booth, introduction in Finney, 1926.

teach, that some are doomed to go to Hell, whether they will or no, or forced to remain in sin whilst they are in the flesh, and who, consequently, got whole populations to repent and be saved.'[59]

In 1926 the Salvation Army published a summary of *Finney's Revival Lectures* (a fact which would seem to emphasise the extent of his enduring influence). Some of the influences on William Booth can be seen in these lectures. While it is not known when Booth first read Dickens or Carlyle, it is known that in his teenage years he was reading Finney's lectures, which Booth himself claimed to have had a powerful influence on him. It contained much that can be traced through to the principles and practices of the organisation that Booth would found. For example:

> A minister may be very learned, and yet not be wise to win souls... On the other hand, a minister may be wise to win souls without being learned. A learned minister and a wise one are two very different things. Churches commonly look out for a learned minister, without stopping to consider whether he is wise to win souls. If he lacks this wisdom he will fail. If he possesses it, the more learning he has the better.[60]

If ever William Booth read something that presaged his work in founding the Salvation Army it must surely have been what Finney wrote on measures to promote revivals:

> In the entire history of the Church, there has never been an extensive reformation except by new measures. When the church gets settled down in some *form* upon which it relies, only by new measures can it be aroused and awakened. It seems impossible for God Himself to arouse people except by new measures; in any case, He has *always* employed them as the best and wisest way of producing a Revival. And they have always met with strenuous opposition, because they were new, but have received His recognition and blessing.[61]

There is no record of Booth ever meeting Finney, but in 1846, in Nottingham, William heard James Caughey, another American revivalist, preach and was greatly impressed by both his methods and his words.[62] He was later to write of the impact on him of the way in which Caughey brought people to a point of making a decision about the Gospel. Booth realised that there were ways of putting forward the message that were more likely to lead to conversions.

Caughey preached in England for seven years between 1841 and 1848 and claimed that 22,000 people were converted under his ministry. He was an American Methodist and caused considerable disagreement among English Methodists about his methods, perhaps another foreshadowing of what was to happen to Booth. Some argued that Caughey had a wonderful gift for bringing people to make a decision about Christ while others claimed he used devices and

---

59 Finney, 1882, title page.
60 Finney, 1926, p. 48.
61 Finney, 1926, p. 37.
62 Rader, 1977, p. 76.

dodges, such as decoy penitents. The Methodist Conference of 1846 resolved to ask the American Methodists to recall him.[63] Nevertheless, as well as Caughey's influence on those who were converted through his ministry, he had also played his part in influencing the future direction that the Salvation Army of William Booth was to take.

In Kent's words, what Caughey and other American evangelists did was to 'demythologize' revivals so that 'it was possible to approach the task of starting a revival as rationally as one would tackle any other problem, and so to think out and apply methods of reaching that goal.' It was a shifting of emphasis from a revival as an 'occasional, spontaneous occurrence', a sign of God's presence in the world, to a revival which could be worked for and organised in advance, taking for granted that 'if enough prayer had been offered, God was bound to co-operate'.[64]

Paul Rader argued that the books of Finney, and the preaching of Caughey, were as influential on the methods of the Army as Wesleyanism was on its theology.[65] Certainly Booth's methods, so repugnant to much of respectable society, were not quite as unique as either his critics or admirers claimed, and his work, like Wesley's before him, was part of a much wider revival on both sides of the Atlantic.

On three further major issues William Booth reached views, during the period 1850 to 1865, that were to remain important to him for the rest of his life: Calvinism, women's ministry and holiness.

Calvinism

William Booth did not remain a pawnbroker's assistant in London for long. He began preaching on Sundays and was soon looking for ways in which he could devote himself full time to preaching. In 1852 there was a possibility of him training for the Congregational ministry. Congregational theology was based on Calvinism which included the doctrine of election, the belief that only those who had been predestined could be saved. Booth received a provisional acceptance at the Congregational Training College but was advised to seek to bring his doctrinal position more nearly into line with the college's own. Catherine Booth, in her autobiographical notes, explained the difficulty:

> We were both saturated, as it were, with the broadest, deepest, and highest opinions as to the extent of the Love of God and the benefit flowing from the sacrifice of Jesus Christ. We were verily extremists on this question. The idea of anything like the selection of one individual to enjoy the blessedness of the Divine favour for ever and ever, and the reprobation of another to suffer all the pains and penalties of everlasting damnation, irrespective of any choice, conduct, or character on their part, seemed to us to be an outrage on all that was fair and righteous, to say nothing about benevolent.[66]

---

63 Chadwick, 1987(a), p. 379.
64 Kent, 1978, pp. 16-22.
65 Rader, 1977, p. 74.
66 Begbie, 1920, Vol. I, p. 141.

However Booth was advised to read either Abraham Booth's *Reign of Grace* or George Payne's *Divine Sovereignty*. William Booth bought a copy of his namesake's book. According to his wife he managed to read between thirty and forty pages before throwing the book across the floor and thus closing the door on the Congregational ministry.

It was only in the second edition of his book, published in 1808, that Abraham Booth added the chapter on election. This chapter stretched from page 21 to page 85 and was without doubt the cause of William's impatience. It is not known which passage, if any one in particular, finally decided William but the three following passages all appear between pages 30 and 40:

But is there any reason assignable why the elect were chosen to life and glory, while others were left in their sins to perish under the stroke of divine justice? None, in the creature. For all mankind, considered in themselves, were viewed as in the same situation, and on a perfect level. Notwithstanding, the great author of all things, and the Lord of the world, condescends to assign the reason when he says: I will have mercy on whom I will have mercy.[67]

Whoever, then, acknowledges any such thing as an election of sinners to future happiness, must necessarily maintain, either, that the sole reason why they were chosen rather than others was their own future worthiness, without grace being concerned at all in the choice; and so their election is an act of remunerative justice; or that they were equally unworthy of the divine regard as any of those that perish; and so their election is an act of sovereign grace.[68]

Hence it appears with striking evidence, that it was Paul's design to prove, not only that some of our fallen race were chosen, in contradistinction to others; but also, that those objects of the divine choice were appointed to glory, not in consideration of any thing which caused them to differ from others; but purely, solely, and entirely, because it was the good pleasure of God to make them partakers of that mercy on which they had not the least claim, any more than those who perish.[69]

It is not difficult to see that exclusive limits on the offer of salvation could never be acceptable to a man who within a few years was to found an organisation with eleven articles of faith of which the sixth stated that: 'We believe that the Lord Jesus Christ has by His suffering and death made an atonement for the whole world so that whosoever will may be saved.'[70]

In rejecting Calvinism, Booth was aligning himself not only with Wesley but also with the main strand of evangelicalism, which followed the Arminian position that all men might be saved and thus accorded to individuals a heavier responsibility for seeking their own salvation, contrary to the Calvinist belief in divine predestination.[71]

---

67 Abraham Booth, 1808, p. 32.
68 Abraham Booth, 1808, p. 37.
69 Abraham Booth, 1808, p. 40.
70 The Salvation Army Act, 1980, Schedule 1.
71 Helmstadter, R.J., 'The Nonconformist Conscience' in Parsons, 1988(d), p. 67.

Thomas Huxley, a close collaborator of Charles Darwin, would be a vitriolic critic of Booth towards the end of the century. Nevertheless a parallel can be drawn in the impact of poverty upon each of them. Adrian Desmond, Huxley's biographer, has argued that Huxley's exclusion from the establishment in early life and the poverty he had known made him loath to agree to the implications of the theory of natural selection. He was unwilling to accept the 'utilitarian shadow of workhouse society ... Even as he championed evolution, he softened selection.'[72] There is a marked similarity between Huxley's youthful sight of poverty leading him to reject the harshness of natural selection and Booth's youthful knowledge of poverty playing its part in his rejection of the harsh doctrine of election. Certainly Booth's acceptance of the wideness of the Arminian doctrine of salvation was an important impetus in his work among the residuum of society.

Women's Ministry

A third American evangelist was to be influential on the Booths during the years between 1850 and 1870. Phoebe Palmer arrived in England after Caughey and Finney. She was preaching to English Methodists in 1859, at a time when William and Catherine were married and William was a minister of the Methodist New Connexion. She has been described as 'decorous and middle-class' and would preach from the nave rather than the pulpit, after her husband had first opened the service. In this way she sought to avoid giving offence.

Nevertheless she was attacked by a Congregational minister, Arthur Augustus Rees, in a tract entitled, *Reasons for Not Co-operating in the Alleged Sunderland Revivals*. It was to counter the arguments he had raised that Catherine Booth first went into print, with a tract called *Female Teaching* (which was to be revised in 1870 and thereafter called *Female Ministry*). According to Norman Murdoch, in his study of the origins of the early Salvation Army: 'Catherine's decision to preach and the Salvation Army's female ministry can be traced to Phoebe Palmer.'[73]

Yet it was not in any sense in imitation of Phoebe Palmer that Catherine began her own female ministry. As Pamela Walker emphasised in her doctoral thesis on the role of women in the Salvation Army, whereas Phoebe Palmer did not justify the right of women to preach per se but only their right to prophesy under the prompting of the Holy Spirit, Catherine argued that for women to preach was part of the natural order.

Nor did Catherine justify her preaching in the terms used by other women preachers, that they were 'the weak, the foolish or the low who would confound the wise. Catherine never described herself in such terms. Indeed she was well aware that she was more widely read and more articulate than most of her congregation.'[74]

---

72 Desmond, 1994, p. 271.
73 Murdoch, 1996, p. 17.
74 Walker, 1992, p. 45.

Nevertheless despite the fact that Catherine moved the argument on considerably there is little doubt that Phoebe Palmer's visit and her preaching were the catalyst for Catherine's preaching career. This would be an important strand in the development of the Salvation Army; in Murdoch's view one that was crucial to its growth. Unarguably it was pivotal to the form of its development.

Holiness

In addition, John Kent, in his history of Victorian revivalism, argued that Phoebe Palmer's teaching on holiness had a greater impact on both William and Catherine Booth than has generally been recognised; claiming that the language they use to describe the doctrine is borrowed directly from Palmer:

> When later writers have paid any attention to the Booths' holiness teaching they seem to have assumed that it was a personal embroidery of John Wesley's teaching; but in fact what the Booths adopted in 1861 was the revivalist holiness doctrine which Mrs Palmer brought with her from the United States.[75]

The church historian, David Englander, made an even stronger claim for Phoebe Palmer's influence, stating that her preaching provided William Booth with an 'off-the-peg doctrine of sanctification'.[76]

All these theological influences were assimilated by the Booths and were the doctrinal basis for their work as it began in the East End. The rejection of the doctrine of election, and thus the acceptance of the availability of salvation to everyone, carried with it the responsibility to tell as many people as possible of the offer of salvation and to seek to persuade them to accept it.

If the one who rejected the idea of election nevertheless retained a belief in Heaven and Hell, as William Booth did, then this added a dreadful sense of urgency to the task. The Salvation Army's eleventh doctrine states: 'We believe in the immortality of the soul; in the resurrection of the body; in the general judgement at the end of the world; in the eternal happiness of the righteous; and in the endless punishment of the wicked.'[77] It was such an urgency from his doctrinal stance that Booth brought to Whitechapel. The Salvation Army was forged in the interaction of Booth's theology and the poverty of the East End.

The East End

The East End and its poverty stood in stark contrast to the opulence of London's West End. In addition there was contrast within the East End itself, certainly in the way the life of its people was viewed and interpreted. Either:

75 Kent, 1978, p. 327.
76 Englander, David, 'The Word and the World: Evangelicalism in the Victorian City' in
    Parsons, 1988(d), p. 30.
77 The Salvation Army Act, 1980, Schedule 1.

> What an attraction ....for the restless and unsteady spirit is the city which asks no
> questions, where old stories are buried and where the secrets of a doubtful past are
> safe; what a fascination for the ambitious is offered by the gigantic lottery of chances;
> what a refuge for the loafer is the 'paradise of odd jobs;' what a home for the
> impecunious is the great sink of 'charities' which in London take the place of
> Charity.[78]

Or:

> [T]o the aesthetic observer [London was] the city where atmosphere was all, where no
> light from whatever source came unfiltered or unenriched by steam, mist, haze, smoke
> or fog; to the psychological contemplative, a city where you could be unutterably
> lonely in the midst of millions.[79]

The importance of the East End as a place of concealment was used by
Wilkie Collins in his novel, *The Woman in White,* when he has Walter Hartwright,
the hero, choose it as a hiding place for the three principal characters:

> The sense of serious peril was the one influence that guided me in fixing the place of
> our retreat. I chose it in the far east of London, where there were fewest idle people to
> lounge and look about them in the streets. I chose it in a poor and populous
> neighbourhood - because the harder the struggle for existence among the men and
> women about us, the less the risk of their having the time or taking the pains to notice
> chance strangers who came among them ... As early as the end of October the daily
> course of our lives had assumed its settled direction, and we three were as completely
> isolated in our place of concealment as if the house we lived in had been a desert
> island, and the great network of streets and the thousands of our fellow-creatures all
> round us the waters of an illimitable sea.[80]

London was pivotal economically as the major port for English imports and
trans-shipment; as a large consumer market; and as 'as a centre of government and
the royal court, it was the focal point of conspicuous consumption and its attendant
luxury trades.'[81] In a way that transcended purely economic power and influence
London was, within England and possibly much further afield at this time, 'the
centre and magnet for all things from luxurious living and High Society to
mendicancy and the criminal underworld.'[82]

At the centre of the 'paradise of odd jobs', and a magnet for 'mendicancy and
the criminal underworld', was Whitechapel where Booth was to begin his mission.
Whitechapel was considered for most of the century as a centre of immigration and
extreme poverty. Mayhew mentioned Whitechapel as one of the localities for low
lodging houses and continued:

---

78 Booth, Charles, 1889, Vol I, pp. 518-9.
79 Best, 1985, p. 25.
80 Collins, 1994, pp. 389-90.
81 Stedman Jones, 1992, p. 19.
82 Waller, 1991, p. 24.

[T]he places I have specified may be considered the *districts* of these hotels for the poor. The worst places, both as regards filth and immorality, are in St Giles's and Wentworth-street, Whitechapel.[83]

In 1868 the Medical Officer of Health for Tower Hamlets stated that Whitechapel was probably inhabited by the poorer classes to a greater extent than any other district in London.[84] It had been estimated in 1865, the exact year Booth chose to work there, that of Whitechapel's 9,000 houses, 5,000 were let out as lodging houses, with each containing an average of three families.[85]

P. G. Hall's research has found that the majority of the tailoring and dressmaking trade in London was centred in Whitechapel, while its furniture making was centred on Bethnal Green. Both trades were carried on with minimal capital investment and a great deal of homeworking and by the 1850s there was a network of subcontracting and sweating. The sweating system in tailoring arose with the introduction of markets for wholesale ready-made clothes in a number of stock sizes.[86]

There were two main reasons why the tailoring industry was centred on Whitechapel. Firstly the workers needed to be near the warehouses because work was often given out to the homeworkers one afternoon for completion by the following midday. Therefore not much time could be lost in travelling to and fro. The second reason for Whitechapel's importance to the industry was the pool of cheap, unskilled labour available in the area.

There were two main groups within this labour pool, consisting, firstly, of the women whose husbands were on seasonal employment or unemployed and, secondly, of the Jewish male immigrants who tended to settle just east of the City limits.

Table 2.1, using figures from the 1851 census, gives an indication of the overcrowding in the East End, and, in particular, in Whitechapel. The areas are divided into Ecclesiastical Districts.

From these figures it is clear that, even within the poverty and overcrowding of the East End, Whitechapel stood out with the highest average number of persons per house and containing the only two Ecclesiastical Districts within the area to have averages of more than nine persons per house.

In addition Whitechapel had the highest numbers and the highest percentages of Irish-born and foreign-born inhabitants within the area, as Table 2.2 shows. The majority of the foreigners in Whitechapel in 1861 came from Germany, Holland, Poland and Prussia.

83 Mayhew, 1985, p. 108.
84 Medical Officer of Health Annual Report, Whitechapel, 1868, Vol. II, p. 12, quoted in
    Morris & Rodger, 1993, p. 228.
85 *Lancet*, 1865, ii: 656, quoted in Morris & Rodger, 1993, p. 228.
86 Hall, 1962 , pp. 59-62, 71, 75-76.

Table 3.1 Overcrowding in the East End in 1851

District/Ecclesiastical Parishes	Persons	Houses Inhabited	Average Persons per House
Bethnal Green			
St. Andrew	10,272	1,591	6.46
St. Barthololmew	10,016	1,472	6.80
St. James the Great	4,503	650	6.00
St. James the Less	2,357	368	6.40
St. John	7,696	1,090	7.06
St. Jude	10,396	1,686	6.14
St. Matthias	8,696	1,078	8.07
St. Peter	5,115	900	5.68
St. Philip	11,418	1,336	8.55
St. Simon Zelotes	4,200	662	6.34
St. Thomas	7,563	1,198	6.31
Total	*82,232*	*12,181*	*6.78*
Whitechapel			
All Saints, Mile End	10,183	1,172	8.69
St. Jude	6,184	686	9.01
St. Mark	15,790	1,737	9.09
Total	*32,157*	*3,595*	*8.94*
St. George-in-the-East			
Christ Church, Watney St	12,497	1,664	7.51
St. Mary, Johnson Street	5,372	725	7.41
Total	*17,869*	*2,389*	*7.48*
Stepney			
St. James, Ratcliffe	1,628	185	8.80
St. Peter, Globe Road	6,403	851	7.52
St. Philip	13,447	1,920	7.00
St. Thomas, Arbour Squ	11,481	1,806	6.36
Trinity, Tredegar Square	6,264	1,000	6.26
Total	*39,223*	*5,762*	*6.81*

Source: 1851 Census pp. 36-7

Table 3.2 Birthplaces of the Inhabitants of the East End – 1861

	Number of Persons	Percentage of Total Population
Whitechapel		
Total Population	78,970	
Born in Middlesex part of London	48,750	61.73%
Born in Ireland	7,626	9.66%
Foreigners born in foreign parts	6,222	7.88%
Bethnal Green		
Total Population	105,092	
Born in Middlesex part of London	83,786	79.73%
Born in Ireland	920	0.88%
Foreigners born in foreign parts	479	0.46%
St. George-in-the-East		
Total Population	48,891	
Born in Middlesex part of London	30,106	61.58%
Born in Ireland	4,004	8.19%
Foreigners born in foreign parts	2,361	4.83%
Stepney		
Total Population	56,572	
Born in Middlesex part of London	34,236	60.51%
Born in Ireland	4,139	7.32%
Foreigners born in foreign parts	829	1.46%
Mile End Old Town		
Total Population	73,064	
Born in Middlesex part of London	46,288	63.35%
Born in Ireland	1,284	1.76%
Foreigners born in foreign parts	1,541	2.11%

Source: 1861 Census Table 13 pp.38-9

The whole question of seasonal employment was crucial to the economy of London. Here was the surplus labour that played such an important part in strengthening the hand of the employer. Within the crowded, poverty-stricken streets of Whitechapel and its environs was an almost limitless supply of labour, particularly for those sectors where little or no skill or training was required. Stedman Jones has described how its very abundance weakened labour's claims:

> Where ... the supply of labour was plentiful, and in some cases, even unlimited, as it was in the docks, and in the semi-skilled or unskilled parts of the building, furniture, clothing, footwear, and food and drink trades, the employer had little incentive to maintain a continuous level of employment. Thus the excess of work at seasonal peaks of production tended to retain within these industries, surplus workers who might otherwise be driven into other forms of permanent employment. Moreover, by the same token, the existence of this surplus pool of labour, always at hand, removed all necessity to iron out irregularity of production and enabled the employer to vary his workforce, solely in accordance with the dictates of demand.[87]

It was the constant threat to lifestyles from employers or competitors that led to what Roberts described as the *leitmotif* of fear that dominated life in the slums. He denies the impression given to outsiders that there was 'a cosy gregariousness' about living there. Having lived in Salford in the early part of the twentieth century he argued rather that '[c]lose propinquity, together with cultural poverty, led as much to enmity as it did to friendship.'[88]

The problem with any judgement about life in the slums of the nineteenth century is that nearly all the information comes from those who 'visited' rather than lived there. Peter Keating has criticized the way in which those who wrote of their visits to the slum spoke of 'penetrating' the slum rather than simply riding there.[89] However there was a sense in which the life of the slum was often impenetrable to outsiders. Kellow Chesney contended that the very way in which buildings were situated added to the impenetrability and the sense of a separate, enclosed world:

> Where dwellings were arranged round a rectangular court, the inhabitants were likely to congest it with water-barrels, pigsties, and lean-to sheds. If adjoining courts were not linked in the builders' plan, connecting runways could soon be established. It is not hard to see how a system of such 'entries', linked to each other, often opening into streets just wide enough to allow for the movements of builders' carts, and tenanted by a degraded and disorderly population, could provide formidable slum-nexuses almost ready-made.[90]

Therefore, there was a gulf in perceptions between the residents and the 'visiting' classes. For example, several philanthropic institutions were appalled at the conditions in low lodging houses and set up 'model' establishments, only to find that very often the poor did not flock to take advantage of them. Those offering a 'service' were not meeting the needs perceived by the 'beneficiaries':

> Even characters not beyond reform might feel more at home by a squalid kitchen hearth than listening to a clergyman's exhortation in a scrubbed day-room; while an

---

87 Stedman Jones, 1984, p. 42.
88 Roberts, 1971, pp. 30, 66.
89 Keating, 1978, p. 16.
90 Chesney, 1991, p. 104.

insistence on early hours kept out many street-sellers whose best hope of custom was the late public-house and theatre crowds.[91]

The public house was an important feature in the life of the slum. Again, for many outsiders looking in, depending on their initial viewpoint, the crowds within the pub were a sign either of the improvidence of the poor or of their 'comradeship, conviviality and companionship'. The facts were that, with working-class homes overcrowded, and often offering little comfort or cheer, the public house was the only meeting place, and the result was that 'for a labouring man to eschew drink ... was more than giving up a single habit; it was a repudiation of important aspects of working class community life.'[92]

Many of the women of the East End made their living by prostitution. The attitude of the upper and middle classes would be at least ambiguous on this issue, but would publicly be one of disapprobation. One prostitute who was interviewed by Mayhew explained the economic and class pressures behind her career choice:

> If I had been born a lady it wouldn't have been very hard to have acted like one. To be poor and honest, especially with young girls, is the hardest struggle of all. There isn't one in a thousand can get the better of it. I am ready to say again, that it was want, and nothing more, that made me transgress.[93]

There was little support or protection in law for those who sought to avoid or leave behind a life of prostitution. Years later, when the Salvation Army was involved in a battle against some of the practices of the prostitution trade, an officer sought to obtain the luggage of a young girl who had been 'rescued' from the brothel. He succeeded because the woman who kept the brothel knew that 'while it would be difficult to bring a case against her for detaining the girl, a very different view might be taken by the police over a tin trunk ... That amounted to theft!'[94]

It was a clinical specialist who overcame the normal prejudices of his class and was prepared to write that the options society offered to women from the lower classes meant that prostitution could prove a logical choice for a woman in the longer as well as the shorter term:

> If we compare the prostitute at thirty-five with her sister, who perhaps is the married mother of a young family, or has been the toiling slave for years in the over-heated laboratories of fashion, we shall seldom find that the constitutional ravages often thought to be a necessary consequence of prostitution exceed those attributable to the cares of a family and the heart-wearing struggles of virtuous labour.[95]

This was the East End in 1865 when William Booth decided he would work there.

---

91 Chesney, 1991, pp. 113-4.
92 Harrison, 1988, p. 78.
93 Mayhew, quoted in Golby, 1992, p. 9.
94 Terrot, 1959, p. 88.
95 Chesney, 1991, p. 376.

Booth's East End Base

In 1865 the level and size of poverty in the East End, with all that it signified, faced William Booth, with his background of Chartism and his experience of years as a Methodist minister and independent revivalist. The East End became the base of Booth's work for the rest of his life. Wherever else his organisation might work, and even when its centre moved from the East End to the city, the fact that it had started in Whitechapel would remain crucial to its activity, focus and development. The tables have shown the level of poverty and overcrowding in Whitechapel. Contemporary descriptions and impressions convey something of what life was like there in the middle of the nineteenth century. It is possible to understand from these descriptions not only the impact of the poverty but also the fact that the people in the area had lifestyles that to Booth underlined their desperate need of salvation.

Henry Mayhew is the most widely read and most prolific on the conditions of the East End at the time and he mentions Whitechapel several times when talking about some of the worst conditions. The thieves who took butcher's meat from the market in Leadenhall knew they had a ready market for what they had stolen in the nearby low lodging houses in Whitechapel.[96] Whitechapel was also a centre for gambling among the many sweeps who lived there:

> [The journeymen sweeps] gamble also, but with this proviso - they seldom play for money; but when they meet in their usual houses of resort - two famous ones are in Back C- Lane and S- Street, Whitechapel - they spend their time and what money they have in tossing for beer, till they are either drunk or penniless. Such present the appearance of having just come out of a chimney ... I am informed that there is scarcely one of them who has a second change of clothes, and that they wear their garments night and day till they literally rot, and drop in fragments from their backs.[97]

Whitechapel was also well known for the number of brothels: 'Shadwell, Spitalfields, and contiguous districts are infested with nests of brothels as well as Whitechapel.'[98] It was peopled by costers or street-sellers or those who worked long hours for poor returns in what were known as the sweated trades:

> The street-sellers in Spitalfields and Bethnal Green are so mixed up as to their abodes with the wretchedly underpaid cabinet-makers who supply the 'slaughter-houses'; with slop-employed tailors and shoe-makers (in the employ of a class, as respects shoemakers, known as 'garret-masters' or middle-men, between the workman and the wholesale warehouse-man), bobbin-turners, needle-women, slop-milliners,...that I might tediously enumerate almost every one of the many streets known, emphatically enough, as the 'poor streets'. These poor streets are very numerous, running eastward from Shoreditch to the Cambridge road, and southward from the Bethnal-green-road to Whitechapel and the Mile End-road.[99]

96 Mayhew, 1985, p. 116.
97 Mayhew, 1985, p. 252.
98 Mayhew, 1985, p. 483.
99 Mayhew, 1985, p. 146.

These descriptions give a flavour of the world of the people among whom Booth decided to work. In Mayhew's words there is a sense of the numbers of poor in the area, the monotony of the streets and the grind of the lives lived there. There are also, in the interviews he conducted, some pointers as to why in working among the poor Booth would find a pressure to address the material problems that could not be separated from the spiritual understanding and perceptions of the people who lived in Whitechapel. There was a coster-girl who said to Mayhew: 'If we cheats in the streets, I know we shan't go to Heaven; but it's very hard upon us, for if we didn't cheat we couldn't live, profits is so bad.'[100] A boy of thirteen, living on the streets, told the following story:

> A boy wanted me to go with him to pick a gentleman's pocket. We was mates for two days, and then he asked me to go picking pockets; but I wouldn't. I know it's wrong, though I can neither read nor write. The boy asked me to do it to get into prison, as that would be better than the streets. He picked pockets to get into prison. He was starving about the streets like me.[101]

In the first ever report of the Christian Mission written in 1867, Booth seemed to suggest that it was the size of the residuum in the East End that had prompted him in starting the mission's work. He spoke of islands of darkness existing in other parts of London and in other major cities, but the East of London stood out as a 'continent of vice, crime and misery'.[102]

It was in this 'continent', with his efforts to bring the gospel to its inhabitants, that William Booth interacted with the poor in a way that would determine the form the Salvation Army would take. While it would not for long remain an organisation *of* the residuum it was intrinsically bound to the idea that brought it into being, that it was an evangelical organisation *for* the residuum.

Collini has argued that the residuum is logically the starting point for religious movements and such has often also been true for denominations and sects. Basing his thesis on the work of Ernst Troeltsch, Collini claimed:

> Great religious movements which base their claim on divine revelation must first take hold among those classes largely unknown and uncared for by the authorities established in Church and State. Only the poor and uneducated unite simplicity and the capacity to believe with primitive energy and an urgent sense of religious need. Their total surrender is unqualified by intellectual training and questioning habits of mind. Members of more reflective and educated classes put complicated queries, opposing human wisdom to divine revelation. Those who demand that belief remain within the bounds of reason tend to regard in relative terms what is absolute and unconditional to true believers of classes below them.[103]

Green has described Booth in 1865 as being 'neither by temperament nor by

---

100 Mayhew, 1985, p. 51.
101 Mayhew, 1985, p. 410.
102 *The Christian Mission Report*, 1867, p. 2.
103 Collini, 1993, pp. 15-6.

theology fitted for the work of the local preacher'.[104] He felt called to preach to the masses as a revivalist. Much the same could be said of him as was said of Booth's contemporary, Gladstone, by his biographer:

> Yet his personality ... and above all his vibrant and declamatory speaking style, began to cry out for the stimulus and indulgence of mass popular audiences ... Gladstone, just in the way that some runners are better at a mile than a sprint, and some reviewers better at 3000 rather than 1000 words, was developing into a natural 5000 - or even 15,000 - arena man.[105]

So the numbers of the poor crowded together in Whitechapel would have offered Booth the one chance to remain in one place and yet have the crowds to listen to him.

While Booth seems always to have had in mind the very poor when he spoke of the masses, he saw their greatest need as being for salvation, meaning an end to their estrangement from God. In comparison with an individual's salvation:

> [A]ny temporal modification of his lot appeared trivial ...What were any of the sorrows of earth when compared with everlasting damnation ... And what were any joys of time when contrasted with the felicities which endure for ever?[106]

Booth was to describe the impact of the poor of the East End as that of people with a false idea of God and religion, as a result of which there was misery and vice everywhere. He seemed to hear a voice saying, 'Why go to Derby or anywhere else to find souls who need the gospel?'[107]

However, not many of the poor would have recognised their need of the gospel. Extreme poverty reduces the parameters of life to a simple struggle for survival that will often force other considerations into the background. Sim claimed that for the poor in London the object of life was attained when 'the night's rent is paid, and they do not have to hesitate between the workhouse or a corner of the staircase in some doorless house.'[108] Booth's methods, therefore, needed to include a way of persuading people of the individual's need of redemption before offering it.

Booth's Early Co-workers

It is not surprising that Booth's reaction to the situation he found in Whitechapel was not unique. He was a part of a much wider movement, the Home Mission Movement.[109] In response to the suffering of the East End others were seeking

---

104 Green, 1989, p. 9.
105 Jenkins, 1995, pp. 232-3.
106 Booth, 'Salvation for Both Worlds' in *All the World*, Vol.V, No.1, January 1889.
107 Editorial, *The East London Evangelist*, October 1868, p. 3.
108 Keating, 1978, p. 74.
109 Horridge, 1993, pp. 8,17.

various ways of bringing social relief, including other evangelists who responded in ways similar to William Booth. Sandall described why people would wish to work there:

> [I]n particular, the East of London - untouched by the revival in any other way and neglected till its people had sunk to appalling depths of irreligious and physical misery - attracted fervent lovers of souls who could find no outlet for their ardour within the churches; it became their special field.[110]

It is necessary to take account of the fact that William Booth was not alone in his efforts at revival and that once he had decided to remain to work in the East End some of these other groups already working there made important contributions to his work.

In fact there had been two earlier occasions when Booth might have begun his work in the East End, but he did not choose at these times to remain. The first was in 1854 when he was second minister for a circuit of the Methodist New Connexion which included a chapel in Watney Street, Wapping. According to Sandall, while he was moved by the misery there, Booth did not feel called to remain, there was no sense of specific identity with the East End at this point and there is no trace of a connection between his work here and his future invitation to take charge of the Quaker Burial Ground Tent Mission in 1865.[111]

The East London Special Services Committee was formed in 1861 to arrange and extend mission work. In that year Booth had some connection with the Committee, having parted company with the Methodist New Connexion and commenced an independent revival ministry. It was suggested that he work with the Committee, but nothing came of the idea at this time. Murdoch claimed that the reason for Booth's not remaining was that he did not feel at home with the crowds of the East End. There was a small audience and he felt that his sermon did not reach them and that it was 'a different affair altogether to what I have ever taken part in.'[112] There is a suggestion here that in the intervening years since Booth left Nottingham he may have grown away from the residuum.

However, in the four intervening years, after preaching in Cornwall for two years, the Booths had worked for a while in Walsall. Finding an initial lack of success they had learnt to gear services to the needs of the poorer people there. Booth spoke outside in the market square, led processions through the slums, and advertised speeches by converted prize-fighters and a poacher. He was thus, by 1865, more experienced and equipped to be able to reach the poor of the East End. In his own words, he had to relearn the lessons of Meadow Platts[113] (the poorest area of Nottingham where he had preached in the open air in the early days after his conversion), when he decided to stay in Whitechapel. The residuum had drawn him back to the focus he had first demonstrated in Nottingham.

---

110 Sandall, 1979, Vol. I, p. 111.
111 Sandall, 1979, Vol. I, pp. 6-7.
112 Murdoch, 1994, p. 36.
113 Sandall, 1979, Vol. I, p. 45.

There were other reasons, related to Catherine, why Booth was more ready to remain in London by 1865. She wanted a more settled life after four years of constant travelling and one preferably near her elderly parents in Brixton. In addition she had been offered several preaching engagements in London. Her earnings from these engagements supported the Booth family, as well as raising funds to support the Mission, during their early work.

By 1865, when Booth decided to stay and work in the East End, the condition of the residuum had not only touched him but touched others who were to play a part in the formation of the organisation he was to found. So it was that members of the East London Special Services Committee were among those missioners who were running the tent mission in the Quaker Burial Ground and at whose open-air service Booth was invited to speak. Two of them, Samuel Chase and John Stabb, invited Booth to take temporary charge of the mission.[114] Other missioners who worked with Booth at the tent were members of the Christian community formed originally by Huguenots, who had fled France at the end of the seventeenth century. Some of the community stayed to become part of Booth's organisation, but right at the beginning they formed a supportive group of like-minded people, involved as they were in mission work, visitation of common lodging houses and work with prostitutes.[115]

The Samuel Chase who had asked Booth to take charge of the tent mission was in partnership with Richard Cope Morgan in a printing business. Among the journals they produced was a weekly paper called *Revival*. It was in the pages of *Revival* that some of the very first reports of Booth's work in the East End were published and so became known to a wider audience.[116]

Another organisation that pre-dated Booth's work in London was the Evangelisation Society. Before his work became established, this society gave grants to some of Booth's mission stations, covering rent, printing and evangelists' salaries.[117] In addition, there were individual benefactors, such as Samuel Morley, whose personal interest in the spiritual life of the East End led them to lend financial support to Booth and his work.

It was often Catherine's West End preaching contacts that gained William Booth access to those groups and agencies, which were frequently connected to each other through 'interlocking directorates of wealthy London evangelicals.'[118]

> The Booths' mission roots were in this non-sectarian mentality. In the 1860s, revivalists expressed their inclusiveness and social concern in extra denominational voluntary agencies which constituted the soil in which Booth planted his mission in London's East End.[119]

---

114 Sandall, 1979, Vol. I, p. 2.
115 Sandall, 1979, Vol. I, pp. 24-5.
116 Sandall, 1979, Vol. I, p. 27.
117 Sandall, 1979, Vol. I, p. 74.
118 Murdoch, 1996, p. 45.
119 Murdoch, 1996, p. 45.

The beginning of Booth's work in the East End was affected, not only by his response to the residuum, but also by the people who were already doing a similar work there. Booth was always adamant that he had not intended to start a new society but the fact that he was now remaining in one place greatly increased the chance of this happening. Added to Booth's personality, the economic and social backgrounds of the poor who were becoming converted would tend to lead to the converts gathering round a leader rather then joining existing churches. Briefly, the converts did not want to leave Booth to join existing churches, the existing churches did not welcome them as a rule and the new converts, as members of the underclass, were just the people needed to win other converts from the same background. All the ingredients were then present for the formation of a new sect.

Once Booth's new organisation began to take shape it branched out from other agencies, such as the East London Special Services Committee. Not everyone who joined with Booth at the start wished to remain with his organisation, either because they had never seen their work with him as long-term or because his style of leadership, or the commitment he demanded, was not to everyone's taste. By the time he had been working a year, his organisation, at that point called the Christian Revival Union, numbered only 60 members.[120] It was branching out in another way, in that it was now no longer merely a revival mission. Because the organisation's converts became members and stayed to work with Booth, there was a need for consolidation, with efforts to care for those already converted as well as to make new converts. This Booth sought to do by classes for members and by setting them to work for others. The significance of membership involvement in terms of working-class community and activity will be discussed below.

It is possible to read into the introduction of membership classes and the resulting activity of members the outline of the organisation of The Salvation Army but the organisation was not an immediate result of the first meeting between Booth and the residuum. In assessing the effect of the Whitechapel residuum on Booth, and his response, it is important to remember that he did not, at this point, imagine that out of his work there would grow an international organisation. What he apparently foresaw was the life of an evangelist within the East End. There were thousands and thousands of individuals with material and spiritual needs to whom Booth wanted to offer the possibility of personal redemption.

Booth's evangelism involved preaching in a tent (that collapsed on the worshippers) and leading services in a dancing academy, or in a hayloft where the ceiling was so low that Booth could only just stand upright inside it. Other meeting halls in these early days included a room behind a pigeon shop where 'the seats had no backs; there was coconut matting on the floor, and the roof was so leaking that when it rained heavily we used to get wet as we sat there'.[121] George T. White was to write of one of Booth's visits there that, on the way back to the

---

120 Sandall, 1979, Vol. I, p. 46.
121 Sandall, 1979, Vol. I, p. 82.

hall from the open-air service, they were baptised with tea slops and had winkle shells thrown at them. [122]

Booth was deeply moved by the needs he saw in the East End and, impelled by the sense of urgency that came from his own evangelical beliefs in the need to offer salvation, he was willing to stay and work there. He did not know at this time that the work would move out from there. There was enough to do in the East End. In Hattersley's judgement, 'He had now become entranced by the magnitude of the challenge which faced him.' [123]

There was plenty of evidence in the East End of London of the need for urgency in persuading people to accept salvation. An article in *Revival,* headed, 'The East London Christian Mission under the Superintendence of William Booth,' spoke of the 'appalling temporal and spiritual destitution of the East of London with its population of nearly one million souls and not one in a hundred of who attend either Church or Chapel.' It spoke of a particular Sunday (perhaps the day of the 1851 religious census) when it was found that, of the 180,000 population in Bethnal Green, only 2,000 attended a place of worship. It also stated that, along the one and a half miles of the Whitechapel Road, 18,600 people entered public houses on a Sunday. [124]

To someone of Booth's temperament and beliefs, the situation in the East End was a spur to the utmost effort. This background needs to be remembered in any assessment of his methods. For Booth and his helpers, the need to work for the salvation of other people was so pressing that it should preclude 'normal' considerations. This sense of urgency was to continue right through his life and it was something he would continue to expect from members of his organisation. So, for example, in *Darkest England*, he wrote about providing field recreations, a reading room and library in the industrial village he hoped to create, adding that: 'These things are not for the Salvation Army Soldiers, who have other work in the world.' [125]

It was an attitude that permeated the work. George Scott Railton was one of Booth's closest co-workers, and during January 1876 he wrote a letter in which he spoke of 'the outrageous theory of an open-air *season*' and said how distressing it was to him that an assumption should be made that open-air evangelical work should cease in September just because it was getting colder. [126] A few months later, Railton wrote to Bramwell Booth about the kind of training needed for workers in the Mission:

> We want to train men to be like us, almost without time alone or for self, always at it, and yet always being fed and stoked up as they fly...All our policy should aim at becoming more and more Apostolic, free from the slightest tie to anything but our Mission. [127]

---

122 Sandall, 1979, Vol. I, p. 83.
123 Hattersley, 1999, p. 152.
124 *Revival*, 6 February, 1868.
125 Booth, 1979, p. 138.
126 Copy of a letter from George Scott Railton dated January 1876, held in Salvation Army Archives, London.
127 Copy of a letter from George Scott Railton to Bramwell Booth, dated 6 November

George Haw quoted William Booth as saying that for some Christians, namely those who did not share his sense of urgency and commitment, Christianity was a 'kind of Worcester sauce to impart a religious flavour to life.'[128]

It is easy to see that this level of single-mindedness could lead to charges of fanaticism and to criticism of style. For Booth and his early workers, the only measure of success was whether people were converted and the question asked of style or method was simply, 'Does it work?'

One of the earliest recorded examples of criticism of Booth's methods is a letter to the Editor of the *East London Observer,* from someone who signed himself 'Anti-humbug':

> I beg to call your attention to the disorderly mob which nightly parade to Mile End Road and its vicinity singing some rude doggerel verses which doubtless they please to style hymns, to the annoyance of the general public. There must be, surely, someone in authority who has power to put a stop to such profanity and vulgarity.[129]

In 1883, Canon Farrar of Westminster Abbey, who in later years came to support Booth's work, preached a sermon in which he accused the Salvationists of dragging their spiritual lives out of the 'gracious shadows wherein God leaves them' and of using 'grotesque and irreverent phraseology.'[130]

Booth, however, would argue that the language and methods which were used were those that were understood by his hearers and therefore most likely to lead to their conversion. Hattersley seconded Booth's argument in a sense by maintaining that it was just those attributes which caused such offence that also caused Booth's success:

> Much of polite society regarded the self-styled General and his Army as fanatical, presumptuous, intrusive and vulgar. Those were the characteristics - described by his supporters as piety, indomitability, determination and simplicity - which made his extraordinary achievement possible.[131]

Long before he started to preach to the East End crowds, while he was a circuit minister in Lincolnshire, Booth wrote to Catherine: 'I want a sermon of the Flood, one on Jonah, and one on the Judgement. Send me some bare thoughts; some clear startling outlines. Nothing moves people like the terrific. They must have hell-fire flashed before their eyes, or they will not *move*.'[132]

This level of commitment and intensity was to continue throughout his life, in the sense that he was willing to do all that might be required to win people for Christ, with his first priority always the offer of salvation. Miss Jane Short, who lodged with the Booths in the 1860s, told Begbie that she heard Booth preach very

---

1877, held in Salvation Army Archives, London.
128 Haw, 1906, pp. 27-8.
129 *East London Observer*, 20 June, 1868, letter to Editor, signed 'Anti-humbug'.
130 Begbie, 1920, Vol. II, p. 30.
131 Hattersley, 1999, p. 2.
132 Ervine, 1934, Vol. I, p. 110.

tender sermons on love, one in particular being on the text 'Acquaint now thyself with Him, and be at peace,' but when praised for this he replied, 'No; the best preaching is damnation; with the Cross in the middle of it.'[133]

The reason for his emphasis was the place of the individual in the scheme of redemption. Among the methods that his opponents criticised were the ways that pressure was put on potential converts in his services. Although he was aware of the possible dangers,[134] he felt impelled to employ almost any method that would lead a person to accept salvation, because of the centrality of individual redemption in his creed. It was in January 1870 that the *Christian Mission Magazine* published an address from William Booth which summed up how he viewed the practical outworking of his evangelical beliefs:

> Whatsoever thy hand findeth to do, do it with thy might. Do it, and do it at once. Your life is uncertain; your days are numbered, and at the longest, in view of what you have to do, they are very few; therefore take the work that God has by His Spirit and providence made evident to be your work, and do it at once, with all the energy you possess of body and soul.[135]

By the time Booth wrote these words he had been working more than two years amid the poorest of the East End, and in embryonic form he had an organisation that was already an ellipse with two foci, the offering of spiritual salvation and practical material help. Faced with the material and spiritual poverty of the East End there would be no diminution of urgency.

An Organisation of the Residuum

There can be little doubt that as an organisation developed around Booth its primary aim was to present the gospel to the poor of London's East End. It was to do this aggressively and to employ methods that were anathema to the more respectable. This aggressive attitude was in part the position that is always taken by revivalists but it was also heightened by the life that the residuum lived, with its only relief being in the garish pubs. There was a need for Booth's organisation to offer something that was equally attractive to these same people. Booth was quoted in the magazine, *The Christian*, in 1871 as saying:

> [F]or every new attack of Satan against our work, I feel the only answer to give him is to open a new mission station. People say we must wait for an open door. The devil will not open the door for us, nor the publican, nor the infidel. We must go and open it for ourselves. So we say, Wherever there is a dark, devil-ridden neighbourhood, go there.[136]

---

133 Begbie, 1920, Vol. I, p. 356.
134 Begbie, 1920, Vol. I, p. 245.
135 *Christian Mission Magazine*, January 1870, page 1.
136 *The Christian*, 20 April, 1871.

In order to open the door, Booth and his co-workers used all that could be used in working-class culture to convey the gospel. Inglis described Booth's evangelists as being ready to use a mixture of evangelical religion and vulgarity, and he argued that what they did was successful just because they were working-class themselves. The workers in Booth's organisation were not in any sense patronising to the poor, with a sense of coming down to their level, because the activities that were 'strategically necessary' in attracting people to their meetings were also what they themselves enjoyed.[137] Inglis described the missioners as being, with minor exceptions, 'the only group of Christian evangelists of their time who approached working-class non-worshippers at their own cultural level'.[138]

Hattersley has argued that Booth himself was temperamentally more suited to evangelising among the poor. In Hattersley's view the early evangelism of Booth in Nottingham would only have been acceptable among the very poor.[139] By this interpretation the relation between Booth and the poor was not purely one-directional:

It was clear enough why the [missioners] were directed towards the largely illiterate poor - a more sophisticated audience would have found [their] behaviour near to ridiculous. William Booth, the super-salesman of emotional Christianity, had identified a growing demand for his product in the slums.[140]

It was in this dialectic between Booth and the very poor that the Salvation Army's embryonic form was forged and strengthened by the extreme reactions from different classes:

Few of [Booth's] followers possessed the slightest capacity for understanding how ridiculous they could sound. The absurdity of much of their publicity attracted support in the slums, but it increased the contempt in which they were held in the respectable suburbs.[141]

The class differences and exclusiveness that existed elsewhere within the churches are underlined by Burnett:

Margaret Cunningham, daughter of the rector of Cranleigh, was forbidden to talk to 'the poor children' who attended the National (i.e. Church) School ... Another clergyman's daughter Ludivina Jackson, was allowed contact with 'the unfortunates' when she became a Sunday School teacher at the age of ten, but here the relationship was clearly one of superior and inferior, not of equals.[142]

In the first volume of *The History of The Salvation Army,* there is a report of a Sunday school outing in 1866. The report gives the words of a song that the

---

137 Inglis, 1963, p. 187.
138 Inglis, 1963, pp. 187-8.
139 Hattersley, 1999, p. 23.
140 Hattersley, 1999, p. 194.
141 Hattersley, 1999, p. 231.
142 Burnett, 1982, p. 48.

children sang while travelling on the train, obviously a song that they knew from
the Sunday school:

> In Three Colts Lane in an old wool-shed
> Glory, Hallelujah!
> We frighten the living and raise the dead,
> Sing Glory, Hallelujah!
> Shout Glory, Hallelujah!
> And while the rats were running around,
> The boys and girls Salvation found.[143]

This is by no means a great hymn of the Church and there are probably few
people who did or ever would sing it, but it is significant in several ways. Firstly,
it underlines the conditions under which Booth and his helpers were working in
the 1860s. Secondly, the juxtaposition of rats and salvation suggests the gospel
being offered to people where they were, and in the words they could understand.
The song itself uses the street-culture that grew out of their poverty so that the
children of Bethnal Green could quite happily sing in this way.

Elijah Cadman is often used as an example of the first workers in Booth's
army. Ervine describes him as 'a pioneer of many of the methods which made The
Salvation Army offensive to cultured people'.[144] A converted chimney-sweep, he
often recited Bible passages by heart, while pretending to read, and on at least one
occasion 'read' the Bible passage, holding the Bible upside down. Significantly he
first heard of Booth's work in the East End as follows: 'Elijah, I've seen a people
in London who live to serve Christ, and they're our class!' [145] Whatever The
Salvation Army was to become later, its roots were firmly among the poorest
working classes of the East End. Whatever later commentators were to deduce and
impute back to those early days, contemporaries clearly saw the organisation as of
the working class. We have the evidence of Cadman's colleague and also the editor
of *The Christian* who ascribed the success of the then Christian Mission to its
working-class preachers:

> It is true these earnest men do their work in a rough way; but men of culture would be
> powerless, with their delicate instruments, to touch the thick trees upon which these
> spirited woodmen wield their axe with wonderful effect. These hard-headed men, by
> their intense energy, bowed their uncultivated listeners like the trees of the wood
> beneath a mighty storm.[146]

Nor did the writer of an article for *The Nonconformist* in 1868 have any doubt
that the Christian Mission had its roots in the working classes:

---

143 Sandall, 1979, Vol. I, p. 63.
144 Ervine, 1934, Vol. I, p. 354.
145 Ervine, 1934, Vol. I, pp. 348-54.
146 Editorial by R. C. Morgan, *The Christian*, 21 June 1877.

Every success of the whole movement has been due to this working class character. The great bulk of its advocates are working people, the language used is that of the working people ... in fact it is rendered so completely working class in all its numerous ramifications, that to all intents and purposes, The East London Christian Mission can be regarded as an essentially working class religious movement.[147]

Much of what was introduced in the 1860s and 1870s has now crystallised into Salvation Army tradition and, in some cases, assumed a middle-class veneer, but its impetus was the spontaneous use of the early missioners' own working-class culture and language to share their knowledge of the Christian gospel. At this point the offer of individual salvation was seen as the best solution for the poor, materially as well as spiritually. The following quote from Booth is an example:

The true Christian is a real self-helper. In bringing the truths of religion before the suffering masses we are also assisting in the great work of social reform. The God-fearing, sober, and industrious man has a better chance of improving his condition than has his ungodly brother, whose evenings are passed in the public house and whose notion of Sabbath observance consists in regular attendance at Sunday markets. When we have taught people to be religious, half the battle has been won.[148]

This philosophy can also be seen in the stories of converts that were printed in the magazines. For example, C. S. Mitchell wrote to *The Evangelist* about a woman who had been converted and was asked if materially her life was now better or worse. She replied 'Worse! oh, no, but a great deal better; for since we have known the Lord, we have never wanted a Sunday's dinner, while last year we had not more than twenty out of fifty two Sundays.'[149] An article by MCB spoke of a converted navvy who said, 'Ah! Miss, the Lord can do anything. He converted me when I'd neither shirt, shoes nor stockings on; and now I've got all I want.'[150]

These illustrations, and many others like them from the early days, seem to underline that Booth and his workers were reaching at least some of the very poorest and that those who were converted often found their material circumstances significantly improved. However, later events were to show that Booth was not satisfied with the numbers that were being reached in this way.

It is also important that the numbers he was reaching were not large enough to have an impact on the social and economic system. The corollary of Booth's later recognition of the possibility of the Salvation Army becoming involved in the redemption of the system is that if a significantly large number of the residuum had had their lifestyles transformed in the early years of Booth's work this would have created its own force for change in the system. It is possible that it was their very minority status that enabled Booth's early converts to improve their lifestyles

---

147 *The Nonconformist*, 4 November 1868, article signed 'P'.
148 Editorial, presumably by William Booth, *The East London Evangelist*, 1 January 1869, p. 63.
149 Booth, 1872, p. 73.
150 Article by MCB in *The Christian Mission Magazine*, January 1871, p. 12.

relative to those around them. They were accepting a personal salvation and, in doing so, were improving their individual social and economic conditions.

Meanwhile, Booth's organisation was in its infancy and did not have the infrastructure that would later give him the confidence to suggest that the Salvation Army was able to offer a solution to huge social problems. Therefore, he wrote in 1868 that only the Government could give effective assistance to those in deep poverty and of the general Christian responsibility to stretch out a helping hand wherever possible.[151]

In 1868 he could not offer more, but it was the very simplicity of his early helpers that played a part in making the Army the centralised, autocratic organisation that would be disciplined enough to feel able to implement a scheme of social redemption. Robert Sandall, the first official Salvation Army historian, wrote that the first members of the movement were 'simple people of limited ability' who were not equipped to share the burden of leadership with Booth. So Booth was 'alone at the head of the Army'.[152] This factor served to increase the autocratic element in Booth's personality. Ervine described him in the early 1860s as beginning to lose a sense of inferiority and acquiring 'an autocratic manner that was often unpleasantly arrogant'.[153] He was living in an age that produced many autocrats since mass poverty and suffering has often called forth an autocratic or dominating response from those who felt that they had found the solution.

Once set in the mould of an autocrat, Booth would not give up his own authority over the organisation. While his organisation, as it grew, attracted people of great ability who shouldered more and more responsibility, Booth was never able to share his supreme authority. He was eventually to take over control from the conference that, at first, made decisions concerning the mission. When he did this he wrote, 'This is a question as between you and me, and if you can't trust me it is of no use for us to attempt to work together. Confidence in God and in me are absolutely indispensable both now and ever afterwards.'[154] The question of William Booth's autocratic leadership was to be raised time and again by those who left the Army and also by those who criticized him in the Press at the time of the *Darkest England* book.[155] But his autocratic nature was part of his dynamism and part also of the charisma that helped to motivate others and it is hard to see how so much could have been accomplished if he had continually waited for consensus to catch up with him. As Leslie Stephen wrote in *The Science of Ethics* in 1882:

> To convert the world you have not merely to prove your theories, but to stimulate the imagination, to discipline the passions, to provide modes of utterance for the emotions and symbols which may represent the fundamental beliefs.[156]

---

151 *The Christian Mission Magazine*, December 1868, p. 47.
152 Sandall, 1979, Vol. I, p. 46.
153 Ervine, 1934, Vol. I, p. 264.
154 Sandall, 1947, Vol. I, p. 207.
155 Huxley, 1891.
156 Stephen, Leslie, *The Science of Ethics,* (London, 1882) quoted in Collini, 1992, p. 79.

Community of Poverty

Glenn Horridge has carried out research on the early Salvation Army and produced statistics which he has used to show that the success of Booth's organisation among the residuum was only marginally significant.[157] However, its focus was fundamentally aimed at the poor and the self-perception of the members of the mission and the perception of others was of a working-class organisation. Because a sufficient number of Booth's early converts and co-workers were working-class the organisation became a working-class community, with working-class mores.

The creation of a working-class community was partly intentional and partly a spontaneous outcome. As Pamela Walker has pointed out, much that the Salvation Army demanded from its members went against what was fairly important in the popular culture of the very poorest, such as visiting the public house and betting.[158] If the Army was to keep its members away from these activities, and if it was to persuade others to leave such activities and join Booth's organisation, then it was necessary to create a community that offered alternative attractions and activities. Therefore, as early as 1867, Booth wrote in the *Christian Mission Report* of opening a room in the Whitechapel Mission Hall that was set apart for 'reading and conversation'. He explained:

> In this room we supply cheap and innocent refreshments. In the East of London, a great barrier in the way of the poor man's rescue from the public house is the want of a place of pleasant resort and profitable and agreeable society.[159]

Booth then went on to explain that the poor often needed to escape because there was little to keep them at home all evening when those homes consisted of usually just one room with six or seven, and even up to fourteen, occupants. Andrew Mearns was to describe the appeal of the public house in his pamphlet, *The Bitter Cry of Outcast London,* in 1883:

> With its brightness, its excitement, and its temporary forgetfulness of misery, it is a comparative heaven to tens of thousands. How can they be expected to resist its temptations? They could not live if they did not drink, even though they know that by drinking they do worse than die.[160]

It was therefore important to create something that would attract the new converts where they would 'meet brothers of kindred sympathy and purpose, who will cheer them on in the way of reformation'.[161] So Booth proposed to open comfortable rooms with books and papers, wherever he had the opportunity. These rooms are just one example of the way in which Booth sought to encourage a sense of community and support within the poor who joined his organisation.

---

157 Horridge, 1993, pp. 152-3.
158 Walker, 1992, pp. 89, 104.
159 *The Christian Mission Report*, 1867, p. 10.
160 Keating, 1978, p. 99.
161 *The Christian Mission Report*, 1867, p. 10.

In addition, Booth followed the example of Wesley in holding classes for the teaching of his new converts and also in setting them to work to seek the conversion of others. This created a sense of community and also a sense of responsibility for each other, but it also had a more practical result. The timetable of activities at the early mission stations shows that in attending the prayer-meetings, Bible classes, open-air meetings and indoor services the new convert could well find most of his evenings and Sunday filled with activity.[162] The convert was thus less likely to enter a public house for lack of anything better to do. It also meant that his social and community identity was almost certain to be centred on the mission.

The important part a mission could play as a centre of community life was shown in Ian Dewhirst's autobiography, in which he reminisced about another Victorian mission:

> [T]he influence of the Mission extended far beyond Sunday worship; its Bibles and hymn books were rivalled in importance by the heavy white crockery and enormous tea-urn in its well-appointed kitchen. The Mission had something to offer everybody. With its Christian Endeavour Society, its choir and Band of Hope and Young Men's Mutual Improvement Class, its rooms blazed with light and activity every night of the week. [163]

---

162 For example the timetable at Bethnal Green, from a report by William Booth quoted in the editorial of *Christian World*, 15 November, 1867:
Sunday Morning:
   8 a.m. breakfast meeting, charge 3d. During breakfast a conversation on the previous week's labours, after that an address on some religious topic and general conversation on the same.
   11 a.m. Preaching in the Hall and in the Open Air
   3 p.m. A breaking of bread or experience meeting and Service in the open-air
   4.30 p.m. Tea for workers and friends, 3d. each. 70 to 90 attend. After tea prepare for the evening's work
   6 p.m. Brothers go out for open air meeting
   7 p.m. Service for young people and preaching in the new East London Theatre
Monday:
   12.30 to 1.30 p.m. Mid-day Prayer Meeting
   2 to 5 p.m. Mothers' Meeting
   7 p.m. Meeting for brothers and sisters engaged in district visitation
   6.30 p.m. Open Air Service
   8 p.m. Preaching in the Hall
Tuesday:
   Mid-day Prayer Meeting
   6.30 p.m. Writing, reading and arithmetic Class
   7 p.m. Believers' Meeting
   8 p.m. Bible Class for young people
   8 p.m. Preaching in the Hall ... and so on through the week.
163 Dewhirst, 1980, p. 4.

The Army's success and impact in this area was assessed by H. Cunningham in his work on leisure and culture among the working classes:

> [T]here was always the possibility of new initiations, the *most significant*, in the late nineteenth century, was the Salvation Army which, in southern towns in particular, fought again the battles for a new leisure culture of the people based on the Christian faith.[164] (Italics added)

Booth was not alone in seeking to build a new leisure culture. Doctor Thomas Barnardo, the founder of the children's homes that bore his name, was also responsible for setting up at least one 'coffee-palace' in a former public house. This was the Edinburgh Castle in Limehouse, which became the People's Mission Church as well as a coffee-palace. He had visited Mrs Hind-Smith, who was running about sixteen 'British Workmen Public Houses without the Drink', in Bradford around 1867-68. Barnardo felt these institutions were both dull and dingy and that to replicate them in Limehouse would be no competition at all to the public houses. Therefore, in creating his coffee-palace he retained and regilded the sign and bar from the original public house and decorated the building to make it more attractive. The coffee-palace worked commercially, supplying good meals, games, newspapers and temperance refreshments to working men.[165]

The working-class community that grew together with the Salvation Army was also crucial in the way in which the Army's first social work began. There is a very real sense in which the earliest social work was a natural outcome of normal working-class sharing. It is easy to overstate the sense of sharing among the working class and there are numerous examples of people seeking to hide the extent of their poverty from their neighbours, such as banging the cooking tins at the time they would be expected to eat Sunday lunch or ironing the brown paper in which the clothes going to the pawnbroker were wrapped.

However, John Burnett's important compilation of working-class autobiographies contains frequent reference to the informal network of help and support that existed within working-class communities, made up of relatives, friends and neighbours. The support was not always offered from generosity and philanthropy but could be simply because those who gave help expected to be able in turn to ask for help when necessary. Nevertheless, whatever the motivation, this kind of network was obviously valued, where people felt free to ask for the loan of sixpence or some food or for someone to mind the baby.

Joseph Terry described his life in Muirfield, Yorkshire, at the start of the nineteenth century and what a support network meant:

> It would take up much time and space to describe every house in 'Kalling Alley' where we now lived separately; suffice it to say that they were all much alike, all being poorly furnished and in some cases at least three beds had to be contrived at nights, and as they were in the constant habit of borrowing all kinds of necessary articles from each other from a hair brush ... or small tooth comb, up to a long brush,

---

164 Cunningham, 1990, Vol. II, p. 300.
165 Mrs. Barnardo & James Marchant, 1907, p. 103.

barrels, dresses, bonnets, soap, candles, tea, sugar, bread, even up to the Sunday, so they were in the constant habit of sleeping over at each other's houses - whenever there was room. And it was no uncommon thing to hear the words, 'Will George be at home tonight? I wanted our Betty to sleep or lie as her father's come home, and she does not like to lie at feet.'[166]

When members of the Christian Mission lived in areas of poverty they became part of the network that existed where they lived. This was true both of those who lived in the East End and joined the mission and, sometimes, those whom the Salvation Army later sent to live in the areas of greatest poverty. Mandler argued that most interpretations of the charity of the period are middle class and that in fact there was a wide gap between the perceptions of the givers and recipients. What the middleclass wanted to give rarely coincided with how the working-class perceived their needs. The working class would adopt strategies to meet the criteria of the donors but still use the help given in the way most suited to themselves. In this way the poor did not see the charity they received as imposing the stigma that most of the donors thought was there.[167]

For the editors of the socialist journal *The Commonweal,* charity was degrading:

> The giving of gifts among equals and friends is a pleasant thing, and good for both giver and receiver, but the doling out of charity is degrading in every way, even when given and received in all honesty and goodwill. When the charity is vicarious, without personal contact and good fellowship; when it is made the vehicle of condescension and class-feeling, a pretence for the preaching of humility, a means of buttressing robbery and preserving the supremacy of property, - it becomes so horrible a blasphemy, so terrible an outrage upon humanity, as to rank, in Socialist eyes at least, along with the most blistering wrongs under which men suffer nowadays.[168]

For the poor the possibility of charity relief was one of the resources that they could bring into the equation of how to care for the family. The decision to adapt to the demands of potential donors, however, was an 'active' one, on the basis of a valuation of the gift, not simply a passive acceptance.

> The relief poor families most needed - a straightforward income supplement - was only rarely available. When it was, in the form of unconditional outdoor doles, it was taken up readily. Other forms of relief were subject to negotiation between donors and recipients. Aid that interfered with survival strategies was shunned. When aid was offered in peculiar but still useful forms, recipients did their best to conform to the donors, expectations ... But the meeting of minds was usually superficial and temporary. The gap between the motives and the uses of charity could be bridged, but it was rarely closed.[169]

166 Jospeh Terry, unpublished autobiography, quoted in Burnett, 1982, p. 71.
167 Mandler, 1990, p. 20.
168 *The Commonweal,* 28 December, 1889, p. 410.
169 Mandler, 1990, p. 23.

To the extent that the Christian Mission, and later the Salvation Army, was really a part of the community and accepted within the network, the help that it gave did not have to become warped by misunderstanding and wrong perceptions. There was certainly much that was offered on conditions that the recipients would not have chosen but there were times when the work the early missioners and Salvationists did was in response to requests from the poor themselves. Examples are missioners who lived within the community and responded to calls for help or when a prostitute asked for somewhere to stay so that she could leave her profession. There was a particular spontaneity about the earliest social efforts that at their best could genuinely have closed the gap between donor and recipient.

Ellen Ross's descriptions of the differing views about the provision of penny meals show the givers investing the meals with the symbolism of friendship and 'communion' with the poor while for the mothers whose children were being fed, 'the meals meant savings of pennies and half-pennies, hours and half-hours, and they raised the subject of bread and meat prices far more often than that of the fellowship of rich and poor.'[170] The Christian Mission also provided meals and the poorer missioners understood that the people who came to eat were there primarily for the food, but they saw within the provision of food an opportunity to evangelise. There was still a gap between the motives and uses of charity but it was more fully recognised and understood by both parties.

Most of the social work that the Salvation Army started prior to 1888 was a spontaneous response to the need that was presented to them specifically because the missioners, and later Salvationists, were working and living among people in great need. In the 1867 *Christian Mission Report,* Booth gave some idea of how the social work started. He spoke of a missioner who was visiting a family of man, wife and four children, living in a home without food, bed or covering. The missioner said to Booth:

> How could I hope to impart any spiritual good, if I could not do something to alleviate the dreadful poverty? Would they not call it a mockery to talk about their souls, whilst their bodies were perishing with hunger?[171]

As early as 2 May 1867, less than two years after Booth decided to remain in the East End, an editorial in the *Christian Times* spoke of his work:

> We are glad to see that Mr Booth unites temporal help with his spiritual efforts. At Poplar means have been provided for giving away 140 quarts of soup and a proportionate quantity of bread four days a week, besides distributing money and clothes.[172]

In the first edition of the *East London Evangelist* in October 1868, there is an example of how the early missioners were inexorably drawn into a social involvement by the areas in which they worked and the expectations raised in the

---

170 Mandler, 1990, p. 182.
171 *Christian Mission Report,* 1867, p. 13.
172 Editorial, *The Christian Times*, 2 May 1867.

minds of others by the words they used. One of the missioners wrote that they had extended their open-air work to Norfolk Gardens, a place inhabited by street-singers, beggars, thieves and prostitutes. As the missioner was about to leave the Gardens a man came up to him and asked for help, explaining that there was a woman in the street whose husband was in gaol and so she was obliged to go out at nights to make money. Her son, almost seven years of age, was running around the streets with a blackened face turning somersaults to earn some money. The man talking said he was a thief himself but he did not want the lad to become one and feared that if the boy was sent to prison once he might keep returning there. Therefore, he wanted the boy to be placed in a reformatory. A note at the end of the article stated that the missioners were trying to get him into the 'Revival Refuge'.[173] It is not hard to see how an aggregation of requests and expectations of this nature would end in the Salvation Army offering its own form of social help to the needs constantly being presented to its members.

Conclusion

The period 1850 to 1870 contained within it a pivotal point in the link between Booth and the London residuum. He came to London first as a job-seeker who found work eventually in a pawnbroker shop. His steps from there could be seen as taking him 'upward' as he eventually trained for the Methodist ministry and worked in communities that were not necessarily the poorest. His theology and his gifts of oratory led him to work as a revivalist and to be able to draw crowds. He, in turn, was drawn to crowds and eventually to the dense, poverty-stricken crowds of Whitechapel. In the size of the residuum of London's East End with its overwhelming poverty and lack of understanding of the Christian gospel Booth found large scope for his revivalist techniques learnt from American evangelists, a focus for his evangelical concerns and increasingly a challenge to face the implications of grinding poverty.

   Although Booth arrived in London in 1849, his decision to remain there was not made until 1865. At this point he was drawn to the East End and in particular his work was first focused on Whitechapel and Bethnal Green. Writing about his decision in 1868 he makes plain the impact made on him by the numbers of people:

> At first sight I felt the *importance* of the sphere. In every direction were *multitudes* totally ignorant of the gospel, and given up to all kinds of wickedness - infidels, drunkards, thieves, harlots, gamblers, blasphemers, and pleasure-seekers *without number*.[174] (Italics added)

It was the size of the residuum that was crucial to Booth's decision to stay in the East End. After his early ministerial work had often been away from the centres

---

173 *East London Evangelist*, October 1868, p. 14.
174 *East London Evangelist*, October 1868.

of poverty, it was the numbers who formed the underclass in the capital that drew him back to his earlier focus on the very poor.

It would be the dialectic of his evangelism and the poverty of the East End that would, in time, create the Salvation Army. Booth had the elements in his Methodism and Chartism from Nottingham but it was the praxis in the East End that led to the particular form the Salvation Army would take. For all his authoritarianism, Booth imbibed the working-class culture to be found there and the poverty of many of the converts constantly drew his attention to social as well as spiritual needs.

The situation in the East End combined with Booth's Nottingham experience of poverty to build organisational foundations that replicated his earliest evangelical and social efforts in Nottingham. The crucial part played by the residuum was in challenging Booth to 'relearn the lessons of Meadow Platts' so that the early Christian Mission was a development of Booth's first Christian work.

The small number, relative to the size of the residuum, of people whose lives were being changed by conversion made it relatively easy for a change in their material conditions to follow. Thus the individual spiritual redemption was often accompanied by a social and economic micro-redemption.

Karl Marx was living in London during this period (from 1849 to 1883) and, in his writings, using examples from newspapers and Government Blue Books that closely resembled what Booth and his converts were meeting. The plight of the residuum also had an impact on Marx's thought just as it did on Booth's although the knowledge was gathered in different ways and led to different solutions being offered, economic theory rather than practical engagement.

Chapter 4

The Revolutionary Philosopher

Introduction

In his biography of London, Peter Ackroyd talks of communism issuing from that city's slums, because Karl Marx was living in London when his most influential works were written:

> So the condition of the mid-nineteenth-century city directly inspired the founders of communism; it might be said that their creed issued out of the slums of London, and those Victorian observers who believed that some great or alarming new reality would emerge from the pervasive presence of the poor were not wholly wrong. The London poor did indeed generate a new race or class, but in countries and civilisations far distant. [1]

London played a crucial role. Clearly, however, Marx's writings were the result of far more than what he saw in London. As the Salvation Army would grow out of the reactive exchange between William Booth and the residuum, so *Capital* and all the other works that Marx was to write in London were the outcome of the interaction of Marx's previous academic and political life with the facts of poverty in urban, industrialised, Victorian London.

Marx's Early Concept of Poverty

Just as William Booth's reaction to the poor of London was conditioned by the poverty he had seen in his youth in Nottingham, so also Karl Marx was first affected by the poverty he saw as a young man in Germany. Marx was first to write about poverty in the journal *Rheinische Zeitung*. He wrote about the poor in the Moselle region of Germany. One of his arguments related to the distribution of wood and the right of the peasants to a share of the timber once the costs had been covered from sales. Even at this early stage, questions of ownership and injustice are evident in Marx's writing:

> The community of several thousand souls to which I belong is the owner of most beautiful wooded areas, but I cannot *recollect* an occasion when members of the community derived direct advantage from their property by sharing in the distribution of wood. [2]

---

1 Ackroyd, 2000, p. 601.
2 *Rheinische Zeitung*, No. 15, 15 January, 1843, in Marx/Engels, 1975-86, Vol. I, pp. 334-5.

Already present here is the idea of communal ownership and his *Rheinische Zeitung* articles reveal Marx's belief that the peasants had a right to a share of the wood. Marx also saw the poverty of the wine-growers as the result of outside competition and trade agreements and not as due to a lack of hard work on the part of the farmers themselves. There was no industrial proletariat and Marx's thought was relatively undeveloped. The time would come, however, when he would totally reject an allocation to the workers, seeing it as a palliative that would hinder the final defeat of private property and capital. Such was not the case in 1842 and 1843 in relation to the particular problem of the Moselle region.[3]

In later years, Marx was to see himself as champion of the proletariat and predicted their pivotal role in the overthrow of capitalism. However, it was in these early articles that he came closest to empathising with the poor as individuals and seeing their immediate needs in terms similar to those that they themselves perceived. Kolakowski has described Marx's articles on timber-gathering as showing a philanthropic viewpoint.[4] At this point in the development of his thought, Marx is prepared to countenance a form of individual redemption for the peasant by granting a right to a share of the property. His thinking could be described as economically naive, but it contains a real sense of compassion for the poor and anger at injustice. It parallels the way in which Booth helped the poor woman of Nottingham and resembles the paradigm through which Booth would continue to see the solution to economic problems: as micro-answers to immediate situations rather than a challenge to the complete system.

However, Marx did not simply argue for the timber-gathering rights of the poor but used the argument as a springboard to introduce themes that he would later develop as important strands in his mature theory. For example, he argued that if every violation of property is theft, then all private property is theft: 'Do I not, by my private property, deprive another person of this property? Do I not thus destroy his right to property?'[5]

Marx also went on to argue that the state cannot simply represent the interests of one class or group, in this instance the landowners, because it would then become the agent of just one class and no longer of the whole community. Here are the first elements of Marx's mature theory of the state as the instrument of class domination.

While Marx's comments on the timber question may seem philanthropic, he later pinpointed this article the start of his focus on economics: 'The proceedings of the Rhenish Parliament on thefts of wood, etc. ... provided the first occasion for occupying myself with the economic questions.'[6] Engels was also to say of Marx: '[I]t was precisely through concentrating on the law of thefts of wood and the situation of the Moselle wine-growers, that he was led from pure politics to economic relationships.'[7]

---

3 *Rheinische Zeitung*, No. 15, 15 January, 1843, in Marx/Engels, 1975-86, Vol. I, pp. 340-3.
4 Kolakowski, 1989, p. 122.
5 Quoted in McLellan, 1972, p. 127.
6 Quoted in McLellan, 1992, p. 11.
7 McLellan, 1972, p. 129.

Paris

In 1843 Marx moved from Germany to Paris where he met Engels during 1844. Engels was returning from a stay in England during which he had gathered the material for his book, *The Conditions of the Working-Class in England in 1844*. It was Engels who recognised the pivotal importance of the English proletariat for any study of economics, both because of the relatively advanced state of industrialisation in England and also because of the availability of statistics for research. Engels wrote in the preface to the first German edition of his book in 1845:

> But proletarian conditions exist in their *classical form*, in their perfection, only in the British Isles, particularly in England proper. Besides, only in England has the necessary material been as completely collected and put on record by official inquiries as is essential for any in the least exhaustive presentation of the subject.[8]

Both of these elements, the advanced industrialisation of England and the official statistics, were to prove of immense importance to Marx twenty years later as he worked in London on producing the manuscripts for *Capital* and *Theories of Surplus Value*.

There is a further idea in Engels' book that foreshadows what was later to become almost a cliché about Marx's thought: his distillation of German philosophy, French socialism and English economics. McLellan claimed that these three constituent elements appeared 'together, if not yet united' for the first time in Marx's writings in the *Paris Manuscripts* of 1844.[9] In 1845 Engels wrote of German philosophy, French socialism and English economics as an important motor in the development of each country:

> The industrial revolution is of the same importance for England as the political revolution for France, and the philosophical revolution for Germany; and the difference between England in 1760 and in 1844 is at least as great as that between France under the *ancien regime* and during the revolution of July.[10]

Marx was to demonstrate a similar dichotomy in his classification of the Paris residuum as the political mob of the lumpenproletariat and the London residuum as the economic victims forming the reserve army of labour.

In *Capital* Marx defined relative surplus population as 'a population surplus in relation to capital's average requirements for valorization.'[11] In defining the various forms of surplus population he wrote that: '[e]very worker belongs to it during the time when he is only partially employed or wholly unemployed.' The lowest sediment of the relative surplus population is pauperism, and within this, according to Marx's definition in Volume I of *Capital*, is found the

---

8 Engels, 1987, p. 29.
9 McLellan, 1992, p. 128.
10 Engels, 1987, p. 61.
11 Marx, 1986, p. 782.

lumpenproletariat. The other groups within pauperism Marx described as either candidates for the industrial reserve army or the dead weight of the industrial reserve army, resulting from the division of labour.[12]

The lumpenproletariat has no economic relation to capital and so cannot be seen as the pool from which the labour army is drawn. The members of the lumpenproletariat (who include beggars, thieves and pimps) are non-productive workers who will not, or cannot, sell their wage labour to capital for the production of surplus value. Such a definition includes other than paupers within the lumpenproletariat and is consistent with Marx's writing in *Eighteenth Brumaire*.[13] Although empirically a man thrown out of work may thieve from necessity and then later return to the workforce in an improved economy, conceptually the lumpenproletariat does not form part of the reserve army of labour. However it is part of relative surplus population.

In his writings about England, Marx put emphasis on the reserve army of labour because the relatively advanced state of the economy meant that capitalist accumulation had created a large reserve from which to draw for its requirements. The size of this pool was both numerically large and proportionately large within the relative surplus population. The lumpenproletariat had relatively little economic or political impact.

In contradistinction Marx gave the lumpenproletariat a high profile within the relative surplus population of France. One reason for this could simply be his motivation for writing about France, which was of great political importance to him, because of the possibility of a revolution there. Therefore, his starting point for his French writings would be a political focus upon the impact of the surplus population and its willingness to sell its allegiance to reactionary forces. However, France was less industrialised than Britain and so the laws of capitalist accumulation, as outlined by Marx, had not produced so large a reserve army of labour as in Britain. Marchand describes France as only half engaged in the industrial revolution, while retaining an excessive agricultural population. In 1851, 74.5 per cent of the French population lived in the countryside and in towns of less than 2,000 people.[14] Although from 1831 onwards urban growth surpassed rural population growth, Fohlen has estimated that even at the period of maximum industrialisation, between 1850 and 1870, the urban population in France never increased by more than 3 per cent per five-year period.[15] The lack of industrialisation gave the lumpenproletariat a greater size and influence relative to the reserve army of labour in France than in Britain, especially prior to 1850.

Empirically the standards of living suffered by both the reserve army of labour in Britain and the lumpenproletariat in France may have been identical as, likewise, may have been their lifestyles in many instances. Louis Chevallier studied the poor of Paris in his book *Labouring Classes and Dangerous Classes*

---

12 Marx, 1986, p. 794.
13 Marx, 1986, p. 797 and *The Eighteenth Brumaire of Louis Bonaparte*, reprinted in Marx & Engels, 1969,p. 442.
14 Marchand, 1993, pp. 69-70.
15 Fohlen, Claude, 'The Industrial Revolution in France' in Cameron, 1970, p. 204.

and quoted from contemporary writings of the day several descriptions that could equally be applied to London; for example:

> If you venture into those accursed districts in which they live, wherever you go you will see men and women branded with the marks of vice and destitution, and half-naked children rotting in filth and stifling in airless, lightless dens. Here, in the very home of civilization, you will encounter thousands of men reduced by sheer besottedness to a life of savagery; here you will perceive destitution in a guise so horrible that it will fill you with disgust rather than pity and you will be tempted to regard it as the condign punishment for a crime ... If you make your way into the old districts now relegated far from the centre, into the Cité, into the narrow, crowded streets of the IXth, VIIIth and XIIth arrondissements, wherever you go you will encounter the image of poverty, even of utter destitution. Indigence in the great cities has a far more disturbing mien than poverty in the country; it inspires disgust and horror, for it assails all the senses at once.[16]

Even the percentage of the population existing in poverty was similar in the two capital cities, although the total number was smaller for Paris, with its population reaching 1 million for the first time in 1846:[17]

> 'The poverty which is crushing a large proportion of the population of our arrondissement goes very deep,' Leuret wrote in his report to the Welfare Office of the XIIth arrondissement in 1836. 'For many of the poor it is one of the misfortunes due to their birth, to illnesses untreated for lack of resources, to the excessive burden of family, to unemployment and to inadequate wages.' This observation clearly identified and brought to the fore the biological determinants ... which placed under a curse a section of the population we now know to have contained at all times, even in the most prosperous periods, nearly one-third of the total population of Paris.[18]

Charles Booth's survey of London at the end of the nineteenth century was similarly to discover around 30 per cent of the population living below the poverty line.[19]

Victor Hugo also wrote about the poor of Paris in his novel *Les Misérables*, which depicted the criminal justice system as one producing criminals. Therefore, Hugo claimed that guilt lay ultimately with society in that societal reform should take precedence over the punishment of individuals. This was not a new theme for Hugo, who expressed a similar idea in his 'documentary' short story written in 1834, *Claude Gueux*. Yet, Hugo had been further influenced by the events of 1848. For his own political reasons, he had turned to what his biographer called the 'peaceful proletariat' of Paris, who 'cherished the image of a socialist Victor Hugo'.[20]

In doing so Hugo gave a graphic description of the poverty in Paris: 'There are in Paris ... whole families who have no other clothes or bed linen than putrid

---

16 Chevallier, 1973, p. 360.
17 Chevallier, 1973, p. 183.
18 Chevallier, 1973, p. 355.
19 Booth, Charles, 1889.
20 Robb, 1997, p. 284.

piles of festering rags, picked up in the mud of the city streets; a sort of urban compost heap in which human creatures bury themselves alive in order to escape the cold of winter.'[21]

This description bears similarities to what Marx would later write of the poor in London. There is a sense in which Hugo was able to see the lumpenproletariat of Paris, at the time of an earlier uprising, in the same way that Marx saw the residuum of London, as victims of the imperfections of society. The connection is best understood by the hidden meaning that Hugo's biographer attributes to the novel's title, *Les Misérables*:

> The title itself is a moral test. It invites a comparison of the human view with the godly-Hugolian view. Originally a *misérable* was simply a pauper (*misère* means 'destitution' as well as 'misfortune'). Since the Revolution, and especially since the advent of Napoleon III, a *misérable* had become a 'dreg', a sore on the shining face of the Second Empire. The new sense would dictate a translation like *Scum of the Earth*. Hugo's sense would dictate *The Wretched*. [22]

However, the function of the underclass was not the same in London and Paris. This was true not only for Marx's interpretation but also for the way in which the unemployed relative surplus population in each capital city saw themselves. The movement from the countryside to the town and particularly to London in nineteenth-century Britain was predominantly economically motivated - there was less work on the land but there was work to be found in towns and cities. However, the dynamic for a similar population movement from the French countryside to Paris was, in part, military and political. While Paris was an industrial centre it was not on a par with London in this regard. Much of its industry was craft-based, with many of the workshops consisting only of one artisan and his apprentice. This was not the kind of industry to attract masses to forsake agriculture for the towns.[23] The reasons for the slower rate of industrialisation were the large numbers of peasant farmers working their own land, the close relationship between the middle class and the state, the difficulty of raising capital because the concept of limited liability took longer to be accepted in France than England, and the fact that France was living through twenty-five years of civil unrest and war at the time when the industrial base might otherwise have been laid.[24]

One motivating force for the creation of a large population that was uprooted from the land and drifted to the city was the militarisation that occurred between 1789 and 1815 with the French Revolution, followed by the wars that were waged to create the French Empire. By the end of this period, the personnel discharged from the army no longer belonged in their home villages. They had an experience of violent internal changes and territorial wars and also a belief in the power of the

---

21 Robb, 1997, p. 284.
22 Robb, 1997, p. 380.
23 Marchand, 1993, p. 19.
24 Fohlen, Claude, 'The Industrial Revolution in France' in Cameron, 1970, p. 221.

mob to change political history.[25]

For those who had moved to Paris for economic reasons it was more a simple escape or flight *from* increased poverty in rural areas than the positive attraction *towards* work in the capital. Bad harvests in 1845 and 1846 led to a rise in grain prices and a sharp reduction in economic activity. This in turn led to some rioting and an increase in people moving to the towns, in search of charity and opportunities for crime as well as opportunities for work. Mendicity grew at this time as it had prior to the 1789 revolution.[26] This was the history of many who formed the lumpenproletariat of Paris and the rest of France. Their cultural identity was intrinsically different from that of the London underclass.

It appears at first as if Marx's changing concept of the lumpenproletariat is a chronological one. As Marx's understanding of the industrial proletariat grew, so he came to see the creation of the underclass as being the result not of personal inadequacies of individuals of the class but of the requirements of capital. However the logic and chronology is not this simple. Marx, over a period of years, was to divide his thinking about the two underclasses of Paris and London so that the residuum of Paris became the lumpenproletariat while the residuum of London became the reserve army of labour.

Like Marx, Engels did not carry his understanding for the poor in England to the downtrodden of Paris, whom he likened to the *lazzaroni* in Naples, and compared them with the *real* workers. Because of their political significance in Paris, Engels made no allowance for the fact that when one is very poor, the opportunity to sell one's allegiance is a similar escape route to that of stealing.[27] The lumpenproletariat of Paris was relatively free to sell political allegiance to either side whereas the reserve army of labour in London had a role that was constrained by the laws of capitalist accumulation. It could therefore be argued that the individual preferences and decisions of the Paris residuum would influence the part to be played by that group in a way that was not true of the London residuum.

In Paris, while experiencing some of the reality of French socialism, Marx learnt more about the situation in England, not only from his meeting with Engels but also from reading the English economists for the first time. The impact of the economists' writing upon his ideas was immediate. This is evident because, in the *Paris Manuscripts* of 1844, Marx quoted from Adam Smith's *Wealth of Nations*:

> In a country which had acquired that full complement of riches ... both the wages of labour and the profits of stock would probably be very low ... the competition for employment would necessarily be so great as to reduce the wages of labour to what was barely sufficient to keep up the number of labourers, and, the country being already peopled, that number could never be augmented.

Marx then added, in his own words: 'The surplus population would have to

25 Marchand, 1993, p. 20.
26 Kemp, 1971, p. 20.
27 Engels, 'The 25th of June' in *Neue Rheinische Zeitung*, 29 June 1848, in Marx/Engels, 1975-86, Vol. VII, pp. 142-3.

die. So in a declining state of society we have the increasing misery of the worker; in an advancing state, complicated misery; and in the terminal state, static misery.'[28]

Many of the ideas which he later developed are to be found in embryo in the *Paris Manuscripts*. Marx's quotation from Smith is found in a discussion of the misery of the working classes which Marx already categorises as a result of the amassing of capital.[29]

In the same notebook Marx also spoke of the way that real material need prevented the sufferer from appreciating anything other than the satisfying of his needs, in a way that paralleled Booth's later realisation that he would often need to offer food and warmth before the poor could absorb the offer of spiritual salvation:

> For a man who is starving the human form of food does not exist, only its abstract form exists; it could just as well be present in its crudest form, and it would be hard to say how this way of eating differs from that of *animals*. The man who is burdened with worries and needs has no *sense* for the finest of plays.[30]

In 1844, Marx had already conceived the concept that he later worked out as the contradictions in political economy, stemming from the value theory of labour: while capital is accumulated labour, the worker is compelled to sell himself and his humanity for a basic minimum income necessary for subsistence. Arthur argued that 1844 marked a turning point in Marx's thinking because from this point material production became pivotal: 'For the first time he attributes ontological significance to *productive activity*.'[31]

It is material production which is the *'mediation'* in which is realised the unity of man with nature, if there is not distortion of the relationship. However, by 1844, as Marx studied the English economists, he had also recognised that the wage labourer was alienated from the object of his productive activity. In capitalist production the labourer was compelled to treat his labour as a commodity and hence had no relation to or interest in his work:

> *The demand for men necessarily regulates the production of men, as of every other commodity.* If the supply greatly exceeds the demand, then one section of the workers sinks into beggary or starvation. The existence of the worker is therefore reduced to the same condition as the existence of every other commodity. The worker has become a commodity, and he is lucky if he can find a buyer. And the demand on which the worker's life depends is regulated by the whims of the wealthy and the capitalists.[32]

Like Carlyle and Booth, Marx drew out a comparison between the lot of the wage labourer and that of a horse:

---

28 Marx, 1992(a), p. 286.
29 Marx, 1992(a), p. 286.
30 Marx, 1992(a), p. 353.
31 Arthur, 1986, p. 5.
32 Marx, 1992(a), p. 283.

It goes without saying that political economy regards the *proletarian*, i.e. he who lives without capital and ground rent from labour alone, and from one-sided, abstract labour at that, as nothing more than a *worker*. It can therefore advance the thesis that, like a horse, he must receive enough to enable him to work. It does not consider him, during the time when he is not working, as a human being.[33]

Marx also quoted from Wilhelm Shulz in his 1843 manuscripts, underlining the different dynamics in creating the underclass in England and France:

Where legislation preserves the unity of large landed properties, the surplus quantity of a growing population crowds together into industry, and it is therefore mainly in industry that the proletariat gathers in large numbers, as in Great Britain. But where legislation allows the continuous division of the land, as in France, the number of small, debt-ridden proprietors increases and many of them are forced into the class of the needy and discontented.[34]

In the second of the *Paris Manuscripts,* Marx made his first reference to the class he would later refer to as the lumpenproletariat. The fact that he was referring to the class in England is made clear by his reference later in the same paragraph to English factory owners and the Amendment Bill of 1834. Marx at this stage seemed to be saying that the residuum had no part to play in the capitalist economy:

Political economy, therefore, does not recognise the unemployed worker, the working man, insofar as he happens to be outside this labour relationship. The rascal, swindler, beggar, the unemployed, the starving, wretched and criminal working man - these are *figures* who do not exist *for political economy* but only for other eyes, those of the doctor, the judge, the grave-digger, and bum-bailiff, etc.; such figures are spectres outside its domain. For it, therefore, the worker's needs are but the one *need* - to maintain *him whilst he is working* and insofar as may be necessary to prevent the *race of labourers* from (dying) out.[35]

It is interesting that the above statement does not suggest the sense of a personal fault leading to membership of such a group or of individual choice being significant, as did his later remarks about the Paris mob, which included the unemployed and starving as well as the rascal, the swindler and the criminal. It could be argued that Marx was simply explaining the view of political economy in the above paragraph and that there is no reason to suppose that he shared such views. However, during 1848, when he joined with Engels to produce the *Communist Manifesto* he used the term 'das Lumpenproletariat', which has been translated into English as the 'social scum' or the 'rag proletariat'. Emphasising its lack of political allegiance, Marx differentiated the lumpen- from the true proletariat:

---

33 Marx, 1992(a), p. 288.
34 Marx, 1992(a), pp. 303-4.
35 Marx, 2nd Manuscript, *Economic & Philosophic Manuscripts of 1844*, in Marx/Engels, 1975- 86, Vol. III, p. 284.

[T]hat passively rotting mass thrown off by the lowest layers of old society, may, here and there, be swept into the movement by a proletarian revolution, its conditions of life, however, prepare it far more for the part of a bribed tool of reactionary intrigue.[36]

Bender suggested that Marx made this distinction because, despite its dire poverty, the lumpenproletariat lacks the condition of entry to the proletariat, through the specific relation to the means of production, that of wage labour.[37] Whether from personal choice, from the conditions of personal life history, from lack of skill that could be of use to a capitalist, or from the conditions of capitalism itself, the members of the lumpenproletariat are not in the relation to capital whereby their labour power, their capacity to work for a given time, is being sold as a commodity under capitalism. Once the unemployed become part of the lumpenproletariat there is an implication that they are unfit to join or rejoin the proletariat via the reserve army of labour. The main significance of members of the lumpenproletariat is political, their willingness to sell their allegiance. Nevertheless, there is implicit in Marx's writings an element of choice that presupposes the possibility of redemption through choosing to fight for revolutionary rather than reactionary forces.

There is an understanding, in the above quotation from the *Communist Manifesto,* that the lumpenproletariat may be the tool of the reactionary forces because of their conditions of life. The conditions that prepare one group of the unemployed to seek the pay of mercenaries and another to wait on the fringes of capitalist production for the chance to sell their labour power are empirically similar. The *Communist Manifesto* was for an international readership and Marx's recognition of the pressures on the lumpenproletariat in its pages is inconsistent with the stance he takes when writing purely about France, notably in *Eighteenth Brumaire.* The lumpenproletariat in France had been paid by Louis Napoleon to fight on the side of the bourgeoisie against the workers' uprising in Paris. Marx had a personal commitment to the workers' revolution. He had an emotional involvement when he wrote about its defeat and, therefore, he was not prepared to allow the historical determinants that led to the actions of the lumpenproletariat, to appear in his French political writings.

The economic significance of the lumpenproletariat is its possible increase. The growth of the relative surplus population, caused by capitalist accumulation, leads to more people living in misery and, thereby, more likely to be recruited or forced into the lumpenproletariat. Marx already recognised that members of the proletariat can be forced into pauperism by the impetus of industrial capitalism. Only a few paragraphs after the above-mentioned description of the lumpenproletariat Marx wrote: 'The modern labourer....instead of rising with the progress of industry sinks deeper and deeper below the conditions of existence of his own class. He becomes a pauper, and pauperism develops more rapidly than population and wealth.'[38]

---

36 Marx, 1988, p. 65.
37 Fredric Bender, footnote in Marx, 1988, p. 65.
38 Marx, *Communist Manifesto*, quoted in Smelser, 1973, p. 85.

Within a year of his arrival in London, Marx wrote *Class Struggles in France,* describing the Mobile Guard, 24 battalions of 1,000 men each, all between the ages of 15 and 20 years, and formed by the Provisional Government to confront the Paris proletariat.[39] That Marx was able to describe 24,000 young men as being part of the lumpenproletariat shows how large a proportion of the population he was able to identify in this group when he was writing a political polemic about France. The total surplus population was politically more important and economically less important in France than in England, a more developed political history and a less developed economy. To Marx, therefore, their significance was political and it was politically negative.

Marx's figures of 24,000 men between the ages of 15 and 20 who formed the Mobile Guard and are drawn from the lumpenproletariat involve 5 per cent of the available population of the cities of France. Assuming that France did not have a higher percentage relative surplus population than Britain, 10 per cent, the lumpenproletariat accounted for half the relative surplus population in France. Marx's writings about Britain, as shown below, described the lumpenproletariat of Britain as one part of one third of the relative surplus population. The lumpenproletariat of France was therefore proportionately numerically stronger than that of Britain.

Marx described the young men as:

> [A] mass strictly differentiated from the industrial proletariat, a recruiting ground for thieves and criminals of all kinds, living on the crumbs of society, people without a definite trade, vagabonds, *gens sans feu et sans aveu,* with differences according to the degree of civilisation of the nation to which they belong, but never renouncing their *lazzaroni* character.....The Provisional Government paid them 1 franc 50 centimes a day, i.e. it bought them.[40]

Marx's disparagement of people who can be bought in this way is obvious. There is no question here of understanding that, at a given level of poverty, to accept payment to fight, for whatever cause, might seem a logical way to meet the need for livelihood. As Worsley has said of a similar criticism made of the poor in modern-day Turkey:

> In fact, the poor, like the established working-class, do not respond to poverty ideologically, but instrumentally: their main aim is to stop being poor. They are therefore vulnerable to a variety of demagogic and hegemonic appeals, promises, blandishments and deceptions ... Yet there is no evidence that the casual poor are any more (or less) susceptible than organised workers to the demagogic appeals of the Right or of the populists, or intrinsically deaf to socialism.[41]

Worsley's words are reminiscent of Marx's about lack of food reducing the

---

39 Marx, n.d., p. 50.
40 Marx, n.d., p. 50.
41 Worsley, 1988, p. 220.

parameters of decision making for the poor,[42] quoted above, but not of Marx's words about the Paris residuum. Marx's attitude is in marked contrast to Engels' understanding that it may be logical for the poor of Manchester to steal. Marx saw the lumpenproletariat of France as a political force because the aim of his writing about France had an immediate political interest.

Marx used the term lumpenproletariat in connection with the finance aristocracy and by so doing communicated their faults and his disapprobation: 'The finance aristocracy, in its mode of acquisition as well as in its pleasures, is nothing but the resurrection of the lumpenproletariat at the top of bourgeois society.'[43]

Marx's description of the finance aristocracy suggests that he imputed to them personal faults and attitudes of which he disapproved. The finance aristocracy is outside the relations of industrial production in a capitalist society. It neither directs wage labour nor adds value by its own labour. It therefore reflects, at the higher stratum, the characteristics of the lumpenproletariat at the lowest level of society.

There are also suggestions in Marx's writing about Paris that those whom he has grouped together as the lumpenproletariat share a degree of poverty as well as the individual characteristics of those who operate outside the system of capitalist production, when he wrote of the lumpenproletariat being led: 'to brothels, to workhouses and to lunatic asylums.'[44] Such a statement, coupled with the numbers Marx includes in the lumpenproletariat in Paris, supports the argument that many members of the Paris lumpenproletariat are empirically comparable to those he would later term as the reserve army of labour in London.

Two years after *The Class Struggles in France* Marx wrote another political polemic on the situation in France, *The Eighteenth Brumaire of Louis Bonaparte*. Once again, he was scathing of the lumpenproletariat, comparing and contrasting them with the working proletariat, just as they had been manoeuvred into actual opposition in France: 'The French bourgeoisie balked at the domination of the working proletariat; it has brought the lumpenproletariat to domination.'[45]

As in his previous book on France, Marx was to concentrate on the political significance of the lumpenproletariat, on their willingness to be bought and on what he clearly saw as personal characteristics which caused them to be part of that group. Therefore, Marx wrote about the proposals of Bonaparte to pay the non-commissioned officers of the Mobile Guard and his proposal for a loan bank:

> Donations and loans - the financial science of the lumpenproletariat, whether of high or low degree, is restricted to this. Such were the only springs which Bonaparte knew how to set in action. Never has a pretender speculated more stupidly on the stupidity of the masses.[46]

---

42 Marx, 1992(a), p. 353.
43 Marx, n.d., p. 36.
44 Marx, n.d., p. 37.
45 Marx, *The Eighteenth Brumaire of Louis Bonaparte*, reprinted in Marx/Engels, 1969, p. 474.
46 Marx, *The Eighteenth Brumaire of Louis Bonaparte*, reprinted Marx/Engels, 1969, p. 437.

That Marx was contemptuous of the people who formed the lumpenproletariat is shown most clearly in the quotation below:

> On the pretext of founding a benevolent society, the lumpenproletariat of Paris had been organised into secret sections, each section being led by Bonapartist agents, with a Bonapartist general at the head of the whole. Alongside decayed *roués* with dubious means of subsistence and of dubious origin, alongside ruined and adventurous offshoots of the bourgeoisie, were vagabonds, discharged soldiers, discharged jailbirds, escaped galley slaves, swindlers, mountebanks, *lazzaroni*, pickpockets, tricksters, gamblers, *maquereaus*, brothel keepers, porters, *literati*, organ-grinders, rag-pickers, knife grinders, tinkers, beggars - in short, the whole indefinite, disintegrated mass, thrown hither and thither, which the French term *la bohème;* from this kindred element Bonaparte formed the core of the Society of December 10. A 'benevolent society' - in so far as, like Bonaparte, all its members felt the need of benefiting themselves at the expense of the labouring nation.[47]

Eighteenth Brumaire is a political polemic against Louis Bonaparte, and Marx sought to underline his disapproval by placing Bonaparte in the lumpenproletariat. The above quotation also gives the most complete list of those whom Marx included in the concept of lumpenproletariat for Paris. Given that he included such people as organ grinders, knife grinders and porters there is further evidence that this is a wider group than those whom he included in the relatively insignificant lumpenproletariat of London when he was writing *Capital*. For Paris, lumpenproletariat is the term Marx used to describe those who were unproductive and parasitic due to personal choice rather than an economic imperative. Marx continued:

> This Bonaparte, who constitutes himself *chief of the lumpenproletariat,* who here alone rediscovers in mass form the interests which he personally pursues, who recognises in this scum, offal, refuse of all classes the only class upon which he can base himself unconditionally, is the real Bonaparte.[48]

Catherine Booth would later draw similar parallels between the parasites at the top and base of society in England, saving her harshest words for those at the top:

> Further, 'the criminal classes' is another of the cant phrases of modern Christianity, which thus brands every poor lad who steals because he is hungry, but stands cap in hand before the rich man whose trade is well known to be a system of wholesale cheatery.[49]

---

47 Marx, *The Eighteenth Brumaire of Louis Bonaparte,* reprinted in Marx/Engels, 1969, p. 442.
48 Marx, *The Eighteenth Brumaire of Louis Bonaparte,* reprinted in Marx/Engels, 1969, p. 442.
49 Booth Tucker, 1912, Vol. II, p. 287.

The two quotations from Marx, when taken together, give the most clear and complete picture possible of his view and understanding of the Paris residuum. There seems to be little overlap with the way Marx viewed the London residuum. There is also no recognition, on his part, that, although he was receiving an income of about three times the earnings of an average skilled workman, Marx was unable to manage financially. His personal situation, which he described in a letter to Engels the same year that he wrote *Eighteenth Brumaire,* involved a lifestyle rather similar to that of the lumpenproletariat. Marx even found himself begging from Engels:

> For 8-10 days I have fed the family on bread and potatoes of which it is still questionable whether I can rustle up any today ... The best and most desirable thing that could happen would be that the landlady throw me out of the house. At least I would then be quit of the sum of £22. But I can scarcely trust her to be so obliging. Also baker, milkman, the man with the tea, greengrocer, old butcher's bills. How can I get clear of this hellish muck? Finally in the last 8 - 10 days, I have borrowed some shillings and pence (this is the most fatal thing, but it was necessary to avoid perishing) from layabouts.[50]

Marx would have seen himself as a victim, a justification he was prepared to share with the residuum of London, but not that of Paris.

London

In 1849 Marx arrived in London, where he was to reside for the rest of his life. He knew about the economic situation in England before he lived there. He had already been influenced by Engels and by his writings. There are two ways in which Engels presaged Booth in the way he wrote about London: in his stress on the particular poverty in Whitechapel and in his calculation of the numbers living in pauperism. In his description of the worst areas of working-class poverty, Engels wrote of the most extensive working class district as being: 'east of the Tower in Whitechapel and Bethnal Green, where the greatest masses of working people live.'[51]

Twenty years after Engels wrote this, Booth chose to stay in the East End of London and work there, because of the size of the residuum in Whitechapel and Bethnal Green. Marx was also to use Bethnal Green as synonymous with great poverty when he wrote in Volume I of *Capital* of 'the notorious district of Bethnal Green' where children from the age of nine years hired themselves out to silk manufacturers at a public market held on Monday and Tuesday morning.[52]

Engels, 45 years before Booth, had estimated that one in ten people were living in dire poverty. In *The Conditions of the Working-Class in England in 1844* Engels approached the calculation from another angle, arguing that: 'ten are somewhat better off where one is so totally trodden under foot by society.'[53] In

---

50 McLellan, 1973, p. 263.
51 Engels, 1987, p. 72.
52 Marx, *Capital,* Vol. I, quoted in Smelser, 1973, p. 43.
53 Engels, 1987, p. 74.

1848, writing for the *Kölnische Zeitung,* Engels was to repeat the same claim: 'One man in every ten in England is a pauper and one pauper in every three is an inmate of one of the Poor Law Bastilles.' [54]

Even more significant for a consideration of the general concept of the reserve army of labour versus that of the lumpenproletariat is the fact that, in writing about London, Engels did not see the predicament of the poorest as being the result of personal inadequacies:

> I assert that thousands of industrious and worthy people - far worthier and more to be respected than all the rich of London - do find themselves in a condition unworthy of human beings; and that every proletarian, every one, without exception, is exposed to a similar fate without any fault of his own and in spite of every possible effort. [55]

Engels was even prepared to accept that theft could be a logical choice where poverty is experienced: 'Want leaves the working man the choice between starving slowly, killing himself speedily, or taking what he needs where he finds it - in plain English, stealing. And there is no cause for surprise that most workers prefer stealing to starvation and suicide.' [56]

That the residuum of England began to have an impact on Marx's thinking before he moved there is shown in an article he wrote in Cologne during January 1849, the year when he was to settle in England. He clearly considered the people living in the workhouses in England as economic victims of capitalism:

> In English workhouses - public institutions in which the surplus labour population is allowed to vegetate at the expense of bourgeois society - charity is cunningly combined with the *revenge* which the bourgeoisie wreaks on the wretches who are compelled to appeal to its charity.....These unfortunate people have committed the crime of having ceased to be an object of exploitation yielding a profit to the bourgeoisie - as is the case in ordinary life - and having become instead an object of expenditure for those born to derive benefit from them. [57]

In 1849, Marx wrote *Wage Labour and Capital,* in which he described the impact of machinery and the division of labour on the conditions of the worker. Marx described in this pamphlet the creation of the reserve army of labour by the capitalist system:

> We have hastily sketched in broad outlines the industrial war of capitalists among themselves. This war has the peculiarity that the battles in it are won less by recruiting than by discharging the army of workers. The generals (the capitalists) vie with one another as to who can discharge the greatest number of industrial soldiers. [58]

---

54 Engels, 'On the State of Affairs in England' dated 31 July, Cologne, reprinted Marx/Engels,1975-86, Vol. VII, p. 296.

55 Engels, 1987, p.74.

56 Engels, 1987, p. 143.

57 Marx, 'A Bourgeois Document' reprinted in Marx/Engels, 1975-86, Vol. VIII, p. 218.

58 Marx, *Wage Labour & Capital,* reprinted in Smelser, 1973, pp. 95-6.

In addition, machinery made it possible for women and children to do work previously reserved for men, thus creating further downward pressure on wages while at the same time people from the higher strata of society were being pushed into the working class. Thus in Marx's graphic words: '[T]he forest of outstretched arms, begging for work, grows ever thicker, while the arms themselves grow ever leaner.'[59]

Wilhelm Liebknecht wrote that *Capital* could only have been written in London. McLellan gives three reasons why this might be so. Firstly, London was the capital of the most advanced industrialised nation, with endless examples of the positive and negative results of the rush to make profit through industrial production, and to capital accumulation. Secondly, the library at the British Museum contained the largest collection of economic writings anywhere at that time and also gave Marx access to Government reports, statistics and the Blue Books, which Marx used amply to support his arguments in *Capital*.[60] Thirdly, during Marx's residence in London there was more tolerance of political exiles than was often the case on the continent, there was little censorship and Marx was allowed to remain without the threat of deportation.

With regard to the impact of London itself, the previous quotations have already shown that Marx was aware, prior to living in London, of the importance of capitalism in England and of the importance of England at the centre of the development of capitalism.

However, to be at the hub must have played a part in directing Marx's thinking although there is no suggestion that, despite his more sympathetic treatment of the London residuum compared with that of Paris in his writings, he ever personally sympathised with the plight of individual members of the underclass. In a sense he allowed the Paris mob more individuality, with their individual inadequacies, their choice to change side for money, than he did the reserve army of labour, whom he saw, en masse, as a necessary condition of the historical imperative of the accumulation of capital.

Nevertheless, Marx was aware of the human plight of the poor in London, referring more than once in his correspondence to the numbers of deaths from starvation. For example in an article written in 1853 and published in the *New York Daily Tribune* Marx wrote:

> Some further cases of starvation have occurred in London during the present month. I remember only the case of Mary Ann Sandry, aged 43 years, who died in Coal-lane, Shadwell, London. Mr. Thomas Peene, the surgeon, assisting the Coroner's inquest, said the deceased died from starvation and exposure to the cold. The deceased was lying on a small heap of straw, without the slightest covering. The room was completely destitute of furniture, firing and food. Five young children were sitting on the bare flooring, crying from hunger and cold by the side of the mother's dead body.[61]

---

59 Marx, *Wage Labour & Capital,* reprinted in Smelser, 1973, p. 97.
60 For example, Marx, 1986 pp. 492-639, the chapter on 'Machinery and Large-Scale Industry'.
61 Marx, 'Parliamentary Debates -The Clergy and the Struggle for the Ten-Hour Day -

The second argument, about the Government statistics and reports available to Marx, is less open to dispute than the first point about the importance of physically seeing London and its industrialisation. Engels himself had made a similar case five years earlier.

The third point about freedom for political exiles in London is also clearly supported. Both the Austrian and Prussian governments had sought to influence the British to act against the refugees who were members of the Communist League, but they were not successful. The fact that Marx did not discover the same opportunity for revolutionary praxis in England and was to some extent marginalised may have led both to the authorities seeing him as less than dangerous and to him having more time to devote to his academic research.

There was to be a similar lack of panic and aggression in the British response to the writings of Marx when they were published:

> British writers found it abnormally easy to maintain their calm. No anti-capitalist movement challenged them, few doubts about the permanence of capital nagged them. The task of disproving Marx was therefore neither urgent nor of great practical importance. Happily, as the Rev. M. Kauffman, perhaps our earliest non-Marxist 'expert' on Marxism, put it, Marx was a pure theorist who had not tried to put his doctrines into practice. By revolutionary standards he seemed to be even less dangerous than the anarchists ... Consequently bourgeois readers approached him in a spirit of tranquillity or - in the case of the Rev. Kauffman - Christian forbearance.[62]

There is a contrast between such reactions to Marx's writings and the furore caused by the publication of Booth's *Darkest England* book, which, while far less threatening to the status quo than Marx's writings, was perceived in England as more of a threat because of the immediacy and practical import of Booth's proposals. More danger was perceived in actions than in ideas. Yet all of Marx's impact came from the power of his ideas and his theory of revolution was formed by study as well as experience:

> It is noteworthy that the idea of the proletariat's special mission as a class which cannot liberate itself without thereby liberating society as a whole makes its first appearance in Marx's thought as a philosophical deduction rather than a product of observation.[63]

His main contact with the proletariat in London was in teaching his ideas as 'the schoolmaster of international socialism' with the General Council of the International Workingmen's Association.[64] Some of the activities at Great Windmill Street bore a striking similarity to those that Booth introduced in his early East End mission halls:

Starvation' printed in *New York Daily Tribune,* March 15, 1853, reprinted in Marx & Engels, 1953, pp. 370-1.
62 Hobsbawm, 1979, pp. 240-1.
63 Kolakowski, 1989, p. 130.
64 Lyon, 1988, p. 127.

On Sundays, there were lectures on history, geography, and astronomy, followed by 'questions of the present position of the workers and their attitude to the bourgeoisie'. Discussions about communism occupied most of Monday and Tuesday, but later in the week the curriculum included singing practice, language teaching, drawing lessons and even dancing classes. Saturday evening was devoted to 'music, recitations and reading interesting newspaper articles.[65]

Marx was someone who had made a personal choice to remain outside wage labour so that he could write. However, although Marx was living in poverty he was not viewed by everyone as sharing the life of the workers. A similar level of income did not lead to identification with the workers. He was viewed by the refugee workers in London as an 'intellectual' rather than a 'practical' man who commanded their respect but not their affection.[66]

Yet Marx emphasised the importance of the fusing of intellectual and practical, what he described in the first of his theses on Feuerbach as 'practical-critical' activity. Despite the fact that he was to a large degree isolated from political and revolutionary activity once he was in England, Marx was aware that 'the question whether objective truth is an attribute of human thought - is not a theoretical but a *practical* question.'[67] It is not clear whether he sensed a danger for himself that in his almost entirely intellectual activity the question of the reality or non-reality of his thinking, isolated from practice, would become 'a purely *scholastic* question'.[68]

Learning from London

During the winter of 1857-58 Marx worked on the notebooks that are today known as the *Grundrisse*. Chronologically, therefore, they occur midway between the *Communist Manifesto* and *Capital* Volume I. The work, which was a 'rough draft' of the series of books that Marx eventually hoped to produce, was written quickly in response to an economic crisis. While many of the themes that were to appear in the six volumes of *Capital* and *Theories of Surplus Value* are outlined in the *Grundrisse,* Marx did not address the effects of the development of modern machinery in any detail.

At the beginning of the notes for 'The Chapter on Capital' in the *Grundrisse*, Marx worked through a definition of a productive worker:

---

65 Wheen, 1999, p. 155.
66 McLellan,1973, p. 247.
67 Marx, 1942, p. 197.
68 Marx, 1942, p. 197.

[Where] one of the contracting parties does not confront the other as a capitalist, [the] performance of a service cannot fall under the category of productive labour. From whore to pope there is a mass of such rabble. But the honest and 'working' lumpenproletariat belongs here as well; e.g. the great mob of porters etc. who render service in seaport cities etc.[69]

The concept of an honest and working lumpenproletariat was a new one. The members of it are still termed lumpenproletariat but such a terminology springs purely from their relation, or lack of it, to capital. Ten years later the working lumpenproletariat was to be differentiated from the 'actual lumpenproletariat' as the reserve army of labour because of the possibility of its members being drawn into productive labour when economic circumstances required.

During the 1860s Marx wrote the three volumes of *Capital* and the three volumes of *Theories of Surplus Value*. He did not use the original outline, found in the *Grundrisse*. The books followed a narrower scope than that outline but with the subjects that remained expanded. The reserve army of labour and relative surplus population are mentioned in every volume but the lumpenproletariat is mentioned only once, in the first volume of *Capital*.[70] The lumpenproletariat as a political force or as a condition of lifestyle had virtually no relevance but the reserve army of labour as a necessary result of capitalist accumulation became crucial.

C. J. Arthur, in his comparison between the *Grundrisse* and *Capital* has emphasised the development in Marx's thinking on the topic of the reserve army of labour between 1857 and 1865:

We thus come to the question of the so-called industrial reserve army, which Marx derived directly from the concept of relative surplus value in the *Rough Draft* (in contrast to *Capital*), without having first described the effect of machinery on the development of the working population ... [T]he *Rough Draft* equates the reserve army with the 'sphere of pauperism', whereas according to *Capital* this sphere, populated by impoverished and lumpen proletarian elements, simply forms the 'deepest sediment of relative overpopulation'.[71]

In Volume I of *Capital*, Marx quoted from a letter from the Chief Constable of Bolton in which he reported that young girls were becoming prostitutes because of being thrown out of work during the cotton famine.[72] Therefore, Marx wrote about a group of people, prostitutes, who, in all his previous writings, he would have automatically categorised as lumpenproletariat, the subject of his disapprobation, and who were here described as the suffering victims of capitalism. Clearly the difference is in Marx's viewpoint, either caused by chronology and the impact of Britain and its economists or a concomitant of a new focus and polemic.

In Volume I of *Theories of Surplus Value* Marx explained how the reserve army of labour could be formed:

---

69 Marx, 1993(b), p. 272.
70 Marx, 1986, p. 797.
71 Rosdolsky, 1977, p. 250.
72 Marx, 1986, p. 587.

The shifting of labour and capital which increased productivity in a particular branch of industry brings about by means of machinery etc., is always only prospective. That is to say, *the increase, the new number of labourers entering industry,* is distributed in a different way; perhaps the children of those who have been thrown out, but not these themselves. They themselves vegetate for a long time in their old trade, which they carry on under the most unfavourable conditions, inasmuch their necessary labour-time is greater than the socially necessary labour-time; they become paupers, or find employment in branches of industry where a lower grade of labour is employed. [73]

Marx used the census returns of 1861 to show the industries in which the total number of people employed had fallen. He included agriculture, worsted manufacture and silk weaving. In describing the areas where employment had increased, Marx referred to the cases of cotton-spinning and coal-mining, where machinery had not so far been employed with much success. Machinery thus helped to create and increase the reserve army of labour, whose function Marx described as follows:

The industrial reserve army, during the periods of stagnation and average prosperity, weighs down the active army of workers; during the periods of over-production and feverish activity, it puts a curb on their pretensions. The relative surplus population is therefore the background against which the law of the demand and supply of labour does its work. It confines the field of action of this law to the limits absolutely convenient to capital's drive to exploit and dominate the workers. [74]

Although Marx's description of the industrial reserve army still included the ideas of weighing down and curbing the industrial proletariat and fulfilling the requirements of the bourgeoisie, he now also saw the unemployed as victims, along with the working proletariat, of the economic forces created by capital accumulation. He wrote of the laws of capitalist accumulation which create and require the reserve army, partly by the wasteful use of the working proletariat:

In line with its contradictory and antagonistic nature, the capitalist mode of production proceeds to count the prodigious dissipation of the labourer's life and health, and the lowering of his living conditions, as an economy in the use of constant capital and thereby as a means of increasing capital ... The capitalist mode of production is generally, despite all its niggardliness, altogether too prodigal with its human material. [75]

This 'contradictory and antagonistic nature' of capitalist production was particularly evident in the ebb and flow of the size of the reserve army, created by the advance in machinery. It was needed for capital's 'free play':

This qualitative change in mechanical industry continually discharges hands from the factory, or shuts its doors against the fresh stream of recruits, while the purely

---

73 Marx, 1978, pp. 217-8.
74 Marx, 1986, p. 792.
75 Marx, 1984, pp. 86-7.

quantitative extension of the factories absorbs not only the men thrown out of work, but also fresh contingents. The workpeople are thus continually both repelled and attracted, hustled from pillar to post, while, at the same time, constant changes take place in the sex, age, and skill of the levies.[76]

Capitalist production can by no means content itself with the quantity of disposable labour-power which the natural increase of the population yields. It requires for its unrestricted activity an industrial reserve army independent of these natural limits.[77]

Marx divided the relative surplus population into three groups: the floating, the latent and the stagnant as well as what he termed the sediment who live in the sphere of pauperism. Within pauperism were to be found: '[V]agabonds, criminals, prostitutes, in short the actual lumpenproletariat'.[78] This was the only time Marx used the term lumpenproletariat in *Capital*.

The categories of pauperism, which were rather reminiscent of Mayhew's,[79] included, first, those able to work; second, orphans and pauper children; and third, the demoralized, the ragged and those unable to work. Of the whole relative surplus population, Marx considered that only this last category did not form part of the industrial reserve army at the upward turn of an economic cycle. He wrote of this category as the *faux frais* of capitalist production, leaving a relatively small and insignificant role for the 'actual lumpenproletariat'.[80]

More recent research has emphasised that often what the politically powerful or intellectually influential refer to as the 'sediment', or by other dismissive terms, has its own subculture that is closed to outsiders and that, were it to be understood, could radically alter the perceptions of wider society concerning the group. To some extent Mayhew had already made this argument for the poor of the East End at the time of Marx, but there is little evidence that society was prepared to view his findings in this way.[81] Worsley's book on the modern residuum has underlined that deviant subcultures have been shown to be as structured and as principled as 'straight' groups:

There were two logical extensions of this line of thought: the relativist one, which argued that *no* group could claim its values to be *superior*, only to be different or *as* good as those of other groups, and the more radical argument that superiority and inferiority were merely outcomes of power, of the capacity of a group to enforce its ideas and practices on others.[82]

Marx would have accepted the second argument on behalf of the working proletariat and even the reserve army of labour, namely that their inferiority within

---

76 Marx, 1986, p. 583.
77 Marx, 1986, p. 788.
78 Marx, 1986, p. 797.
79 Mayhew, 1985, p. 457.
80 Marx, 1986, p. 797.
81 See Stedman Jones, 1992, p.10 footnote 33.
82 Worsley, 1988, p. 52.

the system came from the opposing power of capital, but there was still a stratum in his categorisation that was 'lumpen', who had no part to play in production, no contribution to make to society, because they had no relation with capital. This was the group that William Booth's organisation at its most effective was able to penetrate but which was always opaque to Marx.

The size of the reserve army of labour was part of what Marx termed the absolute general law of capitalist accumulation. The greater the size of the reserve army relative to those employed, the greater is the competition for employment and thus the greater downward pressure on wages. Rosa Luxemburg wrote of the two as being intrinsically linked:

> In representing capitalist wage relations it is quite wrong only to take into account the wages actually paid to the employed industrial workers ... The entire reserve army of the unemployed, from the unemployed skilled worker down to the deepest levels of poverty and official pauperism, enters into the determination of wage relations as an equal factor ... [T]he lowest strata of the rarely employed or totally unemployed destitutes and outcasts are not a kind of excrescence ... but are, on the contrary, connected through all the intermediate links of the reserve army with the topmost and best situated layer of industrial workers by means of internal, living bonds.[83]

Luxemburg argued that the greater the absolute size of the reserve army the greater the spread of misery and pauperism. The residuum is here seen as subject to the laws, and part of the modus operandi, of capitalist accumulation, victims of the system, not members of a stratum defined by personal inadequacies. It is very different from Marx's analysis of the Paris mob but not so different from his view that the Moselle wine-growers were poor because they were the victims of trade agreements. What Marx did was to show that the exploitation of labour was not the result of the acts of individual capitalists against their workers but that it came about from the very logic of the capitalist system: '[M]achinery, while augmenting the human material that forms capital's most characteristic field of exploitation, at the same time raises the degree of that exploitation.'[84]

However, the reserve army of labour had a role to play in capitalist accumulation. In order for the individual capitalist to expand production he needs among other things, additional labour. He cannot himself produce this additional labour, he 'depends upon factors and events beyond his control, materialising, as it were, behind his back'.[85] If the reserve army of labour had been absorbed into the capitalist system by employment, so that it no longer existed as a reserve, then it would become necessary to find other groups to fulfil its function. Rosa Luxemburg stressed the indispensability of 'social reservoirs outside the dominion of capital' from which to recruit into the wage proletariat as necessary.

---

83 Luxemburg, quoted in Rosdolsky, 1977, p. 308.
84 Marx, 1986, p. 518.
85 Luxemburg, 1963, p. 45.

> Only the existence of non-capitalist groups ... can guarantee such a supply of
> additional labour power for capitalist production ... Capitalism needs non-capitalist
> social strata as a reservoir of labour power for its wage system.[86]

Conclusion

Marx's view of the lumpenproletariat of Paris was rather similar to Booth's view
of the London residuum in 1865. They each credited the individual members of the
class with some degree of power and ability to make a choice. Marx emphasised
the choice made by the lumpenproletariat of Paris to be bought by Bonaparte and
his reactionary forces. Booth offered the London residuum a choice in accepting or
rejecting the offer of Christian redemption. Both had their original view broadened
by their increased knowledge and understanding of the making and conditions of
the London residuum.

As Marx studied the workings and results of industrial capitalism in London
he absorbed into his thought the concept that the surplus population was a result of
and necessary to capitalism; that the lumpenproletariat had been squeezed out by
capitalism; and that, like the sea to which the city of London had often been
likened, the surplus population would be drawn into the industrial system and then
discarded again as capitalism followed its cyclical advance.

In later years Booth was to broaden his thought to include the need for
redemption of the system that produced the residuum as well as the individual
redemption for each member of the underclass.

There is a correspondence in the development of their ideas that springs from
their involvement, either academic or practical, with the London residuum. There is
also a sense that Marx had returned to his earlier view of the poor as victims of the
political system, in a similar way to Booth being drawn back to the poor as the focus
of his work. If Booth spoke of relearning the lessons of Meadow Platts, Marx came
much closer in writing *Capital* than in all his previous political polemics to the
sentiments he had expressed about the Moselle wine growers and wood gleaners.
Lyon has made the following judgement about the development of his work:

> [T]he connections between the *Grundrisse* and both Marx' past and future work are
> legion, suggesting that there is a real continuity between the two.... Like most people,
> he clarified his ideas as he grew older and read and experienced more, weaving other
> men's theories into his. But there is a convincing case to be made that he was
> *clarifying* rather than finding new starting-points. If that is so, then the 'total Marx' is
> one always concerned with human nature, alienation and liberation in terms of the
> dialectics of nature. He is a profoundly humanistic and ethical thinker who deserves to
> be evaluated as such.[87]

The relative surplus population produced by capitalism that Marx saw in the
London residuum was not simply a victim, it was a necessary victim, and it had a
crucial function to fulfil in the defeat of capitalism.

---

86 Luxemburg, 1963, pp. 361, 368.
87 Lyon, 1988, p. 112.

Chapter 5

The Philosopher as a Prophet?

Introduction

Marx's writings were not purely economic or political but contained a strong
ethical content. As the previous chapter showed, he was a 'profoundly humanistic
and ethical thinker' who was always concerned with 'human nature, alienation and
liberation'.[1] Leszek Kolakowski, in a study of the history of Marxist thought, has
compared Marx with the utopian socialists in the following way:

> The starting-point of [the utopian socialists'] reflections is poverty, especially that of
> the proletariat, which they are bent on relieving. Marx's starting-point, however, is not
> poverty but dehumanization - the fact that individuals are alienated from their own
> labour and its material, spiritual and social consequences in the form of goods, ideas,
> and political institutions, and not only from these but from their fellow beings and,
> ultimately, from themselves.[2]

Marx, in his writing, would draw attention to qualitative changes brought
about by quantitative change, as well as the quantitative changes brought about by
qualitative change, especially the impact on labour of increases in capital
accumulation:

> The accumulation of capital, though originally appearing as its quantitative extension
> only, is effected, as we have seen, under a progressive qualitative change in its
> composition, under a constant increase of its constant, at the expense of its variable
> capital.[3]

> A necessary condition, therefore, to the growth of the number of factory hands, is a
> proportionally much more rapid growth of the amount of capital invested in mills.
> This growth, however, is conditioned by the ebb and flow of the industrial cycle. It is,
> besides, constantly interrupted by the technical progress that at one time virtually
> supplies the place of new workmen, at another, actually displaces old ones.[4]

These quotes stress that Marx was concerned with far more than the
quantitative issues of economics and was very aware of the stresses suffered by the
worker within the capitalist system. For Marx the resolution of the contradictions

---

1 Lyon, 1988, p. 112.
2 Kolakowski, 1989, p. 222.
3 Marx, quoted in Smelser, 1973, p. 105.
4 Marx, quoted in Smelser, 1973, pp. 131-2.

came internally and not from a transcendent other. Nevertheless, because of his wider, ethical view, the resolution he foresaw can be seen as a redemption, despite his rejection of religion per se.

Marx and Religion

Marx's most famous criticism of religion is that it is the opium of the people. While this is a relatively easy phrase to remember, it is not the most important of his criticisms. Even with the constant repetition of his criticism there are still many people who regard Marxism as a religion. There are also liberation theologians who seek to merge Marxism and Christianity to form a distillation of the two ideologies that will, they believe, answer the needs of the poor of developing nations. So the question of the relation between Marxism and religion is more complex than merely opposition. Peter Worsley argued that Marxism is much more than an intellectual system because it has normative and cognitive dimensions. However 'this does not make it a religion, for it is a humanistic philosophy.'[5]

Marx rejected religion and had claimed that, in his criticisms, he had successfully dealt with the questions it raised. These criticisms serve as an introduction to the Marxist concept of redemption.

Marx came from a Jewish background whose family later converted to the Lutheran faith for what appear to be purely political reasons. While he was studying at the Trier Gymnasium he wrote two essays which, as Robert Kee has argued, show religious ideas and influences that were to stay with Marx for the rest of his life even though he was shortly to reject religion. These ideas, according to Kee, contain the following: first, that Christ's sacrifice has an historical and not merely a metaphysical significance; second, that man's life cannot be fulfilled as an isolated individual; third, that man cannot achieve his historic goal unaided; and fourth, that to the believer the setbacks of this life do not have the last word.[6]

Kee argued that these ideas, while translated from Christianity, remained in Marx's character and are part of the reason for the appeal of Marx and Marxism:

> [Marx] was then what he remained throughout his life: a fervent man of faith. From evangelical Christianity he was converted to neo-Hegelian philosophy. Later he would undergo a further conversion to what is called historical materialism. The content would change in each case, but Marx was never content with a merely intellectual position. He required a faith which at the most general level disclosed the meaning of history and at the most particular gave him the courage to pursue his vocation in life.[7]

Alasdair MacIntyre argued that enough of Marx's earlier ideas remained to enable the secular doctrine of Marxism to maintain the scope of a traditional religion in that it offered 'an interpretation of human existence by means of which

---

5 Worsley, 1988.
6 Kee, 1989, p. 6.
7 Kee, 1990, p. 9.

men may situate themselves in the world and direct their actions to ends that transcend those offered by their immediate situation'.[8] There was within his body of ideas the possibility, if not the inevitability, of societal redemption.

Marx had three main criticisms of religion. The first was that it was an opiate, the second that it was an ideology and the third that it was an inversion.

In Marx's criticism of religion as the opium of the people, he does recognise the validity of religious suffering. However he views religion as a distraction because, while it seems to encompass the aspirations of the poor, it prevents the kind of revolutionary effort that is required to realise those aspirations, for the poor to emancipate themselves. It is like opium in making the unbearable bearable and thereby diminishing the urgency to find a long-term cure. Francis Wheen argued that Marx's point in this criticism is both more subtle and more sympathetic than it has usually been interpreted:

> Though he insisted that 'the criticism of religion is the prerequisite of all criticism', he understood the spiritual impulse. The poor and the wretched who expect no joy in this world may well choose to console themselves with the promise of a better life in the next; and if the state cannot hear their cries and supplications, why not appeal to a higher authority who promised that no prayer would go unanswered? Religion was a justification for oppression - but also a refuge from it.[9]

Leon Trotsky, one of the leaders of the first Marxist revolution, in Russia, was to share the same view of the effects of religion in the 1920s:

> We consider atheism, which is an inseparable element of the materialist view of life, to be a prerequisite for the theoretical education of the revolutionist. Those who believe in another world are not capable of concentrating all their passion on the transformation of this one. [10]

Marx's second criticism of religion was that it was an ideology, that it became identified with the ruling class. As a religion becomes institutionalised there is a danger that its leaders identify with the secular leadership and hence find themselves opposed to the interests of the lower classes. Marx was extremely critical of the way in which the established Church had been identified with the ruling classes, both in history and in his own day. He wrote of the social principles of Christianity justifying slavery in antiquity, serfdom in the Middle Ages and the oppression of the proletariat in the present, of preaching the necessity of a ruling and an oppressed class, and inculcating cowardice, self-contempt, abasement, submissiveness and humbleness.[11] In *Capital* he gave concrete examples of the hypocrisy of Christianity as an ideology, such as the Quaker industrialists who made great claims about their beliefs and yet, in order to increase profits, allowed teenage employees to work thirty hours over the weekend with only one hour for

---

8 MacIntyre, 1971, p. 10.
9 Wheen, 1999, pp. 57-8.
10 Quoted in McLellan, 1987, p. 106.
11 Quoted in McLellan, 1987, p. 23.

sleep.[12] He declared that the established Church would more readily pardon an attack on thirty-eight of its thirty-nine articles than on one thirty-ninth of its income.[13]

William Booth's wife, Catherine, made a similar point in one of her lectures:

> It is inconvenient for ministers or responsible church-wardens or deacons to ask how Mr. Moneymaker gets the golden sovereigns or crisp notes which look so well in the collection. He may be the most 'accursed sweater' who ever waxed fat on that murderous cheap needlework system which is slowly destroying the bodies and ruining the souls of thousands of poor women, both in this and other civilised countries. He may keep scores of employees standing wearily sixteen hours per day behind the counter, across which they dare not speak the truth, and on salaries so small that all hope of marriage or home is denied to them. Or he may trade in some damning thing which robs men of all that is good in this world and all hope for the next, such as opium or intoxicating drinks; but if you were simple enough to suppose that modern Christianity would object to him on account of any of these things - how respectable Christians would open their eyes, and, in fact, suspect that you had recently made your escape from some lunatic asylum.[14]

Because the Church was so identified with the ruling classes, Marx wrote in a newspaper article that the struggle against the Church became part of the class struggle:

> [T]he struggle against clericalism assumes the same character in England as every other serious struggle there - the character of a *class struggle* waged by the poor against the rich, the people against the aristocracy, the 'lower orders' against their 'betters'.[15]

But religion may not always automatically be on the side of the status quo. It could be that the church or individual religious thinkers are responding independently to changes in social reality, that religion's 'character changes in different social and material circumstances.'[16] One example is the growth in the ideas of liberation theology that arose in the twentieth century, where Christians with growing social concerns found that 'the Marxian categories often surface as the most likely alternative to affluent, wasteful and dominating capitalist 'civilization'.[17] In addition, those who reject religion are often influenced in the intensity of their criticism by their experience of religion. Therefore, for example, Engels, with his Pietist background, appeared to consider the criticism of religion more important than did Marx, from a nominal Lutheran background. Lenin, knowing mainly Russian Orthodoxy, was more vitriolic than either against

---

12 Marx, 1986, p. 351, footnote 22.
13 Marx, 1986, 'Preface to 1st Edition', p. 92.
14 Booth Tucker, 1912, Vol. I, p. 288.
15 Marx, 'Anti-Church Movement - Demonstration in Hyde Park' reprinted in Marx/Engels, 1962, p. 437.
16 Lyon, 1988, p. 18.
17 Lyon, 1988, p. 19.

religion, seeing a struggle against religion as an integral part of revolution and declaring that belief in God always blunted feelings of social responsibility.[18]

Thinkers, whether religious or secular, do not merely identify with the rich and powerful. They are influenced by the social reality in which they live. Marx's words about secular philosophies can be applied with equal value to movements in religious ideas:

> Philosophies do not spring up from the ground like mushrooms; they are the product of their age and of their people, whose most subtle, precious and hidden essence flows into philosophical ideas. The same spirit constructs philosophical systems in the heads of philosophers and railways with the hands of workers. Philosophy is not outside the world anymore than the brain is outside man, even though it is not located in the stomach.[19]

So it was that the organisation Booth founded and the particular expression and emphases of his beliefs were specific products of his time and the situation in the East End of London.

Marx's third criticism of religion was that it was an inversion. This was arguably the most important of his criticisms of religion because he went on to use the same idea of reversal in secular criticism. The thrust of his criticism, which Marx inherited from Feuerbach, was that because man has invented God to meet his unsatisfied needs, he therefore projects onto God his own ideals and aspirations. Because a person is unaware of doing this, he is also unaware that the attributes he imputes to God are human attributes, so these human attributes act back on man, in an alienated and reified form to govern him. Feuerbach argued that human thought was not a reflection of Spirit but a mirror of real human existence, that what men have said about God was a 'mystified' version of their knowledge of themselves.[20]

From this argument Marx moved on, as he saw it. The criticism of religion was complete and it was time to consider even more important matters:

> It is the task of history, therefore, once the *other-world of truth* has vanished to establish *the truth of this world*. The immediate *task of philosophy,* which is in the service of history, is to unmask human self-alienation in its *secular form* now that it has been unmasked in its *sacred form.* Thus the criticism of heaven is transformed into the criticism of earth, the *criticism of religion* into the *criticism of law* and the *criticism of theology* into the *criticism of politics.*[21]

McLellan argued that, after 1843, Marx no longer viewed religion as a topic of central interest. Religion became a secondary phenomenon, and any comments

---

18 McLellan, 1987, p. 96.
19 Leading article in No. 179 of the *Kölnische Zeitung*, quoted in Lucien Goldman 'Philosophy and Society in Marx' in Bottomore, 1981, p. 48.
20 Kolakowski, 1989, p. 114.
21 Marx, *Contribution to a Critique of Hegel's Philosophy of Right,* quoted in Smelser, 1973, p. 14.

on it were in future to be peripheral to politics and economics. While criticism of religion per se became secondary it was a useful tool for Marx in building his economic theory. Kolakowski has argued that it was Moses Hess who first suggested in *The European Triarchy* the analogy between religious and economic alienation.[22] In the year Hess's book was published, Marx was drawing out a similar analogy in his dissertation on Epicurus by linking the existence of real pounds in the collective imagination of men and the existence of imagined gods:

> Take paper money into a land where the use of such money is not known, and everyone will laugh at your subjective imagination. Go with your gods into another land where other gods hold sway, and it will be proved to you that you are suffering from fanciful dreams.[23]

By the end of 1843, Marx used Feuerbach's emphasis on realism and his own criticism of religion to proffer the rejection of religious illusion as necessary for the empirical improvement of conditions of life. He had also by this time come to see the role of the proletariat as pivotal in the redemption of society:

> The abolition of religion as the *illusory* happiness of the people is the demand for their *real* happiness. To call on them to give up their illusion about their condition is to *call on them to give up a condition that requires illusions.*

> So where is the *positive* possibility of German emancipation? *This is our answer.* In the formation of a class with *radical chains*, ... a sphere which has a universal character because of its universal suffering and which lays claim to no *particular right* because the wrong it suffers is not a *particular wrong* but *wrong in general;* ... a sphere which cannot emancipate itself without emancipating itself from - and thereby emancipating - all the other spheres of society, which is, in a word, the *total loss* of humanity and which can therefore redeem itself only through the *total redemption of humanity.* This dissolution of society as a particular class is the *proletariat.* [24]

Societal Redemption and the Individual

The need for the redemption of society in the capitalist mode of production arose because the labourer was alienated from the product of his labour. Lyon has argued that Marx could write about alienation from a unique vantage-point because for most of his life he was alienated from society, by his religious background, by his political views or by his financial status. For Marx, full personhood was freedom to develop human capacities through work in a social setting and anything that prevented this was stunting and alienating. The capitalist mode of production had stunted the full personhood of the labourer:

---

22 Kolakowski, 1989, p. 112.
23 Quoted in Kolakowski, 1989, p. 103.
24 Marx, *Critique of Hegel's Philosophy of Right,* in Marx, 1992(a), pp. 244, 256.

What constitutes the alienation of labour? Firstly the fact that labour is *external* to the worker i.e. does not belong to his essential being; that he therefore does not confirm himself in his work, but denies himself, feels miserable and not happy, does not develop free mental and physical energy, but mortifies his flesh and ruins his mind. Hence the worker feels himself only when he is not working; when he is working he does not feel himself ... Finally, the external character of labour for the worker is demonstrated by the fact that it belongs not to him but to another, and that in it he belongs not to himself but to another ... it is a loss of his self.[25]

Marx saw the worker as alienated and he saw deliverance and enfranchisement coming to the alienated worker through a societal redemption. Such a view raises questions regarding the importance of an individual within the process. Hegel, the most important early influence on Marx, saw the individual only becoming truly human through the actualisation of the social and rational nature, by becoming aware of self as not only private and personal but also relational, mutually involved with others.[26] One of Marx's charges against Christianity was that it emphasised individual salvation in a way that was divorced or alienated from the social context. This was seen to be a damning criticism of evangelists such as William Booth, suggesting there is no congruence in aims or practice. However, Esther Reed has argued that there is a correspondence between non-Christian social theory and Christian redemption; non-Christian socio-philosophy could be made part of theological discourse because 'God is the end of all things and is their ultimate desirable good, [thus] all things properly aspire to their good and so to God.'[27]

On a practical level, however, there are real tensions between the good of the individual and the good of society as three of Marx's contemporaries showed in the working out of their philosophies. Each of them saw himself as opposed to authoritarianism and yet in seeking to bring about the utopia envisaged they eventually accepted the concept of force and coercion to bring their utopias into being.

First of these was Pierre-Joseph Proudhon, who had once been admired by Marx but who later rejected Marx's idea of the dictatorship of the proletariat. Instead, he proposed a system of mutualism to promote a free society, with every man his own master, and was depicted by Marx as a petit-bourgeois idealist in his pamphlet *The Poverty of Philosophy*. Proudhon envisaged that 'mutualism' would avoid both laissez-faire and state control, and there would be instead a 'natural' economy based on work and equality.[28]   However, at one point, after seeking to put his plans into practice, Proudhon contemplated the idea of a puritanical elite of vigilantes to enforce public opinion by teaching that the individual conscience should identify with the social conscience. In Peter Marshall's judgement, Proudhon 'never managed to resolve successfully in his ethics the tension between

25 Marx, *Economic and Philosophic Manuscripts of 1844,* in Marx/Engels, 1975-86, Vol. III, p. 274.
26 Reed, 1996, pp. 28-9, 108.
27 Reed, 1996, pp. 187, 189.
28 Marshall, 1993, p. 242.

private judgement and public opinion and between moral autonomy and convention.'[29]

A second thinker of this same period was Michael Bakunin. There was also tension in the thinking of Bakunin, another colleague of Marx's with whom he later disagreed. Bakunin was equally, with Proudhon, in favour of freedom and equality for all and yet was willing to use secret societies to manipulate others in order to bring his libertarian dreams to pass. 'He reveals eloquently the oppressive nature of modern States, the dangers of revolutionary government, and by his own lamentable example, the moral confusion of using authoritarian means to achieve libertarian ends, of using secret societies and invisible dictators to bring about a free society.'[30]

Bakunin disagreed with Marx about the urban proletariat being the most progressive and revolutionary class:

> Bakunin considers the '*flower of the proletariat*' to be the most oppressed, poorest and alienated whom Marx contemptuously dismissed as the '*lumpenproletariat*'. 'I have in mind', he wrote, 'the 'riffraff', that 'rabble' almost unpolluted by bourgeois civilization, which carries in its inner being and in its aspirations, in all the necessities and miseries of its collective life, all the seeds of the socialism of the future.'[31]

Lastly, Peter Kropotkin was a Social Darwinist who believed that evolution was advanced more by co-operation than by struggle for survival. He argued that social progress, like biological progress, depended more on mutual support than force or cunning.[32] This led him to support the replacement of law with public opinion but, like Proudhon and Bakunin, his theory held within it elements of moral coercion and authoritarianism. For example, Kropotkin felt it right for public opinion to oblige all people to do manual work.

In his book, *Making Sense of Marx,* J. Elster pinpoints a similar risk of coercion in what Marx did and did not write about the future:

> Marx never wavered in his view that the main attraction of communism is that it will make possible the full and free realization of the individual; but he did not similarly and consistently place the individual at the centre of the explanation leading up to the communist stage.[33]

Why do those who fight for freedom sometimes think it right to coerce the very people they claim to be liberating? This paradox between wanting mass democracy and fighting for the rights of the masses and yet not welcoming the very conditions that give rise to democracy, namely 'a plurality of social interests and diverse conceptions of the good life' has been explored in detail by Joseph Schwartz. There is a danger that the future envisioned is considered so good that

---

29 Marshall, 1993, p. 251.
30 Marshall, 1993, p. 264.
31 Marshall, 1993, p. 304.
32 Marshall, 1993, pp. 310, 318-9.
33 Elster, 1986, p. 8.

there is no scope for disagreement, and politics will be transcended by the creation of conflict-free societies that fulfil a universal conception of 'true human interests'. He has drawn out the similarity between Hegel and Marx on the future lack of conflict:

> In Hegel ... self-recognition is achieved in a universal state that transcends all conflict through its totalizing bureaucracy. In Marx the bureaucracy withers away, and the agent of total harmony of universal and particular is the mutual interaction of species-beings who simultaneously embody both the particular individuality and the universality.[34]

Marx did not foresee any place for bureaucracy in socialist production perhaps because he considered there would be no need for the state. Schwartz argued that: 'in a democratic society the dialectic between universal and particular, or in more prosaic terms, between the common good and particular interests, never ends.'[35] Because in a truly socialist society the tension between the particular and the universal would be transcended rather than democratised, Marx never addressed how the tension would be resolved in practice.

> Marx's hostility to speculation about the postrevolutionary institutional and political organisations is not solely a product of his materialist opposition to idealist philosophy. It also derives from his faith that 'full communism' would be a classless, conflict-free society that transcends scarcity and thus the need for political and juridical institutions.[36]

Marx would probably not have considered these criticisms worthy of reply. It was only 'crude communism' or 'utopianism' that required explanations of future details. In the societal redemption that he foresaw, the betterment of the individual factory-worker and chimney-sweep was assumed. In Marx's interpretation, communism would be a result of the forward movement of history, it is 'immanent in history'. Schwartz comments:

> Marx's epistemology precluded the separation of facts and values, thereby contributing to his reluctance to make a distinct, *explicit* moral argument for socialism. Although Marx praised communism for producing the first society in which human beings autonomously create and control their social relationships, he appears to conceive of autonomy and freedom as nonmoral goods. [37]

Nevertheless, Marx's writings show that he was aware of the tension between the good of the individual and that of society, which he considered to be a product of the capitalist system. His analysis of the economy underlined this inherent tension for him. Therefore, he explained in *Grundrisse,* when writing about the

---

34 Schwartz, 1995, p. 73.
35 Schwartz, 1995, p. 79.
36 Schwartz, 1995, p. 104.
37 Schwartz, 1995, p. 107.

subordination of all other relations to the money relation in a capitalist economy, that where one individual may succeed in raising his economic status the whole group cannot:

> A particular individual may by chance get on top of these relations, but the mass of those under their rule cannot, since their mere existence expresses subordination, the necessary subordination of the mass of individuals.[38]

A similar contradiction is present within the relations of capital both for one worker versus the mass of workers and one capitalist versus the mass of capitalists:

> Only as an exception does the worker succeed through will power, physical strength and endurance, greed, etc. in transforming his coin into money, as an exception from his class and from the general conditions of his existence. If all or the majority are too industrious then they increase not the value of their commodity, but only its quantity.[39]

> [E]ach capitalist does demand that his workers should save, but only *his own*, because they stand towards him as workers; but by no means the remaining *world of workers*, for these stand towards him as consumers.[40]

When Booth was first writing about the success stories of the Christian Mission he was describing those individuals who, by their personal changes in lifestyle and increased industry, were rising in economic status relative to those around them, for example, those who still spent most of their income on drink. These Christian Mission converts were the exceptions Marx wrote about. When he came to launch the Darkest England scheme William Booth had realised that he must do something to uplift the majority of the group as well. Personal conversion, though essential in Booth's thinking, was not enough to solve the problem of society.

However, the tensions that Marx described were part of the world that he interpreted, the world of capitalist production. As explained above, the tensions between individual and societal good were not to be part of the world that he foresaw. He believed in the possibility of perfect identity between private and collective interests:

> It is above all necessary to avoid restoring society as a fixed abstraction opposed to the individual. The individual is the social being. Therefore, even when the manifestation of his life does not take the form of a communal manifestation performed in the company of other men, it is still a manifestation and confirmation of social life. The individual and the species-life of man are not different.[41]

Marx believed that the sources of antagonism which created the tensions were the result of the capitalist mode of production and therefore purely economic.

---

38 Marx, 1993(b), p. 164.
39 Marx, 1993(b), p. 286.
40 Marx, 1993(b), p. 287.
41 Marx, *1844 Manuscripts,* quoted in McLellan, 1992, p. 138.

Along with his belief in the inevitable overthrow of capitalism he held that a society in which the sources of conflict, aggression, and evil had been removed would be the result.

So what was Marx's idea of personal and societal 'redemption'?

In a higher phase of communist society, after the enslaving subordination of the individual to the division of labour , and therewith also the antithesis between mental and physical labour, has vanished; after labour has become not only a means of life but life's prime want; after the productive forces have also increased with the all-round development of the individual, and all the springs of co-operative wealth flow more abundantly - only then can the narrow horizon of bourgeois right be crossed in its entirety and society inscribe upon its banners: From each according to his ability, to each according to his needs! [42]

Marx used logical analysis in much of his interpretation of history but his view of future society could be compared to a 'religious' conviction, he defended his position on the grounds that the society he envisaged had an inevitability about it because its realisation is immanent in human history.

For any who do not share Marx's belief in its inevitability there is an unreality about the vision of the extirpation of all sources of conflict that continues to suggest the extirpation of the means of expressing disagreement. Schwartz argues that true democracy always involves disagreement; a point which thinkers like Marx fail to foresee:

[E]ven in the most humane of societies ... the social problem of aggregating individual preferences into a collective choice [persists] ... Any final arbiter aiming to eliminate all conflict, be it an omnipotent party or state bureaucracy, will inevitably visit repression on those who dissent from an *a priori* postulated harmony.[43]

Marx, however, argued that the community of revolutionary proletarians was fundamentally different from any previous community, thus negating the arguments of those who seek to impute problems from historical experience:

If the proletariat during the course of its contest with the bourgeoisie is compelled, by the force of circumstances, to organize itself as a class, if, by means of a revolution, it makes itself the ruling class, and, as such, sweeps away by force the old conditions of production, then it will, along with these conditions, have swept away the conditions for the existence of class antagonisms, and of classes generally, and will thereby have abolished its own supremacy as a class.[44]

---

42 Marx, *Critique of the Gotha Programme,* in McLellan, 1992, p. 252.
43 Schwartz, 1995, pp. 104, 124.
44 Marx, *Communist Manifesto,* quoted in Smelser, 1973, p. 90.

The Chronology of Redemption

Marx thought that modes of production would determine the route which he
expected societal redemption to take:

> My view is that each particular mode of production, and the relations of production
> corresponding to it at each given moment, in short 'the economic structure of society',
> is 'the real foundation, on which arises a legal and political superstructure and to
> which correspond definite forms of social consciousness', and that 'the mode of
> production of material life conditions the general process of social, political and
> intellectual life'.[45]

The forces of production would develop as fully as possible under each set of
relations of production until such time as these relations acted as a barrier, when a
period of social turbulence would ensue leading to a new epoch with new relations
of production. Marx believed that the bourgeois relations of production were the
last that would create a divided society and their end would create a new set of
social relations of production: 'In place of the old bourgeois society, with its
classes and class antagonisms, we shall have an association, in which the free
development of each is the condition for the free development of all.'[46] The
capitalist mode of production had been necessary to create the wealth and develop
the productive forces to a level that all members of society could enjoy a life
worthy of human beings.

Charles Fourier had already stressed the importance of a degree of economic
equality to accompany liberty. He wrote, 'When the wage-earning classes are poor,
their independence is as fragile as a house without foundations.'[47] Marx further
recognised that equality of poverty was no real freedom either and that it had
required the wealth-creating possibilities of capitalism to make economic equality
worthwhile. In addition, the development of machinery, which was capitalism's
contribution, while leading originally to the oppression of the workers, would
finally lead to their liberation by a reduction in working time. David McLellan
comments:

> [I]n the *Grundrisse* the nature of the vision that inspired Marx is at least sketched out:
> communal production in the quality of work determined its value; the disappearance
> of money with that of exchange value; and an increase in free time affording
> opportunities for the universal development of the individual.[48]

There was an historical dimension that could not be ignored or avoided. Marx
disagreed with those who spoke or wrote as if the masses had simply to take
power. The progression of capitalism was necessary first before it could be

---

45 Marx, 1986, p.175, footnote 35. The quotations come from the Preface to *A Contribution
   to the Critique of Political Economy*.
46 Marx, *Communist Manifesto*, quoted in Smelser, 1973, p. 90.
47 Marshall, 1993, p. 150.
48 McLellan, 1992, p. 82.

destroyed by its own internal contradictions and superseded by socialism. Marx underlined this historic specificity in his writings on the *Civil War in France*:

> But the working class cannot simply lay hold of the ready-made State machinery, and wield it for its own purposes ... A class in which the revolutionary interests of society are concentrated, so soon as it has risen up, finds directly in its own situation the content and the material of its revolutionary activity: foes to be laid low, measures, dictated by the needs of the struggle, to be taken; the consequences of its own deeds drive it on. It makes no theoretical inquiries into its own task. The French working class had not attained this standpoint; it was still incapable of accomplishing its own revolution.

> The development of the industrial proletariat is, in general, conditioned by the development of the industrial bourgeoisie. Only under its rule the proletariat wins the extensive national existence, which can raise its revolution to a national one and itself creates the modern means of its revolutionary emancipation. Only bourgeois rule tears up the roots of feudal society and levels the ground on which a proletarian revolution is alone possible ... [T]he industrial bourgeoisie did not rule France ... If, therefore, the French proletariat, at the moment of a revolution, possesses in Paris actual power and influence which spur it on to a drive beyond its means, in the rest of France it is crowded into single scattered industrial centres, being almost lost in the superior numbers of peasants and petty bourgeois.[49]

Marx's emphasis on economics and the relations of production as the base of society are thus not a claim that economic self-interest is each individual's only preoccupation but a recognition of the motive power of productive forces in shaping society and of the necessity for them to be developed before a socialist society can come into being. McLellan has argued that the economic doctrines Marx held were not purely economic. His economic theories could not be contained within a narrow definition of economics; for him economics was about how 'the way men produced their means of subsistence conditioned their whole social, political and intellectual life.'[50] Again, economics and ethics are seen to be inextricably linked in Marx's thought.

It is clear that Karl Marx and William Booth offered very different answers to the woes of society. Booth offered an individual redemption that was immediately available and therefore the aim of his socially redemptive programme was to offer an improvement instantly. Such an idea was unacceptable to Marx:

> On our side the old world must be brought right out into the light of day and the new one given a positive form. The longer that events allow thinking humanity time to recollect itself and suffering humanity time to assemble itself the more perfect will be the birth of the product that the present carries in its womb.[51]

A much later writing underlines still more clearly that Marx would be

---

49 Marx, 1933, p. 37.
50 McLellan, 1973, p. 299.
51 McLellan, 1992, p. 19.

opposed to any proposed solution that sought simply to ameliorate particular conditions without overthrowing the whole capitalist system:

> For almost forty years we have stressed the class struggle as the immediate driving power of history, and in particular the class struggle between bourgeoisie and proletariat as the great lever of the modern social revolution; it is, therefore, impossible for us to co-operate with people who wish to expunge this class struggle from the movement. When the International was formed we expressly formulated the battle-cry: The emancipation of the working classes must be conquered by the working classes themselves. We cannot therefore co-operate with people who openly state that the workers are too uneducated to emancipate themselves and must be freed from above by philanthropic big bourgeois and petty bourgeois.[52]

Marx and Engels wrote in *The German Ideology*: 'Communism is for us not a stable state which is to be established, an *ideal* to which reality will have to adjust itself. We call communism the *real* movement which abolishes the present state of things.'[53]   Gajo Petrovic wrote that there was a similar sense of movement in Marx's conception of mankind:

> For Marx, man is an active being, but his activity is not the self-knowledge of the Absolute, but the transformation and creation of the world and of man himself. Therefore for Marx man can be never completed and never finally defined.[54]

Conclusion

For Marx there would be no individual redemption without societal redemption. It was through the active transformation of the world and himself, the interaction of mankind and nature, of philosophy and action, that would come societal redemption. Marx may not have specified the details of a 'redeemed society' but he did specify its agents and the part they would play.

As explained above, the proletarian revolution would not destroy capitalism in a backward move but would move society on beyond the historically necessary state of capitalism. It was not an immediate transformation but involved a long political struggle, in which the two classes of capitalist and worker would be opposed. One of the incentives for the working class to engage in this struggle will be what Rosa Luxemburg named the 'law of the tendential fall of relative wages' which necessarily increases the 'reciprocal distance' between the two classes.[55] Because a fall in relative wages is less obvious than a fall in real wages, Rosdolsky argued that the struggle against such a fall becomes a subversive attack against the concept of labour power as a commodity rather than an open struggle within the parameters of a commodity economy.[56]

---

52 McLellan, 1992, p. 204.
53 Marx & Engels, 1942, p. 26.
54 Petrovic, Gajo, 'Marx's Concept of Man' in Bottomore, 1981, p. 28.
55 Luxemburg, quoted in Rosdolsky, 1977, p. 294.
56 Rosdolsky, 1977, p. 295.

Capital is only powerful enough to enforce the fall of relative wages because of the reserve army of labour. The reserve army strengthens capital's hand in two ways. It allows capital to expand beyond the limits of natural population increase and it acts as a regulator on the wages of the workforce. The capitalist class is therefore enabled to push forward its capital accumulation to the limit and at the same time it pushes the working classes into becoming the class of the proletariat, equipped to take on the struggle against capital. The reserve army of labour thus has a pivotal role in the Marxist conception of societal redemption.

If religious criticism had led the way to secular criticism, economic understanding now did away for any need of religious criticism, which had been superseded:

> Religious alienation as such occurs only in man's interior consciousness, but economic alienation is that of real life, and its abolition therefore covers both aspects.[57]

Societal redemption thus involved the abolition of economic alienation, which would enable individuals to find fulfilment as social species beings and this in turn would enrich society in many ways, for example:

> The employment of the industrial reserve army and the ability to exploit the manifold talents latent in most individuals would make communist society much richer.[58]

The chronology for Marx is that the overthrow of capitalism and the social revolution, that is a societal redemption, would enable each individual, including the members of the residuum, to develop into a 'universal individual'[59], who would in turn help to make society richer.

But while Karl Marx was grappling with these issues in the British Museum a less scholarly activist was offering other solutions. For William Booth at this time redemption was an offer to the individual and was immediate. Even when he later saw the need for a societal redemption, it never precluded any one person from accepting immediate individual salvation.

Booth's work as an evangelist saw him offering salvation to the individual and the stories of his early converts suggested that following acceptance of salvation they were able, spiritually and economically, to enrich society. However, when he launched his *Darkest England* campaign in 1890 he was, in effect, accepting the same cycle as Marx; for the residuum it might be necessary to first change the system to enable the individual member of that class to accept individual salvation and go on to enrich society.

---

57 Marx, *1844 Manuscripts,* quoted in McLellan, 1992, p. 124.
58 McLellan, 1992, p. 244.
59 McLellan, 1992, p. 244.

Chapter 6

The Making of a General

Introduction

The poverty in the East End was a long-standing problem and its endemic nature had a profound qualitative effect on the life of the people. It was the seeming permanence of the problem also that altered how the poverty was viewed from outside the East End and that led William Booth to introduce a programme that sought to address the needs of the residuum at a societal rather than individual level, in his Darkest England Scheme. Like the difference between an epidemic and an endemic disease the long-term poverty of the East End took on a different aspect from a crisis of poverty.

Just as Booth's evangelical initiative in Whitechapel took place when others were seeking to address the same issues, so his social programme was part of the response of many to the seemingly intractable problem of poverty and unemployment. Stedman Jones has stated that 'from the middle of the 1880s there was a growing concern about the survival and extent of casual labour in London.'[1]

The durability of poverty refocused the Salvation Army on the residuum. The organisation was beginning to be upwardly mobile in its membership, like the Methodists before it, a procedure that had brought tensions to Methodism. By institutionalising the focus on the poor the Salvation Army was significantly changed, absorbing some tensions while creating others.

Changes in religious belief and in secular attitudes to poverty were crucial to the form of social work that the Salvation Army commenced around 1890. It was at this point that Booth's integration of atonement theology with incarnationalist social conscience became pivotal. It became the strength of his organisation. His insistence on the Atonement as a central doctrine meant that the Army's social work could never overlook the importance of one individual's redemption and no one could be viewed as irredeemable.

In addition, any organisation that continued to emphasise an individual salvation that involved recognition of personal sin, and an act of atonement by another, could not easily become absorbed into a more general move to welfare provision. Yet, because its social work contained the elements that enabled it to be claimed as incarnationalist by some, it was less likely that the Salvation Army would be marginalised as simply an extreme evangelical sect.

It was the long-term poverty in the East End, as well as the trends in religious and social thought, which worked together with the Salvation Army's own

---

1 Stedman Jones, 1992, p. 92.

development to give the impulse for Booth's Darkest England Scheme and to make him a General.

Many of the leading thinkers of the late-nineteenth century were less prescriptive in their ideas, in both secular and religious circles, than those of previous periods. There was more diffusion, with people choosing their positions along a continuum of choices rather than electing one of two opposing positions. There were more strands of thought that were being vocalised and more information in the public domain.

Within this period, too, there is much more evidence of William Booth becoming aware of trends in religious, social and political thought, and accepting or rejecting them, sometimes out of conviction and sometimes for more pragmatic considerations. It was the diffusion and diffusiveness of ideas within the national culture at just this period that facilitated such an approach by Booth at the time that his organisation was taking form and shape. It was equally true of his social efforts as of his evangelical work that he was a product of his time and was neither as unique nor as original as many of his critics and admirers claimed. He was simply integrating parts of the movements in religious belief and secular understanding into his 'core' creed.

One of Marx's strengths was the way he thought through the implications of his theories. William Booth, to a large extent, did not do this. Booth had, until the late 1880s, only considered his organisation's social work in entirely micro-redemptive terms, a human, Christian response to the material needs of individuals who were also being offered salvation. His training did not allow him to envisage a truly macro-redemption in economic and political terms. Large as his scheme was in scope, it was never on a scale to threaten an overthrow of the system. It remained, in essence, a summation of a myriad of micro-redemptions.

Permanent Poverty in the East End

By 1890 the problem of the vast number of members of the residuum in the East End of London had remained effectively untouched for nearly half a century.[2] Some of the efforts to address the problem had served only to intensify it, for example the Artisans' Dwelling Act of 1875:

> In fact the operation of the Act was disastrous. Instead of alleviating overcrowding, it intensified it. Instead of penalizing slum owners, it rewarded them substantially. Instead of yielding a profit, or even paying for itself, it resulted in a huge financial loss. The failure of the Act was to a considerable extent responsible for the crisis of overcrowding in London in the 1880s.[3]

It was forty years since William Booth had first arrived in London. The length of time that the poor had remained apparently unreached and unhelped in

---

2 Stedman Jones, 1992, p. 66.
3 Stedman Jones, 1992, p. 200.

appreciable numbers had a qualitative impact both for the poor and for those who were trying to help them. The size of the residuum was static. Poverty thus became an oppressive, grinding condition, an insoluble, intractable problem, qualitatively different from the poverty that is a short-term crisis. Table 5.1, drawn from census returns, underlines the seeming permanence of the problem.

Table 5.1 Overcrowding in the East End 1851-1891

	1851	1881	1891
Whitechapel			
Houses per acre		19.92	21.68
People per acre	196.45	188.79	196.99
People per house		9.48	9.11
Bethnal Green			
Houses per acre		21.99	22.66
People per acre	118.68	168.16	171.04
People per house		7.65	7.55
St. George-in-the-East			
Houses per acre		23.79	22.43
People per acre	199.08	194.06	187.43
People per house		8.16	8.36
Stepney			
Houses per acre		17.32	16.79
People per acre	88.13	126.72	124.67
People per house		7.31	7.42
Mile End Old Town			
Houses per acre		20.68	20.81
People per acre		155.54	158.42
People per house		7.52	7.61

Source: 1851, 1881 and 1891 census returns

There is a suggestion in these figures that Whitechapel and St. George-in-the-East had reached saturation level in terms of people per acre by 1851 and that there was no room under the living conditions of the time for it to increase. As can be seen Whitechapel had the highest figures of people per house within the area.

Table 5.2 compares the percentage figures of occupants of different size dwellings in Whitechapel with the whole of London. In each size of dwelling the median occupancy figure is at least one person higher for Whitechapel than for all of London.

Table 5.2 Occupancy Rates in London and Whitechapel 1891

Number of occupants:	1	2	3	4	5	6	7	8+
	%	%	%	%	%	%	%	%
1 room tenements								
All London	34.85	32.33	16.81	9.34	4.30	1.66	0.51	0.20
Whitechapel	17.99	29.31	22.10	14.89	8.35	4.37	2.05	0.94
2 room tenements								
All London	8.49	24.29	21.17	17.12	12.66	8.18	4.67	3.42
Whitechapel	3.14	14.18	16.92	15.96	16.13	13.51	9.22	10.94
3 room tenements								
All London	3.60	17.79	19.03	17.49	14.79	11.29	7.80	8.21
Whitechapel	1.56	7.64	12.38	13.25	16.38	14.27	11.50	23.02
4 room tenements								
All London	1.62	10.46	14.45	16.41	15.78	14.15	11.11	16.02
Whitechapel	0.88	6.68	8.17	14.59	13.09	12.65	13.80	30.14

Source: Census 1891, Table 5

The conception of the intractability of poverty and its attendant problems entered the language of those who discussed it. George Sims wrote about *How the Poor Live* in 1881. The illustrations he used were extremely dramatic and were designed to cause the maximum impact, on the basis of making people take notice of what was happening. For example one of the most evocative descriptions he wrote was as follows:

> [T]he attic is almost bare; in a broken fireplace are some smouldering embers; a log of wood lies in front like a fender. There is a broken chair trying to steady itself against a wall black with the dirt of ages. In one corner, on a shelf, are a battered saucepan and a piece of dry bread. On the scrap of the mantel still remaining embedded in the wall is

a rag; on a bit of cord hung across the room are more rags - garments of some sort, possibly; a broken flower-pot props open a crazy window-frame, possibly to let the smoke out, or in - looking at the chimney-pots below, it is difficult to say which; and at one side of the room is a sack of heaven knows what - it is a dirty, filthy sack, greasy and black and evil-looking. I could not guess what was in it if I tried, but what was on it was a little child - a neglected, ragged, grimed and bare-legged little baby-girl of four. There she sat, in the bare, squalid room, perched on the sack, erect, motionless, expressionless, on duty.

She was 'a little sentinel', left to guard a baby that lay asleep on the bare boards behind her, its head on its arm, the ragged remains of what had been a shawl flung over its legs. That baby needed a sentinel to guard it, indeed. Had it crawled a foot or two, it would have fallen head-foremost into that unprotected, yawning abyss of blackness below. In case of some such proceeding in its part, the child of four had been left 'on guard' ... It is one of the saddest pictures I have seen for many a day. Poor little baby-sentinel! - left with a human soul in its sole charge at four - what will its girl-life be, when it grows old enough to think?[4]

However, just a few pages later Sims deplored the difficulty of finding 'that element of picturesqueness' and spoke instead of 'monotony'.[5] In the same way Andrew Mearns in *The Bitter Cry of Outcast London,* a book that played a major part in publicising the problems of the East End, wrote: 'We might fill page after page with these dreary details, but they become sadly monotonous.'[6] What really made the poverty monotonous was not so much that there was so much of it but that it had become in Stedman Jones's word 'chronic and endemic',[7] rather than an acute crisis situation. Sims and Mearns were not the only people to become affected by this aspect of East End life: Morrison described 'each day in the life of the East End being like every other day'[8] and the Reverend James Adderley, in his introduction to *East End Idyll,* wrote of 'a dullness and a sadness in East London, peculiarly its own.'[9] These words: monotony, dreary, dullness, speak of and are associated with a time span, not simply a level of poverty or a geographic area of poverty.

The ways of life which often accompanied poverty were also becoming endemic. That William Booth had become aware of the effects of long-term poverty can be seen in his speech on 'The Future of Missions' in 1889 where he spoke of the slums and the 'brutal wife-beating and savage treatment of women and children in general that is becoming quite an institution with us'.[10] There was a very real sense growing that the problem was not being tackled in an adequate way. So Mearns wrote: 'We are simply living in a fool's paradise if we suppose that all [the] agencies combined are doing a thousandth part of what needs to be

---

4 Sims, George R., *How the Poor Live,* in Keating, 1978, pp. 71-2.
5 Sims, George R., *How the Poor Live,* in Keating, 1978, p. 77.
6 Mearns, Andrew, *The Bitter Cry of Outcast London,* in Keating, 1978, p. 101.
7 Stedman Jones, 1992, p. 99.
8 Briggs, 1990, p. 315.
9 Adderley, James, preface to Adcock, 1897, p. 2.
10 Booth, 1889, p. 7.

done.'[11] There was also a suggestion that those who were there were 'trapped', another evocation of a long-term problem. Collett spoke of the home workers who could not travel for better wages, in particular '[t]he married woman can never have the freedom of movement without which population cannot follow industry.'[12]

Part of the reason that the situation 'dragged' on and on was that any efforts at improvement were more than counteracted by the new immigrants. Whitechapel was a focus for immigration so that any who improved their lot were more than replaced in numbers by those who were coming in:

> By 1881 nearly 20 per cent of the population of parts of Whitechapel was foreign-born. But the great wave of immigration followed in the years 1881- 6, arising from the persecution in Russia and Poland. In these between 20,000 and 30,000 East European Jews entered London, and most went to Whitechapel ... [I]n 1891 82 per cent of the Russian- and Polish-born inhabitants of London were enumerated in Whitechapel, St George's in the East and Mile End Old Town, covering a total area of about two square miles.

> Whitechapel's population by 1901 was 32 per cent alien. The proportion of foreign-born in the total population of London was 3 per cent; in 1881 it had been 1.5 per cent ... The old East End - Whitechapel, Stepney, and St. Georges-in-the-East - contained an unusually high percentage of Irish-born.[13]

Immigration was helping to increase the supply of casual labour in the East End where there was a decrease in demand due in large part to the changes in dock and riverside employment. The pervading sense of doom was increased by slum clearances and the transformation of the City itself into an almost entirely commercial centre, which led to an immense increase in overcrowding in the housing areas that remained. The impressions of people who lived through the late 1880s in the East End are the most telling evidence:

> [In 1888] Mr. Karanelli, member of the Whitechapel District Board of Works, voiced the alarm of his colleagues at the change in Whitechapel during the last few years from the influx of homeless outsiders. 'Whitechapel [is] now the resort of the residuum of the whole country and the refuse of the Continent.'[14]

> In a letter of appeal at the beginning of [1888], the old campaigner Barnardo warned that 'more homeless children are now to be seen wandering about or asleep at night in our streets, *than ever before.* Each day crowds of starving little ones besiege our gates.'[15]

---

11 Mearns, Andrew, *The Bitter Cry of Outcast London,* in Keating, 1978, p. 92.
12 Collett, Clara E., 'Women's Work', in C. Booth, 1889, Vol. I, p. 449.
13 Waller, 1991, pp. 26-7.
14 Fishman, 1988, p. 10.
15 Fishman, 1988, p. 126.

Public Knowledge of Poverty

Within the monotony of grinding poverty there were crises that would attract more public attention to the plight of the poor. The cyclical depression of the 1880s stemmed mainly from price deflation and thus benefited the employed workers but A. M. McBriar has argued that it had two further effects. It dented the Victorian confidence in the certain and stable success of capitalism and it drew attention to the problem of unemployment in the modern sense of the term, in that it did not simply involve those who did not want to work.[16] At the same time:

> Socialism reappeared in the 1880s, and recruited an elite of active and able workers who in turn created or transformed the broader-based mass labour movements.[17]

> The emergence of the idea that poverty could be eradicated ... owed more to new socialist propaganda than to old working-class culture.[18]

Richard Shannon argued that it was also during the 1880s that as they learnt of the poverty in the East End 'people now found such evils intolerable whereas in earlier times they had accepted them as inescapable.'[19]

Meanwhile, individuals were being brought face-to-face with the poverty of the East End. Such was the case of the Reverend Samuel Barnett, whose wife described her first impression of their home in the vicarage of St. Jude's, Whitechapel:

> The people were dirty and bedraggled, the children neglected, the street littered and ill-kept, the beer-shops full, the schools shut up. I can recall the realisation of the immensity of our task, the fear of failure to reach or help these crowds of people.[20]

Some people were getting their first sight of the poverty of the East End from railway carriages. By 1900 railways in the central zone of London accounted for 776 acres; 5.4 per cent of the land of the central zone was owned by the railways.[21]

> The cutting of railway lines, underground tunnels and sanctioning of improvement legislation proved disastrous for the casual workers and tenement dwellers of central London. As Victoria Station, Charing Cross, Farringdon Street, Liverpool Street, as well as Euston and St Pancras, were scythed through the city an estimated 120,000 of the 'labouring classes' were evicted from their homes between 1840 and 1900. In the frenetic period 1859-67 alone, some 37,000 displacements took place. And up until 1874 there existed absolutely no requirement upon railway companies to rehouse the homeless.[22]

---

16 McBriar, 1987, p. 47.
17 Hobsbawm, 1990, p. 165.
18 Shannon, 1976, pp. 221-2.
19 Shannon, 1976, p. 201.
20 Barnett, 1918, p. 69.
21 Morris & Rodger, 1993, p. 185.
22 Hunt, 2004, p. 293.

This had caused still further cramped conditions for those who had been evicted to make way for the railways. In addition, the railways:

[C]onfined the inner districts into which migration from the centre took place, by their network of main line, viaducts, yards and works, and, as it were, *suggested* areas where, because residential values had been frozen, the overflow might accumulate. Unlike other areas, for which the process of gradual improvement and residential replacement was always a possibility, however remote, the inner districts intersected by the railways were fixed in dereliction.[23]

It was this dereliction which was brought into the light of day by the railways and to the eyes of those who travelled in the trains.

As more people became aware of the poverty, and contemporaneously with the insecurity of the mid-1880s, there was a growing concern about casual labour and poverty in London. There was an increasing number of books written, including one by Henry George the title of which, *Progress and Poverty,* drew attention to the association of progress with poverty, which for many was becoming 'the great enigma of the times'.[24]

Where the conditions to which material progress everywhere tends are most fully realised - that is to say, where population is densest, wealth greatest, and the machinery of production and exchange most highly developed - we find the deepest poverty, the sharpest struggle for existence, and the most enforced idleness.[25]

Boyd Hilton has argued that the introduction of limited liability for the joint-stock company may have pushed some of the middle class towards a more caring concern for the poor:

More people would be admitted to the share-holding elite, but the elite itself would be cushioned against danger. To this extent limited liability can be stigmatized as a gross example of middle-class selfishness. Yet this in itself forced many of the more conscience-stricken to seek another mode of justifying, or at least rationalizing, their social advantages, and this in turn impelled some of them to take a more positive attitude to working-class conditions.[26]

There were other ways in which the lives and demands of the poor were coming to the attention of the public. Three events that played their part in raising the profile of the underclass were the Trafalgar Square demonstrations, the strike of the match-girls at Bryant & May and the Dock Strike.

Firstly, the Trafalgar Square demonstrations were in response to the suffering of the destitute and unemployed who were to be found loitering there. These culminated in a march on the square on 13 November 1887, protesting at a ban that

---

23 Morris & Rodger, 1993, p. 197.
24 George, 1932, p. 9.
25 Harrison, 1990, p. 13.
26 Hilton, 1991, p. 267.

had been placed on assemblies there. The demonstration was broken up by truncheon-waving police:

> One hundred and fifty people were taken to hospital with injuries received as a result of the confrontation in the Square, and 300 odd were arrested; the incident quickly became known as 'Bloody Sunday'.[27]

More publicity followed when one of those injured, Alfred Linnell, died from his injuries and he was given a spectacular funeral:

> Annie Besant directed the arrangements with an eye to ceremonial worthy of the Earl Marshal. To the solemn music of the Dead March from *Saul*, fifty wand bearers, veterans of the Chartist agitation, preceded the coffin ... According to Annie the steps of St Paul's were black with spectators; 'the chimney pot hats stayed on but all the others came off as the coffin with its escutcheon, "Killed in Trafalgar Square" went by.' She thought close on 100,000 people followed to Bow Cemetery.[28]

In the second event, Annie Besant was also active, raising publicity for the working conditions of the match-girls working at Bryant & May. An article she wrote about their conditions was called, 'White Slavery in London' and brought the following details to the attention of the public:

> The splendid salary of 4s is subject to deductions in the shape of fines: if the feet are dirty, or the ground under the bench is left untidy a fine of 3d is inflicted; for putting 'burnts' - matches that have caught fire during the work - on the bench 1s has been forfeited ... If a girl is late she is shut out for half a day ... and 5d is deducted out of her day's 8d ... These female hands eat their food in the rooms in which they work so that the fumes of the phosphorus mix with their poor meal and they eat disease as seasoning to their bread. Disease I say; for the 'phossy jaw' that they talk about means caries of the jaw, and the phosphorus poison works on them as they chew their food, and rots away the bone.[29]

Seven hundred match-girls went on strike in 1888 for better conditions and won, in large part due to the public attention that had been drawn to their cause.

Thirdly, in 1889 there was a larger strike, the Dock Strike, which again won the day because of the force of public opinion with the increased understanding of the living standards of the poorest strata of society:

> [T]he London Dock Strike ... was a 'prosperity strike'. That is to say it was a case ... of workers with low standards revolting against their continuance in the face of swelling and obtrusive prosperity. And it occurred at a time when the educated and reflecting classes had but lately come to realize how very low many working-class standards of life still were. The Dockers struck to obtain a standard wage of 6d an hour that spoke for itself. It was well known that their work was hard and their casual earnings

---

27 Taylor, 1992, p. 194.
28 Taylor, 1992, p. 196.
29 Taylor, 1992, p. 208.

extremely precarious, since far more 'stood by' in the Port than could ever be employed simultaneously. Public sympathy, therefore, was with the men; who then, perhaps, represented with their families the largest single mass of chronic poverty in the Metropolis ... After a month's struggle public opinion proved too strong for the dock companies. They conceded the main demand, the 'docker's tanner'.[30]

As knowledge of the lives of the poor became disseminated, so attitudes slowly changed. One who did a great deal to increase such knowledge was the 'social explorer', Charles Booth. He felt that simply to convey the size of the problem 'en masse' was to take too gloomy a view. Charles Booth wanted to share the detail of the actual people who formed the mass. He used 'questionnaires, interviews, personal observation; collection of statistical data; collation of data; sampling; and statistical tabulation of data in his work'.[31] He worked on premises that were antithetical to those of the political economists, namely that 'empirical evidence, properly analysed, was essential before one could draw generalisations or, more importantly, move on to considered policy'.[32] Whether people accepted his thesis or not, Booth's work drew an immense amount of data and information into the debate and increased the general level of 'knowledge' about the conditions of the poor.

While there was undoubtedly much that remained hidden from Charles Booth and his helpers, and their own perceptions and priorities coloured what they reported, the very dissemination of information brought light and publicity to the whole topic of poverty in the East End and in particular had an impact on the investigators themselves. Charles Booth wrote: 'what I have witnessed has been enough to throw a strong light on the materials I have used, and for me, has made the dry bones live'.[33] It was also Charles Booth who underlined both the advantages and the dangers of obtaining the statistics concerning the poverty of the East End, what statistics conveyed and what mere statistics could never convey. He used the evocative term, the 'arithmetic of woe':

There are two different ways of looking even at mere figures by which very different impressions may be produced by the same facts. It may with some show of reason be regarded as not so very bad that a tenth of the population should be reckoned as very poor, in a district so confessedly poverty-stricken as East London; but when we count up the 100,000 individuals, the 20,000 families, who lead so pinched a life among the population described, and remember that there are in addition double that number who, if not actually pressed by want, yet have nothing to spare, we shrink aghast from the picture. The divergence between these two points of view, between relative and absolute, is itself enough to cause the whole difference between pessimism and optimism. To judge rightly we need to bear both in mind, never to forget the numbers when thinking of the percentages, nor the percentages when thinking of the numbers. This last is difficult to those whose daily experience or whose imagination brings vividly before them the trials and sorrows of individual lives. They refuse to set off

---

30 Ensor, 1992, pp. 205-6.
31 O'Day & Englander, 1993, p. 18.
32 O'Day & Englander, 1993, p. 18.
33 O'Day & Englander, 1993, p. 49.

and balance the happy hours of the same class, or even of the same people, against these miseries; much less can they consent to bring the lot of other classes into the accounts, add up the opposing figures, and contentedly carry forward a credit balance. In the arithmetic of woe they can only add or multiply, they cannot subtract or divide. In intensity of feeling such as this, and not in the power of statistics, lies the power to move the world. But by statistics must this power be guided if it would move the world aright.[34]

The statistics were the important element in Marx's view of macro-redemption. William Booth's scheme would concentrate on improving the specific conditions of the individuals leading 'so pinched a life'.

Where was Religion?

With the widening gulf in beliefs there was no longer one Christian response to social problems. The degree to which evangelical Christians became involved in working for the improvement of social conditions depended in part on their understanding of the millennium, the return of Jesus Christ to reign on earth. The nineteenth century was one in which the concept of the millennium was still important. There was a division among churchmen between premillennialists and postmillennialists. Premillennialists argued that improvement in this world would occur only after the Second Coming of Jesus, which would be preceded by chaos and disorder. There was thus little point in working for social improvement. The postmillennialists by contrast saw the need to work to build the New Jerusalem, the result of the work of Christian agencies, before the Second Coming. William Booth was a postmillennialist. The postmillennialists were likely to be more interventionist in politics and economics as a result of their beliefs.[35]

By 1890, not only did Booth believe in the coming of God's Kingdom on earth but he saw the Salvation Army as having an important part to play in bringing this about. By this time his view of the Army's role included its work of social reclamation but it should not be assumed that the Army's view of its role in reaching around the world came only from its social involvement. Of all the Army's songs about 'winning the world', what was probably the most optimistic was written in 1879, just after the change of name from Christian Mission to Salvation Army, and well before the more organised social work began:

> Salvation Army, Army of God,
> Onward to conquer the world with fire and blood.[36]

As the variations of belief and unbelief increased and widened there were not just differences within Christian denominations but sects and groups began that were

---

34 Booth, Charles, *Life & Labour of the People in London,* quoted in Keating, 1978, pp. 136-7.
35 Hilton, 1991, p. 17.
36 Song Book of the Salvation Army.

on the outside of mainstream religion. Some were aggressively atheistic and secularist. Charles Bradlaugh fought to become the first atheist to sit legally in the House of Commons. After being elected five times and fighting for five years, nine months and eleven days he finally took his seat on 13 January 1886.[37]

However, with the exception of those who were so determined to be outside anything that resembled church life, many of the so-called heretics still maintained much that owed its existence to the church. The church's beliefs and influence did not simply evaporate when people rejected mainstream beliefs, they were transmuted. So that for a period there was something similar to a Church community for unbelievers, because many of those who rejected the demands of Christianity still required the social support and trappings of a Church-like organisation.

The London Positivists believed that 'Humanity' was the embodiment of all that was good and beautiful, and that religion, science and art were all one. 'Humanity' was the Great Being to replace God, who should be worshipped by prayer and meditation. Positivism would have its own priesthood who would not only preach but administer the Positivists' Utopia, which seemed to J. S. Mill among others to be dangerously rigid and open to abuse.[38] Huxley referred to Positivism as 'Catholicism minus Christianity'.[39]

Even Huxley himself, who is credited with introducing the word agnostic to England, walked in to sacred music played on a booming church organ, when he started his 'Sunday evenings for the People'. Accustomed to using biblical language, his lecture proved to be:

> A revivalist meeting with its ecstatic highs; the 'Kingdom of Nature' was at hand, and 'a noble discourse on a nobler theme was never delivered'. Lost amid the hallelujahs was its serious function, as Darwin's laity imputed the old moral laws to the cosmic fabric itself. Jenny Marx exulted in this 'genuinely progressive' sermon.[40]

John Trevor formed the Labour Church, which was once described as a Socialist Salvation Army.[41] Trevor ruled out theology but considered it was possible to still have 'a kernel of religious faith,' without theology. No dogma of any kind was accepted but Trevor believed his movement was a church, which left every man free to develop his own relations with the Power that brought him into being. Trevor saw his church as 'God in the Labour Movement - working through it as he once worked through Christianity, for the further salvation of the world'.[42]

All this questioning had thus led to a much wider spectrum of belief with far more choice available to people in religious and quasi-religious organisations.

---

37 Inglis, 1963, p. 215.
38 Sylvester Smith, 1967, pp. 90-1.
39 Desmond, 1994, p. 373.
40 Desmond, 1994, p. 345.
41 Inglis, 1963, p. 215.
42 Inglis, 1963, p. 221.

Within that spectrum were vague beliefs and ideas, but also more entrenched and dogmatic beliefs held by those who felt threatened or challenged by what was happening around them. At the other end of the spectrum were those, like Charles Bradlaugh and Thomas Huxley, who, as aggressively as the evangelicals, fought for their right to proclaim no religious belief at all. As the century drew to its close people felt freer than ever before to openly choose their own place on the continuum of belief/unbelief.

Diffusive Christianity and Secularism

Jeffrey Cox has coined the term diffusive Christianity to explain the influence of the churches in their philanthropic activity, that led in many people's minds to an acceptance of the work of the Church as a civilising influence. According to this view, the Church played its part in presenting an ideal and a code of moral practice but no longer made the kind of demands membership of an orthodox religion made. Diffusive Christianity, according to Cox's definition, was what remained when any element of the supernatural or superstition had been removed from earlier ideas of 'popular' Christianity.[43] With the change of emphasis from the atoning Christ to the incarnate one in the Church's teaching, he was less likely to arouse hostility but perhaps also less likely to arouse any reaction at all. Once the evangelical doctrine had been superseded as the central belief, some of the underpinning of the Church's earlier work was demolished along with the urgency and activity.

Added to the changing role of the Church was the fact that many of its philanthropic works were being taken over by the State,[44] at a time when the churches, in an effort not to give offence, were watering down their teaching, and were concentrating, instead, on good works. This led to the danger that when these good works were later performed by others the churches could become marginalised.[45] The two Reform Acts had indirectly reduced the political influence of the churches by giving the vote to those classes who were proportionately less likely to be church-goers.[46]

Chadwick argued that as the country became more urbanised, it was likely to become more secular because cities were more removed from the structure of church-going than villages.[47] However there was a very real movement to seek to do the good of Christian idealism without the constraints of Christian doctrine and dogma. Perhaps the most public presentation of this dilemma was a character in fiction, the hero in Mrs Humphrey Ward's novel, *Robert Elsmere*, published in 1888, which became 'the best-seller of the century'.[48] Elsmere left the church

---

43 Cox, 1982, p. 95.
44 Kitson Clark, 1973, pp. 232-3.
45 Cox, 1982, p. 253.
46 Helmstadter, R. J. 'The Nonconformist Conscience' in Parsons, 1988(d), p. 62.
47 Chadwick, 1987(b), p. 425.
48 Sutherland, 1991, p. 108.

where he had been a clergyman because he had lost many of his beliefs, and went to do the work of the Church among the poor without the doctrinal underpinning. Although a character in fiction, he was not lacking in authenticity for his lectures were based on the lay sermons of T. H. Green and his work was based in part on that of Edward Denison, a founder of the settlement movement.[49] The novel's success indicates that the novel articulated the changing beliefs of much of the population.

Jose Harris has argued that in addition to people who sought to remove doctrine from good works, for those who did not reject the Christian faith, religious belief was a much more individual thing and in many instances much more private. As religious belief became more diverse and also often more nebulous, less dogmatic, so there was less reason for it to be publicly declared or to impinge on business and commercial life. In this way, the apparent secularisation of society was greater than the actual diminution in private and personal belief.[50]

Among those who both influenced and articulated the ideas of the time were the members of what became known as the Idealist school. One of their leading thinkers, whose influence continued through the rest of the century, had been T. H. Green. The Christian Socialist, Hugh Price Hughes, attended a course of lectures given by Green and described them as the 'the philosophical expression of the good old Methodist doctrine of entire sanctification'.[51]

Green had an evangelical inheritance but did not retain an evangelical faith in the face of the dilemma caused by the question of science and biblical scholarship.[52]   Richter assessed the place of Green by applying the hypothesis of Ernst Troeltsch which suggests that 'it is only the poor and uneducated who unite simplicity and the capacity to believe with primitive energy and an urgent sense of religious need,'[53] and so it is among them that the great religious movements begin. However these submerged classes do not hold political power and so the movement will either be confined to the lower classes or it must be rationalised and therefore taken over by the educated classes. There are dangers in the two extremes that either the rationalisation will go too far and the essentials of faith will be lost or, if there is no rationalisation, the believers will not be able to answer sophisticated criticisms. Booth and Green were at opposite ends of this continuum.

However what they were trying to do was not so different. Booth saw himself as carrying on Wesley's tradition, without any dilution of his creed, and seeking to do for the poor of his century what Wesley had done for the poor of the previous century. Jowett suggested that the Idealists were seeking to do for the educated middle-classes what Wesley had done for the poor. They sought to encourage a secularisation of evangelical fervour, retaining the energy and dedication of the Evangelicals, but stripped of belief in the miraculous. Just as Dickens had secularised sin to become crime, so Green transmuted sin to self-indulgence, which

---

49 Sutherland, 1991, pp. 114-5.
50 Harris, 1993, pp. 176-7.
51 Norman, 1987, p. 147.
52 The next section relies on information in Richter, 1964.
53 Richter, 1964, p. 14.

was then capable of being overcome by an act of will, negating the need for the Atonement.

> [Green] sought to replace fundamentalist Evangelicalism by a metaphysical system that would transform Christianity from a historical religion. This would turn the attention of those disciplined in Evangelical families away from the means of personal salvation in the next world to improving the condition of this one. In politics as in theology, the doctrine of citizenship and reform developed by Green can best be understood as a surrogate faith appealing to a transitional generation.[54]

It was the fact that Booth worked to improve the condition of this world that made him appear to people like the Reverend Campbell to have altered his theology; but he had not turned his attention away from the means of personal salvation.

Although Idealism belonged to the middle classes it was a doctrine of altruism and so sought to encourage and nurture philanthropic impulses. The beneficiaries would therefore be the working classes. Green believed in the capacities of all men for development and self-improvement. He also believed in the right of all men to express their opinions, in the belief that the views of all men would produce superior ideas to many of those provided by the ruling classes alone. This was the secular counterpart of Booth's belief in the equal value of men that sprang from his evangelical faith in the Atonement.

Green's philosophy of history was one of progress. He was an optimist because he believed in the possibility of the transformation of the world. Booth also believed in the possibility of progress and transformation. The bases of their beliefs were secular and evangelical equivalents. There is evidence here of the truth of Stephan Collini's thesis, that ideas are the product of the time and the people who become known as the 'founders' are often simply articulating what is a more general atmosphere of thought at that time.[55]

Richter described Green as being in tune with his age by his 'optimistic conception of human nature'.[56] Booth, by contrast, was optimistic from belief in a transcendent, powerful God, but did not share the optimism about human nature, and the motivation for his work was that humanity was not progressing as it should and could in his judgement. Booth's criterion for judging the progress of humanity was the spread of Christianity and, in 1889, he had reached the following conclusion:

> A great many of us have been living for a long time in a sort of fool's paradise. We had been supposing that the banner of Christ was winning its way in every direction, that the world was being gradually subdued to Christ ... but instead of this speedy and universal victory over the powers of darkness ... Christianity has been actually losing in the race ... There are fewer Christians in the world today, in proportion to the population, than there were twenty years ago.[57]

---

54 Richter, 1964, p. 19.
55 Collini, 1993, p. 4.
56 Richter, 1964, p. 109.
57 Booth, 1889 (b), pp. 3-4.

There were many who shared Green's optimism about moral progress, which was reinforced by the signs indicating increased concern for the welfare of others. Collini has argued that the speed with which the word 'altruism' became assimilated into the language in the 1870s suggests a 'significant landmark in the history of thought and sensibility'.[58] However such an improvement in social care can be explained as a result of the loosening of the hold of evangelical religion in the 'transitional generation' before the habit of evangelical discipline was also loosened:

> The representative Victorian intellectual, whether believer or sceptic, did not have a constant impulse to serve: he had a constant anxiety about apathy or infirmity of the will. The prevailing moral scheme, when internalized, meant that 'selfish' purposes, whether religious or secular, could not sustain the necessary load. Thus, it was *because* altruistic aims were assumed to motivate that Victorian intellectuals found social work an antidote to doubt, and not that, already having the motivation, they 'transferred' its direction from God to man.[59]

Christian Socialists

Booth was not alone during the nineteenth century in uniting social action and Christian belief. He was part of a more general movement that led to widespread acceptance of the Church's role in social criticism and action. Some of the personalities who were part of the movement towards social involvement were known by the collective name of Christian Socialists.

Christian Socialism was another outcome of the move to Inca nationalism. One of its main proponents was Stuart Headlam who applied the parable of Jesus about sheep and goats in the following way:

> Jesus Christ said that if they were taking pains to see that the people were properly clothed, fed, and housed, however much they might say that they did not know God, God knew them and claimed them as His. Now, what I have to suggest is that modern English Christians need not presume to be more religious than Jesus Christ was; and if He said that the goodness of a nation consisted in seeing that the people were properly clothed, fed, and housed, then surely it is the bounden duty of every minister of Christ from the Archbishop of Canterbury down to the humblest Sunday school teacher, to be doing their best to see that the men, women, and children of England are properly clothed, fed, and housed. I hope, then, that I have said sufficient to make it clear that, so far as Christ's works and teachings are concerned, not only is there no contradiction between the adjective 'Christian' and the noun 'Socialism', but that, if you want to be a good Christian, you must be something very much like a good Socialist.[60]

This is some way from the evangelical ethic of individualism and perhaps even further still is the remark of Hugh Price Hughes that Jesus legislated not only

---

58 Collini, 1993, p. 60.
59 Collini, 1993, pp. 84-5.
60 Headlam, 1892, reprinted in Fabian Socialist Series no. 1, 1908.

for man but also for states.[61] It was a relatively short step from these ideas to that of the Welfare State, with the churches handing over their philanthropic and educational activities to the state.

Edward Norman has described the leaders of the Christian Socialists as neither political nor socialist. In fact there was no consistent body of theory to justify referring to Christian Socialism as a movement.[62] Yet the personalities who influenced it during the nineteenth century did have a cumulative effect on the views of many Christians. Booth would have had much in common with them although he has rarely, if ever, been seen as part of the Christian Socialist tradition.

Many of the personalities of Christian Socialism were ministers in the Anglican Church. Christopher Hill has described how radicalism was almost inevitable in a state church that had survived for so long. As a state church it has to fulfil many functions in relation to the different classes: to console the downtrodden and yet maintain the mighty, to convince the rich to be charitable as well as the poor to be patient. The church, in the balancing of these demands, chose to interpret many of the sayings of Jesus in terms of the after-life:

> But this is sometimes difficult to square with the Biblical text. As the Bible became available in English after the Reformation, and as literacy sank down the social scale, so men and women began to take literally the more subversive texts of the Bible which their betters preferred to read allegorically.[63]

Christian Socialists also took biblical texts literally. For example, Stuart Headlam said the miracles of Jesus were significant acts to show the kind of person he was and how his followers should act. Headlam added that it could be deduced from the miracles of Jesus that his followers were to fight against disease and premature death, to see that people were properly fed and to seek to bring mirth and joy into their lives. This was the aim of Christian Socialism, according to Headlam, and it was an aim with which Booth would have been in total agreement.[64]

On one point, however, Booth would have disagreed with all the Christian Socialists. They had all rejected evangelicalism, and were incarnationalists. Headlam, for example, referred to the doctrine of eternal punishment as a monstrous libel upon God and a horrid doctrine. Headlam was influenced by the teaching of F. D. Maurice, an early Christian Socialist, whose rejection of the evangelical emphasis on individual salvation was for him a way to make his Christianity more centred on the needs of people.[65] Booth, however, found his own motivation for a similar social involvement from his own experience of poverty allied with a Christian faith that encompassed incarnationalism, while remaining

61 Helmstadter, R.J. 'The Nonconformist Conscience' in Parsons, 1988(d), p. 89.
62 Norman , 1987, p. 3.
63 Hill, Christopher in Olbelkevich et al., 1987, pp. 394-5.
64 Dearmer, 1908, in Fabian Socialist Series No. 1, p. 45.
65 Norman, 1987, p. 102.

firmly convinced of the doctrine of atonement. Whatever the difference in doctrine, in practice there were many similarities. Norman placed Carlyle as one of the Christian Socialists' leading intellectual sources, the others being Coleridge and Thomas Arnold. Perhaps because of Carlyle's influence, many of them, for example Charles Kingsley[66] and Maurice,[67] were in favour of emigration schemes.

Norman argued that the Christian Socialists, far from being truly socialist, were only dimly aware of all the currents in the political socialism of their day. Their socialism was a moral rather than a political programme and they emphasised voluntary solutions to social ills rather than collectivist ones.[68] They did not have a programme for changing the structure of society but only to improve the quality of human relationships. Norman has defined Thomas Hughes' Christian Socialism as:

> [A]n attempt to humanize the new world with the values and personal styles of the old. It was, to put it simply, even obviously (but accurately), to convert the whole of England into a kind of Rugby School, with the social reformers, like Arnold, teaching manly virtues to the emergent masses.[69]

Such programmes are not the kind of radical socialism which made Booth appear conservative. However, the concern for improvement of the conditions of the poor was radical for its time. Just as Booth's life was fundamentally affected by the residuum in the East End, so many of the Christian Socialists were influenced by their knowledge, either direct or indirect, of the plight of London's poor. Maurice, for example, was drawn to the ideals of Christian Socialism from reading Mayhew's accounts of London life, and Headlam was influenced by his time as a curate in Bethnal Green.

Booth was close to the Christian Socialists in his recognition of the importance of economic conditions for a person's moral life. This was acknowledged several times in *Darkest England*. He gave the illustration of a man who is tempted to steal because his family is starving, stating that the man desires to be good and probably would be if the path were easier for him.[70] Booth was even more explicit in the following quotation:

> But what is the use of preaching the Gospel to men whose whole attention is concentrated upon a mad, desperate struggle to keep themselves alive? You might as well give a tract to a shipwrecked sailor who is battling with the surf which has drowned his comrades and threatens to drown him. He will not listen to you. Nay, he cannot hear you any more than a man whose head is under water can listen to a sermon.[71]

---

66 Norman, 1987, p. 40.
67 Norman, 1987, p. 18.
68 Norman, 1987, p. 6.
69 Norman, 1987, p. 90.
70 Booth, 1970, p. 255.
71 Booth, 1970, p. 45.

Booth was not here rejecting his previous stance. He still wanted to preach the Gospel. However experience had shown him that hunger could preclude a person from listening. It was an intensely practical response. He did not follow through his evangelical belief in the way that Samuel Barnett, working as a curate in the East End, would do, by refusing to help people who were not prepared to change their ways, fearing that charitable alms would prevent them ever changing. Booth's evangelical beliefs were always softened in practice by his own experiences of poverty.

In the same way Ludlow, another member of the Christian Socialist movement, recognised that, crucial as he considered an inner transformation of individuals for any transformation of society, yet there had to be a certain level of social conditions reached before such a change in a person became possible.[72] Chadwick judged that 'among the clergy and ministers of the left - whether they were radical by temperament, or slum pastors moved by the poverty of their people, or evangelists bridging the gulf between themselves and the working man - the social gospel reached its Victorian culmination about 1891, 1892, 1893.'[73] That is, Booth launched his 'Darkest England' campaign just as Christian social action was at a zenith.

The Christian Socialists were intellectuals and this gave their social concerns what Norman called a vicarious quality because they did not reach the threshold of a social experiment.[74] Booth, by contrast, was more pragmatist than intellectual and became deeply involved in social experimentation, leading Huxley to write:

> Mr Booth's scheme appears to me, and, as I have shown, is regarded by Socialists themselves, to be mere autocratic Socialism, masked by its theological exterior. That the 'fantastic' religious skin will wear away, and the Socialistic reality it covers will show its real nature, is the expressed hope of one candid Socialist, and may be fairly conceived to be the unexpressed belief of the despotic leader of the new Trades Union, who has shown his zeal, if not his discretion, in championing Mr. Booth's projects.[75]

There is an irony in Booth's being 'claimed' by the Socialists, apparently in a way they did not claim the Christian Socialists, especially in view of Booth's statement that Socialism was anti-Christian, compared with Headlam's statement that to be a good Christian you must be something very much like a good Socialist.[76]

The Churches and the Working Classes

One of the forces leading to the creation of the Christian Socialists was the sense that the Church would only be attractive to the working classes when it was seen to

---

72 Norman, 1987, p. 70.
73 Chadwick, 1987(b), p. 279.
74 Norman, 1987, pp. 183-4.
75 Huxley, 1890, p. 7.
76 Headlam, 'Christian Socialism', 1892, reprinted in Headlam et. al. ,1908, p. 9.

be working for justice and dignity for the working man. The churches were becoming more aware in the second half of the nineteenth century that they were not attracting members of the urban working classes to worship. The Catholic Church had a large working-class congregation, mainly due to the large number of immigrants from Ireland.

The Church of England was hampered by its pew rents system. Those churches that had most need of pew rents to keep the churches maintained were those where the congregations were least likely to rent pews. However, K. S. Inglis has argued, in his book on the history of the churches and the working classes, that the pew rent system was just an obvious excuse for the poor to stay away, one the churches could latch on to as a reason. However, there was much more than this one issue which made the churches seem middle-class in the eyes of the poor and prevented them attending worship.[77]

Many priests in the Tractarianism tradition (the Anglo-Catholic wing of the Church of England) went to work in the slums, believing that life there was so drab that by using 'every artifice of colour, music and dramatic action' their ritual would mean more to the people there than the more 'reserved, dull and cold' conventional Church of England worship.[78]

George Haw argued that the working classes were not shut out by being forbidden to enter but that, by 'caste and respectability, by hypocrisy and ecclesiasticism', the Church was seen as a capitalist organisation and thus the enemy of labour.[79] Andrew Mearns had no doubt that a gulf existed between the churches and the poorest of the working class:

> [T]he churches are making the discovery that seething in the very centre of our great cities, concealed by the thinnest crust of civilization and decency, is a vast mass of moral corruption, of heart-breaking misery and absolute godlessness and that scarcely anything has been done to take into this awful slough the only influences that can purify or remove it ... We are simply living in a fool's paradise if we suppose that all [the] agencies combined are doing a thousandth part of what needs to be done, a hundredth part of what could be done by the Church of Christ.[80]

Not all the denominations and/or their leaders sought to reach the urban working classes. Jabez Bunting told the Methodists in 1854 to cultivate country areas, remembering that Methodism was a rural system.[81] R. W. Dale of the Congregationalists thought that as William Booth was ministering to the poor the other denominations could leave him to it and devote themselves to the 'vigorous and cultivated'.[82]

Booth felt called to preach to the poorest of the working classes in the East End of London and obviously people like R. W. Dale felt he was managing to do

---

77 Inglis, 1963, pp. 56-7.
78 Vidler, 1990, pp. 158-9.
79 Haw, 1906, pp. 28-9.
80 Mearns, Andrew, *The Bitter Cry of Outcast London,* quoted in Keating, 1978, p. 92.
81 Inglis, 1963, p. 12.
82 Inglis, 1963, pp. 104-5.

this. On 16 May 1882, in a House of Lords debate on the Salvation Army, the Archbishop of Canterbury 'declared his full support for the aims of the Army and hoped that the Movement might do a great deal of good among "uncultivated minds".'[83]

Since then, historians such as McLeod and Inglis have denied that Booth did reach the poorest classes. However, Pamela Walker, in her research on the Salvation Army, compiled biographies of over 60 women officers who were named in the early editions of the *Christian Mission Magazine* and *War Cry* and found that well over half of them were from poor, working-class backgrounds.[84]

It is true that the Salvation Army was not to remain a purely lower working-class denomination and that from the start it attracted some middle-class people to work with it. It is also true that like the Methodists before them, the Salvationists' new life-styles tended to result in pushing them up the social scale.

The Growth of the Salvation Army

As well as the background in religious and social thought in which Booth launched his Darkest England Scheme the development of his own organisation up to that point was of vital importance. The Christian Mission had its name changed to the Salvation Army in 1878 and William Booth took control over the mission from the committee to which he had previously been answerable, at least nominally.

Some of the Army's activities became more high-profile as the area of activity spread, some of the methods became more aggressive, its members wore uniform and used military terminology. Nowadays this is often seen as anachronistic but it was part of a general trend:

> 'Armies' were noticeably common about then; thus a 'Blue Ribbon Army' (teetotal) had a great vogue from 1878; and in 1883 a 'Skeleton Army' was formed to fight the Salvationists. The Boys' Brigade, also, dates from 1883.[85]

Eric Hobsbawm has emphasised the battle at the time for the control of symbols and rites, of which he judges the two most powerful to have been music, both national anthems and military music, and the flag.[86] The Salvation Army was to appropriate military-style music and a flag as symbols of its own.

Judith Walkowitz has assessed the importance of the uniform particularly for the women members of the Army:

> [T]he Salvationist woman ... dressed in 'military' uniform, topped by a 'Quaker-like bonnet,' ... presented herself as an androgynous figure, whose liminality allowed her to travel through a range of social spaces in London. The Army uniform enabled her to

---

83 Horridge, 1993, p.114.
84 Walker, 1992, pp. 132-6.
85 Ensor, 1992, p. 163.
86 Hobsbawm,1995(b), p. 107.

cross over to the West End; it also marked her off visually from the 'dangerous' fallen women of Piccadilly and protected her from 'male pests' while serving on midnight patrol.[87]

It was not only the woman Salvationist who was protected by her uniform. Ellen Ross made a similar claim for the nurses' uniforms at the same time and in the same areas:

The soberly uniformed nurses (the Metropolitan and National nurses in the 1870s wore a 'brown holland gown and black bonnet with blue ribbons,' and the Ranyard nurses from the 1890s on wore a gray-blue dress with a dark blue cloak and bonnet) enjoyed much popularity and relative safety as they moved about even the poorest streets, protection that was attached to their liminal position.[88]

These changes to Booth's organisation were accompanied by growth of members and centres but there was a negative side in terms of some early supporters:

Many people who had supported The Christian Mission when it was confined to the East End and could be viewed as a worthwhile charity from a distance were now offended when the Army came to public attention. Many of these supporters were now embarrassed by the Army's means and methods - they thought of them as antics. They had been happy, and perhaps not a little satisfied, to support a small mission in a part of London where neither they nor their friends visited. But they could not support these religious zealots dressed in military uniform who were now marching in significant numbers in the main streets of the cities and towns of England disrupting the traffic and making a mockery of religion.[89]

One further result of the change of name was that individual members became more noticed for their denominational affiliation, in a way that would probably not have occurred with the name Christian Mission, and may well have thereby given the impression that the Army's membership was higher in proportion to other churches than was perhaps the case. The story recounted by A. St. John Adcock about an early-day Salvationist is a typical example: 'Everybody in and about Binney and Co.'s coal-yard at Stratford called him "Salvation", because, by some incredible process, he had become converted and joined the Army of that name.'[90]

Perhaps the best measure of the kind of impact the Army had is to be found in the level of criticism of it. The abuse poured upon the Army by G. W. Foote in *The Freethinker* in 1882 suggests that it was not giving the impression of being about to slip quietly into middle-class respectability:

87 Walkowitz, 1992, p. 75.
88 Ross, 1993, p. 173.
89 Green, 1996, p. 199.
90 Adcock, 1897, p. 11.

In one respect Salvationism excels all previous revivals. It is unparalleled in its vulgarity. The imbecile coarseness of its language makes one ashamed of human nature ... Its metaphors are borrowed from the slaughterhouse, its songs are frequently coarser than those of the lowest music hall and the general style of its preaching is worthy of a congregation of drunken pugilists. The very names assumed by its officers are enough to turn the stomach. Christianity has fallen low indeed when its champions boast such titles as, Hallelujah Fishmonger - Bloodwashed Miner - Devil Dodger - Devil Walloper - Gipsy Sal.[91]

Both Peter Keating[92] and Norman Murdoch[93] have argued that Booth only commenced social operations because he felt that he was not being successful in reaching the very poor with the gospel. This is too simplistic an approach. Booth, from his personal compassion, and members of his organisation, from the needs of the people they worked among and their own sense of Christian responsibility, were engaged in the practical working out of a social gospel long before the launch of the Darkest England campaign.

Table 5.3 Salvation Army Corps 1878-95

Year	Total	U.K.	Abroad
1878	50	50	
1879	130	130	
1880	172	172	
1881	251	251	
1882	442	442	
1883	634	528	106
1884	910	673	273
1885	1,322	802	520
1886	1,749	1,006	743
1887	2,297		
1888	2,413		
1889	2,714	1,445	1,269
1890	2,874	1,375	1,499
1891	n/a		
1892	n/a		
1893	3,134	1,211	1,923
1894	3,200	1,210	1,990
1895	3,456	1,273	2,183

Source: Salvation Army Archives

Nevertheless, whether one accepts the argument of Keating or the argument that Booth only started to tackle the social issues in a systematic way when he felt

---

91 Foote, G. W., letter published in *The Freethinker*, 23 April 1882.
92 Keating, 1978, p. 19.
93 Murdoch, 1996, p. 113.

he headed an organisation that was strong enough to encompass this work, the numbers are important. It was not a time when statistics were a preoccupation and the first Salvationists would never have dreamt that the numbers they did collate would be used over one hundred years later to back or refute arguments about success and motivation.

The statistics are further complicated by the fact that they are not always gathered consistently. For example, the numbers for corps sometimes include smaller centres known as outposts and sometimes do not; the numbers for officers sometimes include all employees of the Salvation Army and at other times distinguish between those who were officers and those who were lay staff. These facts make it difficult to draw conclusions from the statistics.

Table 5.4 Salvation Army Officers 1878-95

Year	Total	U.K.	Abroad
1878	127	127	
1879	195	195	
1880	382	363	19
1881		533	
1882		1,067	
1883	1,541	1,340	201
1884	2,332	1,644	688
1885	3,076	1,780	1,296
1886	4,192	2,260	1,932
1887	5,619		
1888	6,391		
1889	8,012	4,314	3,698
1890	9,416	4,506	4,910
1891	n/a		
1892	n/a		
1893	10,874	4,499	6,375
1894	10,671	4,166	6,505
1895	11,694	4,371	7,323

Source: Salvation Army Archives

The earliest statistics available, held in the Salvation Army archives, London, are presented in tabular form in Tables 5.3 and 5.4. Plotting the figures for both corps and officers on time-graphs shows a strong increase in officers and corps in the early years. There are many years for which worldwide figures are also given. However interpolation in the numbers given suggests that 1889 was the year when corps reached their highest number for the UK for the period covered by the table, although were to be higher in both 1898 and in the years 1927-1930. In 1889 the number was 1,445, and after that there was a slight reduction.

As far as number of officers is concerned, the highest number available for the UK is 4,506 in 1890. The next available figure is for 1893 when there were 4,499. If the log-graph of the figures is produced, this shows extremely steep growth at first. For example from 1881 to 1882 the number of officers in the UK rose from 533 to 1,067 and the number of corps in the UK from 251 to 442. From 1883 the figures available include work outside the UK and the numbers for all work show the corps continuing to rise consistently until at least the time of Booth's death in 1912, while the figures for officers, although more likely to fluctuate, show an overall upward trend. However the plotting of the log-graph for worldwide figures does underline the dramatic rate of growth at the start of the organisation which, by 1890, has flattened out considerably.

This data could have meant that Booth felt a new impetus was needed in the form of a new social scheme. It could also mean that the organisation had reached, as many organisations do, a consolidation plateau. The nature and size of the statistics suggest an organisation that was now 'established' with the advantages and disadvantages that this brings. When coupled with the speeches showing Booth's frame of mind at the time of the launch it would seem to give weight to the argument that the 'Darkest England' scheme was started from a feeling of strength rather than weakness or failure.

Failure in the East End?

Despite these arguments, there remains the fact that the Salvation Army was not growing fast in the East of London, whence the impetus for its existence had come. The first numbers for attendance in London to be discussed in the public domain were in the *British Weekly* census of 1887. At this point, the Army's reputation and self-confidence were high and it was believed, within and without the organisation, to be successfully reaching the residuum, according to Hugh McLeod.[94]   The census revealed that nearly 54,000 people had attended Salvation Army services, a fact that received the judgement of 'most disappointing' from the editor of the *British Weekly*.[95]

In fact, McLeod claims that these figures were overstated due to the Salvation Army's poor geography and the *British Weekly*'s poor arithmetic. He states that the Army incorrectly included places such as Hounslow and Canning Town and that the figures were not added up correctly. This brings the figures down to 42,200 and McLeod goes on to argue that numbers for afternoon services should be excluded, thus reducing the figures still further to 30,000. This would make the Salvation Army attendance in London 0.7 per cent of the population in 1887, which McLeod compares to 1881 figures showing attendance as the following percentages of population in other areas: - 11.1 per cent in Scarborough, 7.4 per cent in Hull, 6.8 per cent in Barnsley, 5.3 per cent in Bristol, 4.2 per cent in Barrow, and 3.3 per cent in Portsmouth.[96]

---

94 McLeod, 1974, p. 38.
95 Horridge, 1993, p. 119.
96 McLeod, 1974, p. 89.

Horridge has done further work on the geography of the Army's success in the UK during the 1880s. According to the tables he has produced, the areas with the highest number of corps were, respectively, Lancashire 45, West Riding of Yorkshire 43, Durham 30, London 26, South Wales, Somerset and Gloucestershire 22 each. In addition he has calculated corps seating capacity as a percentage of county population to show the highest counties, which respectively were North Riding of Yorkshire 6.18 per cent, Durham 5.06 per cent, East Riding of Yorkshire 4.88 per cent, while London stands at 0.93 per cent.[97]

The facts contained in these statistics are not in dispute. It is however possible that the figures for attendances and seating capacity fail to convey the impact of the Salvation Army among the residuum. This may be suggested by the surprise of the editor of the *British Weekly* when the figures were printed. What is certain is that Booth himself was aware that London was not the 'flagship' in terms of numbers as early as 1878, when he wrote in the *Christian Mission Magazine*: '[S]ome of our friends, I know, are a little disappointed that we don't do more in London. They cannot be more so than we are.'[98]

Murdoch has calculated that there was a large decline in membership of the mission stations in the East End between 1871 and 1877. The Shoreditch station with 325 members in 1871 had ceased to exist by 1877, Poplar declined from 199 in 1874 to 34 in 1877, Limehouse from 183 to 75 and Whitechapel from 372 to 221.[99] Nevertheless, the very earliest report of organised opposition to the Army was in Whitechapel in August 1880,[100] which suggests very strongly that the organisation was still having a considerable impact in the area.

It can be seen from the above data, that the Darkest England Scheme, launched in 1890, was hardly a knee-jerk reaction to poor success among the residuum. In fact, a more immediate response to the perceived failure was the creation of the Cellar, Gutter and Garret Brigade in the mid-1880s. Nevertheless, it is an irony that the poor of the East End of London, while having so much influence on the form the Salvation Army was to take and providing such a focus for it, did not become members in large numbers.

The poorest of the residuum were to prove the catalyst again, however, in deciding how the Salvation Army would develop. Despite the low membership figures, the Christian Mission and then the Salvation Army was becoming known as an organisation for the poor and a part of the working-class scene. For example, a woman wrote to the *Christian Mission Magazine* in 1873:

> On the following Sunday I was anxious to attend a place of worship, but not having suitable clothes I was at a loss to know where to go, when I remembered having heard the 'Christian Mission' people say at one of their open-air services they invited people to attend in their working attire.[101]

---

97 Horridge, 1993, pp. 58-9.
98 Horridge, 1993, pp. 58-9.
99 Murdoch, 1996, pp. 84-5.
100 Horridge, 1993, p. 101.
101 *Christian Mission Magazine*, July 1873, p. 107.

Pamela Walker's research into the class and cultural background of the Army led her to conclude:

> [The Salvation Army's] influence extended far beyond its membership. In the 1880s it was not unusual for three thousand spectators to crowd into one of the London halls to hear a speaker, and the *War Cry*'s weekly circulation of 400,000 far exceeded the number of active Salvationists. Moreover, in the 1880s, Salvationists became representative figures in comic magazines and music hall performances, suggesting that while the movement was small it nevertheless had a recognised place in working-class communities.[102]

By the mid-1880s, with the growing sense within the Salvation Army that they were not reaching the very poorest, the work of the Cellar, Gutter and Garret Brigade, otherwise known as the slum sisters, was commenced. These women were not simply making forays into the areas of poverty; they lived there.

Nor were they like the settlement movement such as Toynbee Hall, for they adopted to a large extent the living conditions of their neighbours. The aim of the settlements was the very laudable one of promoting understanding between classes by having the middle-class men living and working within the working-class community. Barnett in the 1890 Toynbee Report wrote: 'Every settlement assumes that men of education settle in some industrial centre, and there undertake the duties which naturally arise.'[103]

There was an underlying assumption that middle-class ways were better and that, while the middle class would learn from meeting the working classes, the main benefit would be to the workers as they were able to see and maybe imbibe middle-class values and culture. In a way the same was true of the slum sisters in that they were also proselytising, but this was in terms of religion without an overt class element. Such an equality of background was the strength of many early Salvationists and eased their relationship with their neighbours in the slums in a way that could not be forced.

Mary Ward's biographer said of her that: 'her touch faltered when it came to dealing with the poor on an equal footing, without the ceremonies of organized philanthropy.'[104] By contrast:

> [F]emale Salvationists in East London practised rescue and slum work in their own neighbourhoods well before it had become an important program of the Army in the mid-1880s. To be sure, there were significant differences between the Army 'slum saviours' and middle-class female philanthropists - slum saviours lived among the poor, on approximately the same material level, they performed domestic chores for their poor neighbours, and they could speak in their idiom.[105]

---

102 Walker, 1992, pp. 10-1.
103 Barnett, 1918, Vol. II, p. 24.
104 Sutherland, 1991, p. 221.
105 Walkowitz, 1992, p. 76.

Margaret Harkness was a cousin of Beatrice Potter and wrote articles for *Justice*. Using the *nom de plume* John Law, she wrote a novel entitled *Captain Lobe*, based on her own experience of watching the Army's work in the slums. Harkness wrote of the slum sisters that they would go into lodging-house kitchens where policemen and others were afraid to go but where they seemed to be accepted. This apparently unbiased report, for no record has been found of Harkness having a previous connection with the Army, would seem to suggest that the slum sisters were accepted as part of the working-class network of support and that possibly the social action and help they gave began to approximate to the needs of the poor. However, it is also true that her own judgements were middle-class:

> They go to the slummers with a Bible in one hand, with the other free to nurse the sick and help the helpless. No room is too filthy for them to work and pray in; no man or woman is too vile for them to call brother or sister. They penetrate into cellars where no clergyman or priest has ever ventured, and spend hours among people who frighten policemen.[106]

Therefore, the Salvation Army was perceived by itself, and by a substantial number of others, as 'belonging' to the poorest classes. It was influenced by their culture, it used methods aimed at drawing them into a specifically Salvation Army working-class community. To some extent it became accepted by those who lived in the slums that the members of the organisation were there for them and so it was almost inevitable that long before Booth officially 'launched' a social wing the organisation was involved in a work of social and material relief.

The Springboard for Darkest England

The early social work grew from the requests of others and became, by force of circumstances, more institutionalised until the forms of social work became in turn some of the building blocks from which Booth created his Darkest England Scheme. This was the case in the work with prostitutes and the work with newly released prisoners.

Work with Prostitutes

The creation of a refuge for prostitutes who wanted to leave their way of life was already a project in 1868 when Mrs Flora Reid began to work for the Christian Mission for just this purpose. However her health gave out and there were insufficient funds, so the project was abandoned.[107]

---

106 Harkness, writing as Law n.d. The book was republished in 2004 as *In Darkest London* by Margaret Harkness.
107 Fairbank, 1987, pp. 10-1.

In February 1881 a Salvationist at Whitechapel called Mrs Cottrill spoke to a young prostitute who asked, 'How can I be a Christian - the life I'm living?'[108] Mrs Cottrill replied that she must give up prostitution. However it was nearly eleven o'clock at night and Mrs Cottrill was about to discover how hard it was in practical terms for a prostitute to give up her way of life. She took the young girl first to a home she knew where other girls had been accepted but the matron said it was too late, they did not keep open all night. She then took her to a coffee-house where the charge was 2s 6d but Mrs Cottrill had only 1s and they would not trust her until the morning. After trying and failing to find accommodation at another coffee-house, Mrs Cottrill took the girl to her own home, where her husband and six children were sleeping, and fed her and made up a makeshift bed for her in the kitchen. The next day she took the girl back to her mother in Brighton.[109]

This was the start of a whole new field of work for Mrs Cottrill who opened up two rooms in her house to receive prostitutes who wanted to leave their way of life. She often had four, and even up to eight women, staying there at one time. Eventually, Mr Cottrill's patience and generosity were exhausted and he said his wife must cease to bring the girls into the house. She went to see Bramwell Booth who immediately agreed that the Salvation Army should provide rooms for this rescue work. It was Mrs Cottrill who herself found a house for the Army to rent and eventually officers were appointed to run the work.[110]

It was as a direct result of the requests from people among whom the Army was working and the sense of responsibility for them among its members that the Army began to provide social care. As the numbers of people helped grew in size and were no longer containable as an offer of individual help in someone's home, the Army was to channel both financial and personnel resources into the running of social work.

At the Prison Gate

The first prison work began in Australia. Major James Barker was invited by Dr. John Singleton to help him in leading meetings in gaols. As the officers of the Army began to work with the prisoners they soon realised that if they were to reform, a change of environment was needed on their release.

Right at the beginning, Barker was visited by a man who at the age of sixty had spent forty years in gaol. He pleaded for help because he did not want to die in prison. Barker's assistant, Horsley, took the man into his own home. Barker himself took another prisoner into his home.[111]

However, as the Army's official historian has pointed out:

Wonderful as it was that many Salvationists should follow the example of the Horsleys and Barkers, there were difficulties in the way of this being made a general

---

108 Fairbank, 1987, p. 11.
109 Fairbank, 1987, p. 12.
110 Fairbank, 1987, p. 13.
111 Sandall, 1979, Vol. III, p. 4.

practice. *An institution was obviously needed* to which such men could come when released and where they could stay while being fitted to face the world and its temptations.[112] (Italics added)

Once again a similar pattern was followed. The Army's name for working with the poorest in society led Dr. Singleton to choose them to help with his prison work. The words the Salvationists used as they spoke about the Gospel led prisoners to expect their practical help in trying to change their lifestyles. While at first individual Salvationists opened their homes to meet the need, the work eventually grew to require an institution.

The work with released prisoners was known as prison gate work because, in the beginning, an officer went to meet the released prisoners at the gate of the prison to invite them to go with him to the home. This work was carried out in other countries, including Britain, where the following stunning comment was made by an early Salvationist writer, Major Susie Swift, when comparing a prison gate home with the conditions of ordinary hostels for homeless men:

> The dormitories, dining-room, etc. are rather more comfortably appointed than those of the shelter. Whether this is correct or not, from a reformatory point of view, it is an absolute necessity. English criminals are accustomed to so much more comfort than English poor, that an ex-prisoner really cannot 'rough it' like a poor man who has always been forced to depend on what his two hands could earn, or on the alternative scant and chilly hospitality of his parish.[113]

This is an indictment of the living conditions of the residuum but also backs up Booth's statement at the beginning of *Darkest England* when he introduced his cab-horse charter: 'Some time, perhaps, we may venture to hope that every honest worker on English soil will always be as warmly clad, as healthily housed, and as regularly fed as our criminal convicts - but that is not yet.[114]

The Army's first involvement in the national political arena also arose from the way in which those who were victims in society saw the organisation as being on their side. The work of the organisation was obviously making enough impact for people to perceive Salvationists in this way.

The 'Maiden Tribute' Case

The Army's political involvement began in 1885 when a young girl came up to London from the country in answer to an advertisement for general work in a house. Soon after her arrival she discovered that she had been trapped in a brothel and was held there against her will. She managed to escape one night and because she had attended one or two Salvation Army meetings in her home town she had in her trunk an old Salvation Army song book with General Booth's address printed on its cover. It seemed to her that he was the one person in London she could trust

---

112 Sandall, 1979, Vol. III, p. 5.
113 Quoted in Fairbank, 1983, pp. 14-8.
114 Booth, 1970, p. 19.

and she fled to the Army's headquarters to await his arrival.[115] In fact, it was to his son, Bramwell Booth, that she told her story and, after seeking corroborative evidence, he was instrumental in persuading W. T. Stead, editor of the *Pall Mall Gazette*, to expose the horror of the white slave traffic in his newspaper.[116] The methods used to obtain evidence led to them both standing trial at the Old Bailey, charged with the abduction of a young girl whom they 'bought' and took to France to prove their story. Booth was acquitted and Stead sentenced to three months' imprisonment. According to Charles Terrot, this trial and the attendant publicity resulted in the almost immediate suppression of the white slave traffic, with vice rings all over Britain being ruthlessly smashed by the police and courts being filled with traffickers and procurers.[117]

This was rather a different social involvement from the previous examples. It was more activism than practical action and had more political overtones. The Salvation Army was challenging society for the first time in a way that was not purely in terms of personal religion. In doing so, it raised its own national profile and also attracted to itself allies and opponents whose positions were drawn on account of considerations other than their personal opinion of Huxley's 'corybantic' Christianity. This was in some ways a foretaste of the Army's challenge to the establishment in the Darkest England Scheme, which would once again involve Stead.

It was also different in that it drew the Army into an arena where the lines of battle and the motives of the protagonists were blurred. It can be argued that each time Salvationists offered practical assistance they were involved in a political act, for example by making the actual conditions more bearable. Motives are always difficult to define. Nevertheless the 'Maiden Tribute' campaign, as Stead's newspaper campaign against child prostitution was named, had a more dubious pedigree, not so much in the aims of seeking to prevent the white slave traffic, or raise the age of consent, but in the manner in which the case was presented. Walkowitz has specified several ways in which historians have addressed the events of the campaign in the *Pall Mall Gazette*, concentrating either on Stead's reliability as a narrator, on his sexual psychology, or on the impact of the campaign and the legislation that resulted.[118]

Walkowitz argued that although Stead sought to present the story as political melodrama it contained many genres, with Stead himself playing differing roles within the drama, including 'Chief Director' of the 'Secret Commission', voyeuristic explorer and shadowy villain.

In addition, Stead's writing, by the 'theme, language and self-presentation', came close to resembling late-Victorian pornography: 'The "Maiden Tribute" not only mapped out the same social geography as late-Victorian pornography, it also replicated, in a moralizing frame, many of the sadistic scenarios that filled pornography's pages.'[119]

115 Booth, Bramwell, 1925, p. 119.
116 Booth, Bramwell, 1925, pp. 119-123.
117 Terrot, 1959, p. 216.
118 Walkowitz, 1992, p. 83.
119 Walkowitz, 1992, pp. 94-5, 99.

One of the main criticisms launched against Stead was that *Maiden Tribute* had created an appetite for obscene literature:

> Readers of the *Pall Mall Gazette* during the first week of July 1885 were warned not to buy the issue of 6 July, since it would contain matters to upset the squeamish. Even without these inducements, 'The Maiden Tribute of Modern Babylon' would have been a sell-out – a full account of the sale or violation of children, the procuration of virgins, the international trade in little girls and the unnatural vices to which they were subjected. Headlines such as 'THE FORCING OF UNWILLING MAIDS' and 'DELIVERED FOR SEDUCTION' had all the hallmarks which this type of journalism has had ever since. That is, while professing to deplore what it describes, it offers the readers the pornographic thrill of reading all about it.[120]

There was also a class element in the way that Stead presented the story. The working-class women in his narrative were either victims in a melodrama or they were the working-class mothers, 'transformed into the principal villains.'[121] Three years later Stead was to repeat these stereotypes when he reported the Jack the Ripper killings in Whitechapel. The working-class prostitutes were either depicted as victims of seduction or dehumanized women who were willing to sell their bodies for a night's lodging. The economic exploitation that forced women to weigh 'the advantages of one form of work against another, the work of the jam factory against the work of the streets', was completely ignored.[122]

It is therefore possible that, while its campaign started as a response to a cry for help from a prostitute, the way in which the campaign advanced had class-identification implications for the Salvation Army. The campaign developed its own momentum that took it out of the sphere where it began.

However, for all the differences there are clear similarities with the beginnings of the work with prostitutes and released prisoners. Once again it was the Army's work among the poor that led to the young girl knowing of its existence and it was what she had seen and heard at the meetings that led her to believe that Salvationists were people she could trust and who would help her. Yet again it was a work of charity in the broadest sense that grew out of a response to the need and expectations of those on whose salvation the Army was focused.

The Darkest England Scheme

The event that is seen as triggering a change in William Booth's view of social work in the Salvation Army, and would lead on to the Darkest England Scheme, is dated by the Army's historian, Robert Sandall, as 30 November 1887, the only engagement in Booth's diary for that period that would have necessitated his crossing the Thames late at night. Booth was returning from opening the corps hall

---

120 Wilson, 2002, pp. 474-5.
121 Walkowitz, 1992, p. 119.
122 Walkowitz, 1992, p. 114.

at Whitstable.[123] He was shocked by the sight of men sleeping rough on the Embankment. The next morning his son, Bramwell, was to find him in a state of great agitation about their plight. The following, in Bramwell's own words, describes the first steps to follow from the next important 'meeting-point' between the London residuum and William Booth:

> (W)hat he had seen on that midnight return accounted for this morning's tornado. Did I know that men slept out at night on the Bridges?
> 'Well, yes,' I replied, 'a lot of poor fellows, I suppose, do that.'
> 'Then you ought to be ashamed of yourself to have known it and done nothing for them,' he went on, vehemently.
> I began to speak of the difficulties, burdened as we were already, of taking up all sorts of Poor Law work and so forth. My father stopped me with a peremptory wave of the brushes.
> 'Go and do something!!' he said. 'We *must* do something.'[124]

There is a telling parallel with the first person Booth helped, the old woman in Nottingham, who had also been sleeping rough. That had been 40 years before and Booth may well have been confronted with the seeming permanence of the problem. All those years, all that had happened, all he had seen and done, and still people were forced to sleep in the open.

This can be taken as simply another illustration of how the Salvation Army social work, especially the men's shelters, began. However, it is far more significant. The story in Bramwell's own words shows that Booth was personally moved by the plight of the homeless and now felt in a position to order that his organisation 'do something'. Booth would brook no arguments but that the Salvation Army should get hold of a warehouse, warm it, and make it a shelter for the homeless. He did not mention their spiritual salvation. Their physical suffering was such that Booth wanted the Army involved in relieving it. Whatever the work might eventually become, this was not simply a means to maintain a spiritually motivated change of life style, but a practical solution to a practical need. In this, it differed from the commencement of work described in the previous section.

It was also different because it did not arise as the result of someone who was specifically seeking help from the Salvation Army, or as the result of a Salvationist trying to help an individual. This was the leader of the organisation pledging it to meet a specific need that had become known to him. It was a top-down process of implementation. Therefore, there was more danger that it would be an offer of help that was imposed by the giver rather than sought by the recipient, as had been the case for the Salvation Army's social work until that point. The Army ran the risk of being part of the charity culture that Frederick Coutts, a former Salvation Army General who wrote a history of the Army's social work, described:

> [M]uch well-intentioned charity was offered *de haut en bas*. 'Thank you, your leddyship,' ran the script under a cartoon of an unemployed labourer's wife receiving

---

123 Sandall, 1979, Vol. III, p. 67.
124 Booth, Bramwell, 1926, p. 67.

an alms. 'God bless you; we shall meet again in Heaven.' 'Goodness gracious, I hope not,' was the tart reply.[125]

Charity that was offered at the instigation of the middle-class donor, even when given in a more caring spirit than that of the woman in the cartoon, rarely 'matched the needs' of the recipients. This meant that would-be recipients had 'to fit themselves into the positions required by the donors at the moment of the transaction and then apply the gift (so far as they were able) to their own real needs.'[126]

For example, working-class women had to perform acts of considerable ingenuity in seeking to make their needs and characters appear to meet the prejudices of the middle-class philanthropists. There is little evidence that the recipients felt the stigma in receiving charity that their donors imputed to them. Indeed it would appear that making the best use of the charity that was available was an integral part of their survival strategy:

> Free meals for schoolchildren...in London provide a striking case study in the gift relationship. Throughout the period 1870-1918, the providers of the meals were volunteers, whose impulses were on the whole generous, even loving, toward the poor, especially toward their children. Their soaring hopes for the feeding had sacramental overtones; volunteers spoke of the 'spiritual beauty' of the feeding and of the meals as moments of 'human communion' ... The caregivers' colourful fantasies ... clashed with the gray, instrumental hues of the mothers' approach to the meals; the parents simply wanted decent food for their offspring at some saving to themselves. To them, the meals represented no sacramental linking of the classes invoking reverence and gratitude but a household resource.[127]

What Charles Booth said of interpreting the life of another individual or class was also true for those who wanted genuinely to help. One needed to 'lay open its memories and understand its hopes'.[128] What William Booth was now doing was seeking to offer a solution, but the organisation of it was now from his own ideas and its success would in part depend on the extent to which, in responding previously to expressed needs from the poor, the Salvation Army had truly imbibed the residuum's 'memories' and its 'hopes'.

In less than three years from the night Booth had seen the 'niche-dwellers' of the Embankment he had a whole scheme of social redemption to present to the public, one which he felt the Salvation Army was uniquely qualified to put into practice. It did not hold many totally new features. Much that was included had already been suggested or was already being tried by others. The unique feature was that it incorporated so many features into what Booth hoped would be a complete system of social improvement. This was seen as its strength by some, but also caused fear and bitter opposition in others.

---

125 Coutts, 1978, p. 32.
126 Mandler, 1990, p. 2.
127 Ross, Ellen, 'Hungry Children: Housewives and London Charity, 1870-1918' in Mandler, 1990, pp. 175-6.
128 O'Day & Englander, 1993, p. 56.

Booth described the aim behind his Darkest England Scheme as being to raise all people to at least the standard of the London cab-horse. There were two main points to this charter. The first was that if a cab-horse fell down in the street, then, if only to prevent an obstruction to traffic, the horse would be picked up again. The other was that every cab-horse in London had 'a shelter for the night, food for its stomach, and work allotted to it by which it can earn its corn'. [129] So Booth proposed now a scheme for all people to be helped up when they were down and to be allowed food, shelter and work. Each was to be helped individually to reach the 'cab-horse level'.

William Booth worked on Charles Booth's figures in *Life and Labour in the East End of London* and, assuming that the rate of destitution was twice as high in the East End of London as in the rest of the country, he calculated that there were about three million people in the UK who were not reaching the standards of the cab-horse charter. These three million people he termed the submerged tenth. There was inevitably controversy over his figures, but in reaching his conclusion he also quoted from others, Samuel Smith, Lord Brabazon, Joseph Chamberlain and Robert Giffen. [130] Samuel Smith estimated that there were between two and three million who were either pauperised or unable to support themselves, describing the vast majority as drunken and profligate in their habits, and stated that it was difficult to say whether misfortune or folly was most responsible for their plight. Smith used these figures as back-up for his proposal for emigration, mainly child emigration. [131] Lord Brabazon also wrote in favour of emigration, what he termed State Directed Colonisation, and seems to have culled his figures from Samuel Smith, quoting him in regard to 'two to three million pauperised and degraded people, including in that number the 900,000 persons in receipt of pauper relief'. [132]

The others from whom Booth quoted, Giffen and Chamberlain, gave widely divergent estimates, with the difference in their data undoubtedly influenced by their status and political stance. Giffen's estimate was very low, showing a fall in the number of paupers from 1,676,000 in 1849 to 1,014,000 in 1881 but, as a Government statistician, he would include only those people who were registered as being in receipt of relief. [133]

Chamberlain was a radical politician. Booth quoted his estimates of the numbers living in 'destitution and misery' as between four and five million. How Chamberlain reached the figure is clearer from a speech he gave in 1885:

> [B]ut continuously and concurrently with that there was always one million, or very nearly a million, of persons in receipt of parish relief. There are more than one million others on the verge of pauperisation, who, in times of depression like these, and at any

---

129 Booth, 1970, p. 20.
130 Brabazon, 1886, p. 102.
131 Smith , 1884, p.9 It was Smith's work which was so influential on Barnardo in his
    work with child emigration.
132 Brabazon, 1886, p. 102.
133 Giffen, 1884, p. 18.

moment of bad trade, are subject to the most desperate privations. The whole class of the agricultural labourers of this country is never able to do more than make ends meet, and they have to look forward in the time of illness or on the approach of old age to the workhouse as the one inevitable refuge against starvation ... The ordinary conditions of life among a large proportion of the population are such that common decency is absolutely impossible.[134]

Booth declared himself content to take the figure of three million already arrived at as being midway between Mr Giffen and Mr Chamberlain.

Booth had several main aims for his scheme, by which he said it should be judged. These aims were (1) that the scheme had to be such as would change the man, when it was his own character and conduct that had caused his degradation; (2) that it must change his circumstances where these were responsible for his condition;   (3) that the scheme must be as large as the evil it was seeking to combat;   (4) that the scheme must offer a permanent remedy;   (5) that it be capable of being implemented immediately;   (6) that it should not inadvertently injure those it was seeking to help, and finally (7) that it should not benefit one class to the detriment of another.[135]

William Booth's proposal for the residuum can be seen to proceed directly from his evangelical faith, with its emphasis on the atonement and the equality of all men before a transcendent Redeemer. This is what made William Booth see the residuum as both redeemable and worthy of the offer of redemption, in contrast to Charles Booth who was concerned with the 'repression of the residuum',[136] and in whose view special action was required to safeguard the working class from the residuum. 'The segregation of the inefficients,' Charles Booth explained, 'is not for their sakes but for the sake of those who are left.'[137]

The central core of the Darkest England Scheme proposed three colonies: the city colony, the farm colony and the colony overseas.   All this was united pictorially in the chart at the front of the *Darkest England* book.   The chart shows the submerged tenth drowning in a sea of want and sin.   Salvationists are dragging them out and manning lifeboats to take them to the city colony.   In this city colony were shelters for men, with the offer of food.   There were also factories for those who were out of work. Here they would learn a trade so that they could earn enough to pay for their food and shelter.   There would also be a labour bureau for those with other trades.   In addition, others of those rescued would be put to work in the household salvage brigade, collecting recyclable rubbish from the houses of the well-to-do and putting it to better use.   From this city colony many would find work and be able to return to their families or build a new life.[138]

However, those who did not find work would move on to the farm colony. Here, they would not only learn farming techniques that would equip them to

---

134 Chamberlain, 1914, p. 163.
135 Booth, 1970, pp. 85-7.
136 O'Day & Englander, 1993, p. 151.
137 O'Day & Englander, 1993, p. 152.
138 Booth, 1970, pp. 94-123.

become independent but they would regain physical strength in the process. Many would remain in the UK, some of them to work on small-holdings or co-operatives, originally financed by the scheme, until enough money was raised to buy the land themselves. Others, once they were fit and knowledgeable enough, would emigrate from England to the overseas colony also to be run by the Army. As part of the scheme, there would be an emigration bureau and even a salvation ship to take them to the colony.[139]

In addition to the core scheme of three colonies there were proposed numerous other 'Missions into Darkest England' that included some schemes already in operation such as the slum sisters and the prison gate brigade, as well as new schemes such as the poor man's bank, a matrimonial bureau and Whitechapel-by-the-Sea, where the poor from the East End could go on holiday.

The Theology behind 'Darkest England'

There have been several theories put forward as to the link between Booth's theology and his social work. Because of the publication of *Darkest England* with its scheme for social regeneration in 1890, Keating[140] and Murdoch[141] have tried to show a break in Booth's work at this point. Campbell[142] argued that this increase in social involvement indicated a change in Booth's theology of which even he was not aware. In fact this supposed break is a false one; the real change brought about by the publication of Booth's book was the increase in publicity given to his work and the way in which the social involvement of the Salvationists became more institutionalised and 'professionalised'.[143]

Very early after Booth's conversion, he was noted for seeking to bring the 'roughs' of the district to church and to get them saved and for making the effort to meet the material needs of someone suffering from poverty and want. In a sense all he did for the rest of his life was to continue to bring the 'roughs' to church and meet the material needs of the poor. Because Booth was both a doer and a pragmatist, experience was to change form of his work but not its basis. The organisation he founded grew and with it grew Booth's own understanding of what could be achieved. The organisation then developed its own dynamic. However, as Begbie pointed out, in 1894, after the Darkest England Scheme was in full swing, Booth, in an interview, described his life and work as being in a straight line developing from his conversion up to 1894. He did not talk of a break or a turn or a significant change to suddenly include social work.[144]

There is evidence from early writings of the Christian Mission to justify Booth's view of a straight line development. Social involvement was not an 1890

---

139 Booth, 1970, pp. 124-155.
140 Keating, 1978, p. 19.
141 Murdoch, 1996, p. 113.
142 Campbell, n.d., p. 147.
143 Walker, 1992, pp. 263-4.
144 Begbie, 1920, Vol. II, p. 200.

addendum nor were the principles a change of direction from the early work of Booth's organisation. In an article published in the *Christian Mission Magazine*, on 1 June 1869, of which Booth was editor, a description was given in which the wife of a new convert, 'The Wooden Legged Dancer', was welcomed at the Mission: 'She was clothed, which was first necessity, and fed; and then an effort was made to touch her heart.'[145] Twenty-one years later, in describing his plan to raise the conditions of the poor, Booth would write of a similar order: 'As a first step we will say to him, 'You are hungry, here is food; you are homeless, here is a shelter for your head'.'[146]

The order that Booth described was in contradistinction to Canon Samuel Barnett, who had begun his work in the East End in 1872 and who, at this time in his life, demanded a change in a man's life before help would be given. According to his wife, Barnett held to his belief in these principles, at great personal cost:

> From his 'principles' Mr Barnett never parted, costly as it was, and indeed it is impossible to convey the long-drawn-out pain of obeying them. Often has a well-cooked dinner become nauseating because one knew the Jones's children and their mother were famishing; but Mr. Jones was a drunkard, and the 'principles' forbade the stealing of his duties as a father, lest an incentive to his reform should be removed.[147]

The order insisted on by Barnett was never Booth's way. In a sense there is parallel between the way in which his social work stopped short of leading his theology to that of the Christian Socialists, and the way in which his evangelical views of personal responsibility stopped short of leading his social outlook to the conclusions of Canon Barnett. In 1877 Barnett explained the reasoning and belief behind his work:

> [W]e aim at decreasing not suffering, but sin. Too often has the East End been described as if its inhabitants were pressed down by poverty, and every spiritual effort for its reformation has been supported by means which aim only at reducing suffering. In my eyes the pain which belongs to the winter cold is not as terrible as the drunkenness with which the summer heat seems to fill our streets, and the want of clothes does not so loudly call for remedy as the want of interest and culture.[148]

Booth would always have agreed with Barnett that the best improvement in social conditions comes from a change in behaviour, namely from an individual's conversion. In January 1869 Booth wrote the following editorial in the *East London Evangelist*:

> The true Christian is a real self-helper. In bringing the truths of religion before the suffering masses we are also assisting in the great work of social reform. The

---

145 *East London Evangelist*, 1 June 1869, p. 3.
146 Booth, 1970, p. 106.
147 Barnett, 1918, Vol. II, pp. 229-30.
148 Barnett, 1918, Vol. I, p. 75.

god-fearing, sober, and industrious man has a better chance of improving his condition, than has his ungodly brother, whose evenings are passed in the public house and whose notion of Sabbath observance consists in regular attendance at Sunday markets. When we have taught people to be religious, half the battle has been won.[149]

Twenty years later, in an article called 'Salvation for Both Worlds', Booth spoke of all the things he could have aimed for in social improvement and spoke of the way in which the Salvation Army, before the Darkest England Scheme, was, by its work of spiritual reclamation, bringing about some of these social improvements. Then he wrote of the way in which Christianity added far more to people's lives than merely social improvement.[150] He was to return to the theme that Christianity encompasses social improvement and more in his last public address, given in the Royal Albert Hall, in 1912:

And the object I chose all those years ago embraced every effort, contained in its heart the remedy for every form of misery and sin and wrong to be faced upon the earth, and every method of reclamation needed by human nature.[151]

For Booth, there was a crucial inter-relationship; not only did personal faith lead to good works, including care for the poor, but the sharing of Christian faith was the best form of social work. Social work was religious and religious work was social. The Salvation Army's official view has been that there is no tension between the religious and social work:

To William Booth and his soldiers the work of redemption embraced the whole man ... He understood the biblical word salvation as bringing health - physical, mental and spiritual - to every man ... No radical is more true to his name than the biblical radical who sees that the salvation of society must include the salvation of the individual, and that the one will never be accomplished without the other. No genuine radical will turn a blind eye to the obstinate fact of human egoism, supposing that it will go away because he chooses not to notice it.[152]

However, there were tensions that arose, not as a result of any incompatibility between the two goals but because of organisational questions arising from the best use of men, money and effort. Begbie claimed that in later years when Booth looked at the social work of the Army with its success stories, he still wondered whether he had been right 'to have diverted any of the energies of the Army from the strictly evangelical responsibilities of the preacher's vocation'.[153]

The ministry of women was an important part of the Salvation Army's programme and one of the most innovative sides of the organisation. Much of the early social involvement was at the instigation of the women members and

149 *Christian Mission Magazine*, 1 January 1869.
150 Booth, 'Salvation for Both Worlds', in *All the World*, Vol. V, No. 1, January 1889.
151 Begbie, 1920, Vol. II, p. 460.
152 Coutts, 1978, pp. 20-1.
153 Begbie, 1920, Vol. II, p. 88.

Victorian women generally were at the forefront of philanthropic activity. Octavia Hill was such an example, as her biographer, Gillian Darley, suggested:

> Octavia's religion, a strong core to which she held with increasing faith, was not a questing one; it laid down principles, of service, duty and of individual responsibility which she applied to herself and her family and those with whom she worked. The idea of service was often the way in which Victorian women philanthropists expressed their religious impulses, rather than in more contemplative or purely doctrinal fashion.[154]

The Army benefited from the fact that its work began at a time when such ideas were prevalent and there were not many avenues of service of this kind open to women to choose from.

There has been considerable disagreement over Catherine Booth's input into, and opinion of, social work being made part of the Salvation Army's agenda. Her contribution was especially difficult to judge because of her death in 1890, as *Darkest England* was being prepared for publication. An article written by Catherine and published in *War Cry* of 7 July 1881 included the following lines:

> What does it matter if a man dies in the workhouse? If he dies on a doorstep covered with wounds, like Lazarus - what does it matter if his soul is saved?[155]

Robert Roberts quoted these words in his book, *The Classic Slum,* to support his mother's view of the Salvation Army. Her opinion was, 'So long as you're saved, they don't give a damn why you're starving.'[156]

Nevertheless, many of Catherine's sermons to the richer people of the West End related the poverty in the East End and their responsibility to help alleviate such suffering. She was often more closely involved in social campaigns than William, as for example with W. T. Stead over the 'Maiden Tribute' campaign. Roger Green, a recent biographer of Catherine, has adjudged that 'at times she felt conflicted and fretful about the relationship of social work and spiritual work, while at other times she had a calm settled view as to their perfect harmony and unity'.[157]

In 1903 Booth wrote to his son, 'As to whether we get as much real benefit out of the time and labour and ability bestowed upon feeding the poor as we should do if spent in purely spiritual work is a very difficult question to answer.'[158] In his history of the Salvation Army's social work, Coutts wrote that 'it can be argued that on this relationship between men's spiritual and social needs [Booth] was not wholly consistent.'[159] However, what was totally consistent was that Booth never accepted the condition of the poor as 'divinely ordained, from which state they

---

154 Darley, 1990, pp. 47 -8.
155 Roberts, 1971, p. 119, footnote 2.
156 Roberts, 1971, p. 119, footnote 2.
157 Green, 1996, p. 271.
158 Begbie, 1920, Vol. II, p. 288.
159 Coutts, 1978, p. 19.

could be no more protected than from the east wind'.[160] He once said: 'There may be a godly poverty which is hallowed by God's presence, but that is not to say that God approves destitution.'[161]

Booth was aware of the danger of people claiming conversion in the hope of thereby gaining a material advantage and he specifically sought to reduce that risk. On the opening of the Food and Shelter Depot in 1888, a notice appeared in the Salvation Army magazine, *The War Cry*:

> [N]o Salvation Army officer will be allowed to give away ... tickets. This regulation will prevent the danger of 'charity' being the hindrance it too often is to ascertaining the genuineness of professed conversions. No one will come to our penitent forms for soup and coal any more than before![162]

Green argued that Booth was not always clear in his explanation of the exact relationship between social and spiritual salvation. At times he described personal and social redemption as two sides of the same coin but at other times he spoke of social redemption as a way to make it easier for people to accept personal redemption.[163] With this lack of consistency Booth left his organisation to work out the implications of any tensions it produced in very different areas and decades. It could be a creative tension.

Saved from Poverty or from Sin?

In his study of the East End in 1888, Fishman wrote of a 'quartet of great philanthropists' who directed their life-long efforts to improving the life of the residuum of the East End and in the process 'projected the East End of London on the international scene'.[164] One of these four was William Booth. He projected the East End on the international scene because his organisation became an international one and it was formed and shaped by Booth's own meeting-points with the residuum. The level of urban poverty so marked him when he was young that he could never see poverty of the East End through purely middle-class eyes and take the objective view of, for example, the Charity Organisation Society. The size of the residuum caused him to stay in the East End, thus enabling the formation of an organisation. The seeming permanence of their poverty then led directly to the formation of the 'social wing' of the Salvation Army, giving the organisation two 'foes' to fight, poverty and sin. By 1890 the organisation was formed from these meetings with the residuum, its two foci the core around which ideas and theories would be tried and either implemented or rejected. And between

---

160 Coutts, 1978, p. 19.
161 Coutts, 1978, p. 19.
162 *The War Cry*, 25 February 1888, quoted in Fairbank, 1987, p. 7.
163 Green, 1989, p. 94.
164 Fishman, 1988, p. 235.

the two, sometimes unity and harmony, but at others enough creative tension to drive it forward to assimilate or reject other new ideas.

Conclusion

As Chadwick emphasised, the Incarnation has always been an important part of Christian doctrine. The talk of a move from atonement to incarnation theology was, for many, more a change of emphasis. The Incarnation was also part of Salvation Army theology from the beginning; its fourth doctrine states:

> We believe that in the person of Jesus Christ the Divine and human natures are united, so that He is truly and properly God and truly and properly man.[165]

Booth saw Jesus as an example, as did the incarnational theologians, but he never saw Him only as an example. He would never preach about Jesus without preaching of Him as saviour. If his entry into social work was interpreted as an increased emphasis upon the Incarnation it was never for Booth at the cost of less emphasis on the Atonement. For Booth, Christ as a teacher of ethics, as a model for men, never replaced Christ as the way toward salvation. If there was any major difference in his theology it was not a shift or a change of direction but a broadening to include the idea of a plan of social redemption, and then not so much an ideological change, more an acceptance of the Army's work within that plan.

To continue in the same language, William Booth combined the theology of the Atonement with the social conscience of the Incarnation. As suggested above, such a combination was not without its tensions, for example, the allocation of resources between different functions. However the two were not a contradiction in the generally used sense of the word. What they may have been is an Hegelian contradiction in the sense of creating tensions and pressures because they did not always produce a simple solution.

This would mean that the Army was more responsive to historical trends, more equipped for transformation and development than an organisation fixed upon a set of Utopian formulae. A denomination that needs to come to terms with the organisational stresses of an atonement theology and a social conscience of the Incarnation, in each new generation and geographical area, is more adapted to change and survival than one whose pattern is set once and for all.

Jeffrey Cox described the evangelical revival of the nineteenth century as being 'dissipated in the various movements for 'Social Christianity' in the very late nineteenth century'.[166] William Booth fought hard to ensure that social salvation would not break loose from its ties to spiritual salvation within his organisation, which in his eyes would render the Salvation Army merely an ineffectual social agency.[167] He was aware of the movements and trends around him that were

---

165 The Salvation Army Act, 1980, Schedule 1.
166 Cox, 1982, p. 5.
167 Green, 1989, p. 94.

tending toward this for other agencies: 'You dreamers, you Robert Elsmere people. You people who have these humanitarian wishes and schemings on your brain ...You have stolen the idea of our heaven, and now you want to get men and women into it without Jesus Christ.'[168]

The continuing emphasis on the Atonement can be seen from a headline in *War Cry* in 1908 concerning William Booth's address to the delegates at the British staff council: 'The General's chief note: "We must hold on to the Atonement".'[169] In a book of his sermons from 1907-8 is one entitled 'The Blood of the Lamb', that begins:

> Comrades and friends, - We Salvationists are always glorying in the death of Jesus Christ, and testifying to the benefits that have flown from it to mankind. Perhaps no text is more frequently quoted than the words of John, 'The Blood of Jesus Christ, God's Son, cleanseth us from all sin.' And, perhaps, no song more popular in our ranks than the one commencing:-
> There is a Fountain filled with Blood
> Drawn from my Saviour's veins;
> And sinners, plunged beneath that flood,
> Lose all their guilty stains.[170]

Booth's own insistence on the centrality of the Atonement prevented the loosening of social and spiritual ties in the Salvation Army. At the same time the social work the organisation was involved in greatly enhanced its total witness. Social involvement gave Booth and his organisation a high profile and recognition far beyond its actual numbers.

The two, social and spiritual, were not working in opposition. The social activity of the Army presented to its members a possibly unrivalled opportunity at the time for the practical expression of their Christianity. In the opposite direction, new members were joining the Salvation Army who first knew it through its social work. However, there were not always simple answers to questions about the application of resources and priorities. Individuals and groups would continue to resolve these tensions in their own ways.

Percy Dearmer wrote, of Christian Socialism, that if Jesus had taught a specific form of economics in which to practise the brotherhood of man it would have become out of date when mankind grew beyond it. The kind of socialism Jesus taught, so Dearmer argued, was far greater than simply the particular form of collectivism and so did not become outdated.[171]

On a much smaller scale, William Booth, by failing to reach a formulaic resolution of the tensions created by the link between a theology of atonement and the social involvement of the Incarnation probably, quite unknowingly, helped to prevent his organisation becoming locked in a time warp and being only applicable to certain areas and cultures. The tensions were creative ones that gave it the

---

168 Booth, 1889 (b), p. 10.
169 *The War Cry*, 20 June, 1908, p. 9.
170 Booth, 1921, p. 73.
171 Dearmer, Percy, 'Socialism and Christianity' in Headlam et al., 1908, pp. 55-6.

impetus to adapt. Its commitment to social reclamation prevented it from becoming marginalised as a corybantic sect while its evangelical theology prevented it being lost in a diffusive, social Christianity that was ripe to be taken over by the welfare state.

Chapter 7

The Making of a General's Mind

Introduction

William Booth's first biographer, Harold Begbie, claims that in the literature of political economy Booth was influenced by W. H. Mallock[1] and by Robert Flint's *Socialism*.[2] The question is whether Booth ever fully subscribed to one school of thought or whether he 'cherry picked' those parts of a person's thinking which suited his main purposes and which he could adapt around his own core beliefs.

Booth himself recognised his own pragmatic tendency to acquire and discard ideas and programmes according to their usefulness to his main aim. He wrote of his method:

> Beginning, as I did, so to speak, with a sheet of clean paper, wedded to no plan, and willing to take a leaf out of anybody's book that seemed to be worth adopting ... I have gone on from step to step ... We tried various methods, and those that did not answer we unhesitatingly threw overboard and adopted something else.[3]

Imre Lakatos's theory of scientific research programmes is that there is a 'hard core' of essential beliefs surrounded by the 'softer' auxiliary assumptions that can be absorbed or discarded without threat to the central tenet.[4] Pictorially this can be likened to an amoeba and is a useful paradigm through which to view the development of Booth's work and his ideas. The core of Booth's thought and programme was his evangelical concern for the spiritual salvation of the poor and his humanitarian concern for the material condition of the poor.

Because so little is known of Booth's understanding of political economy it is not straightforward to draw out the influence these writers had. While Booth remained committed to the central core of his belief and work, he could lecture his officers against socialism and then later declare himself to be a socialist. He was apolitical in this sense, with no loyalty to any political theory or programme, despite the fact that he was leading his organisation into the political arena by the launch of his Darkest England Scheme.

---

1 Sandall, 1979, Vol. III, p. 79; Begbie, 1920, Vol I, p. 378.
2 Begbie, 1920, Vol. I, p. 378.
3 Sandall, 1979, Vol. I, p. 208.
4 Worrall, John. 'Imre Lakatos (1922-1974): Philosopher of Mathematics and Philosopher of Science' in Cohen et. al., 1976, pp. 5-6.

Mallock

Mallock is better known than Flint. Harris described him as a 'conservative intellectual', who, during the 1890s defended the large landed estates as a rational allocation of market resources.[5] George Bernard Shaw wrote a Fabian pamphlet in opposition to some of his ideas. Entitled *Socialism and Superior Brains* it was published in 1909.[6] Mallock wrote a book on *Social Equality* that received the praise of Schumpeter who judged Mallock to have been overlooked by the economics profession because he had the courage to tell an unpopular truth.[7]

To read Mallock's arguments against democracy and radicalism in *Social Equality* is to wonder at Booth's approval of it. Some of the language is highly dismissive of the poor:

> I shall show that the principles of modern democracy or radicalism, being deduced, as they are, from an absolutely false generalisation, tend inevitably, in proportion as they are acted on, to increase the very ends which it is their avowed object to remedy; and that by fixing the imagination of the masses on an impossible kind of progress, it is really directing them backwards towards a second barbarism, the horrors and privations of which are now hardly conceivable.[8]

Mallock appears to oppose the redistribution of wealth on the grounds that it can only be done by changing the institutions, which would lead to a change in the structure of society, thus threatening civilisation. As Mallock stated this at a time when he was accusing radicals of seeking a total equalisation of wealth it is not clear whether he was predicting the same result from any degree of redistribution.

Mallock argued that man only labours when he has some motive to do so and that this motive is the result of a combination of a man's character and his circumstances, the wants he has and the means he finds to satisfy them.

Booth's lecture on socialism was given to Salvation Army officers. He stated that under socialism:

> There would be the removal of the present and most powerful incentive from a large part of the Community to produce their best work, or indeed to engage in any work at all. A certain class of motives, as society is now constituted, form the inducement to those studies and those labours, or to those inventions which so far as human influence goes, are essential to the forward march of mankind ... Now under the reign of Socialism this class of inducement would be alienated and it will be seen that its loss would run through all the ramifications of society from childhood to old age. Men, women and children of every station in society would lose the force of this motive, that is the bettering of themselves, if Socialist principle were to be dominant.[9]

---

5 Harris, 1993, p. 119.
6 Shaw, 1909.
7 Schumpeter, 1986, p. 789.
8 Mallock, 1882, p. 47.
9 Booth, 1904, pp. S20-1.

In a later book, *The Limits of Pure Democracy*, written in 1917, Mallock took his argument further, arguing that people who argued for democracy did not really want pure democracy at all:

> [I]f the ideal of pure democracy were realized, and the social conditions of all men made equal by force of law, there would be no such thing as opportunity, equal or unequal, for anybody ... The desire for equality of opportunity - the desire for the right to rise - in so far as it is really experienced by the morally typical man of all ages and nations, is a desire that everybody (he himself, as included in 'everybody', being a prominent figure in his thoughts) shall have an opportunity of achieving by his own talents, if he can, some position or condition which is not equal, but which is, on the contrary, superior to any position or condition which is achievable by the talents of all.[10]

Williams paraphrased Mallock's ideas as: 'What is demanded is an equal opportunity to become unequal'.[11] He went on to write: 'A large part of democratic sentiment, therefore, is in Mallock's view merely a demand for the right to become a member of the oligarchy'.[12]

Booth would probably have accepted Mallock's views of enforced equality. In Booth's lecture on socialism his first objection to it was that it was unnatural because it deprived a man of the right to work for himself, which Booth saw as an instinct born in him, and forced him to work for the community.[13] However, these ideas were not merely imbibed from Mallock. They had been a part of Christian Mission thinking back in the 1870s. George Scott Railton, one of Booth's closest assistants at the time, had written in the *Christian Mission Magazine*:

> Surely no one who was not bereft of reason, for the time being, could advocate the reduction of every member of society to some level of equality in outward circumstances. To make and to preserve perfect equality in men's outward circumstances, there would evidently have to be at once an enormous inequality in their power, for only by absolute force could the men of property be induced continually to share it with their poorer neighbours, and the ignorant to keep up to the level of even moderate education, in order to understand the uses of such property. Indeed, we can scarcely conceive of the possibility of producing anything like outward equality amongst a number of people, without making and keeping them all prisoners.[14]

Booth used an illustration in his lecture that was very similar to that used by Mallock in *Social Equality*. Mallock was arguing against the labour theory of value and quoted from a socialist lecturer, addressing working men, as follows:

---

10 Williams, 1975, p. 168.
11 Williams, 1975, pp. 168-9.
12 Williams, 1975, p. 169.
13 Booth, 1904, p. S24.
14 *Christian Mission Magazine*, September 1875, p. 221.

Just now as I was on my way to this place to speak to you, I watched in the street a magnificent carriage pass me; and in that carriage were two splendidly-dressed ladies. Who made that carriage? - You did. Who made those splendid dresses? - You did. Have your wives any such carriages to drive in? Do your wives ever wear clothes of that kind? I watched that carriage farther, and I saw where it stopped. It stopped before a stately house, with an imposing portico. Who built that house? - You did. Do you and your wives live in any such houses as that?[15]

Booth's illustration was very similar:

The following may be taken as an average denunciation of Capital as heard at a Socialist meeting:

Look at the Aerated Water King. He is a thief and a robber.

He takes away and uses for his own profit your brains, your labour and your character (hear, hear.) I'll prove it to you. He made 50% on his Capital last year!

And who made his buildings? It was you!

His machinery? You!

His carts and waggons? You!

His Offices and mansions? You!

All has been done by labour. Labour has made him what he is. [16]

Mallock's book, *Classes and Masses*, with the sub-title 'Wealth, Wages and Welfare in the United Kingdom', was published in 1896 but the title page shows that the chapters had originally appeared at intervals in the *Pall Mall Magazine*. The book contained more factual economic information than his other writings and could well have been the book that most influenced Booth. It was in the form of an economic tutor. In the preface Mallock described the book as 'addressed to practical people who realise how closely social problems are now connected with the political.'[17] It would seem to be meant for Booth who was a practical man and who in seeking a practical solution to the social problems around him was finding himself drawn into the political arena.

Mallock disputed Karl Marx's claim that the majority of the community was getting poorer. Mallock stated that there was a growing belief, based on the writings of Marx and others, that 'the rich are getting richer, and the poor poorer, and thus the middle classes are being crushed out'.[18] It was his aim in writing the book to show the total fallacy of such a view. The following is a summary of the arguments he used in trying to do so:

Mallock claimed that the number of people on or below subsistence was three million. Although this number had grown absolutely it was a reduced proportion of the total population compared with 1850, a fact which Mallock seemed to feel made a residuum of three million acceptable. He calculated that in 1850 there were 9 paupers to every 200 inhabitants whereas by 1890 that number was only 5.[19]

---

15 Mallock, 1882, p. 43.
16 Booth, 1904, p. S34.
17 Mallock, 1896(a), p. 1.
18 Mallock, 1896(a), p .2.
19 Mallock, 1896(a), p. 4.

Mallock also gave figures to show that the numbers of the working classes increased by 15 per cent between 1850 and 1880 while the middle classes increased by over 300 per cent.[20] He argued that the wealth of the working classes in 1860 was equal to the wealth of the whole country in 1800 and that a similar rise had happened again over the next 30 years. In his opinion he thereby proved that the working classes had all the wealth they would have had if the wealth of the country had been divided equally between all the members of the population in either 1800 or 1860. Implicit in this argument was his belief that the working classes were incapable of creating wealth themselves.[21]

Mallock maintained that the three million people who formed what he termed the unfortunate class were not a product of capitalism for they existed before capitalism. The real problem therefore for philanthropists and reformers was not to interfere with the present economic system but to find a way to bring the residuum into the system. He did not appear to view the actual level of poverty as important as well as the percentages. Instead he wrote:

> [W]e must put the unfortunate class altogether on one side: that it is to say, out of the 37,000,000 inhabitants of this country we must put aside the exceptional case of 3,000,000, and confine our attention to the representative case of 34,000,000.[22]

There is no recognition here of the value of an individual or the reality of his suffering. Mallock does not appear to subscribe to Charles Booth's emphasis on the 'arithmetic of woe' or to accept the implications of the Atonement for the importance of each person. He thinks purely in terms of a macro-redemption:

> It is idle for philanthropists, true or false, to attempt to disprove these facts by citing the cases of misery to be found in every town in the kingdom. London alone possesses an unfortunate class, which is probably as large as the whole population of Glasgow, and an endless procession of rags and tatters might be marched into Hyde Park to demonstrate every Sunday. But if the unfortunate class in London is as large as the whole population of Glasgow, we must not forget that the population of London is greater by nearly a million than the whole population of Scotland; and the great practical lesson which requires to be instilled into social reformers is that the tendencies of a civilisation must be studied in its effects for good on nine-tenths of the population, rather than in the absence of any such effects upon one-tenth; and that the real problem to be solved is not how to alter these tendencies, but to bring those under their influence who have hitherto remained outside it. To attempt to interfere with the progress of the nine-tenths because the one-tenth has not hitherto shared it, would be like attempting to wreck a great steamer with six hundred passengers merely because sixty of them had bad accommodation in the steerage.[23]

There is further evidence here that William Booth was quite prepared to accept and use parts of theories without embracing all the implications. Like

---

20 Mallock, 1896(a), p. 18.
21 Mallock, 1896(a), pp. 28-9.
22 Mallock, 1896(a), p. 6.
23 Mallock, 1896(a), pp. 32-3.

Charles Booth, he had seen the real numbers of those in deep poverty and could therefore no longer think purely in percentages. He was, however, prepared to learn from Mallock the economic theory of how the underclass could be brought within the economic system if that was the most effective way of meeting their material needs.

'To bring the residuum into the system' was the aim of several labour colony schemes like Booth's, such as that written about by George Lansbury to Beatrice Webb when they were both members of the Poor Law Commission:

> [H]e announced his intention of fighting to include in the Commission's report a scheme of labour colonies in three grades. These were: (1) for vagrants ('The proposal to hand over the tramp to the police will meet with my very strenuous opposition, even if I am alone on the Commission in taking that line of action'); (2) for ordinary able-bodied paupers regularly applying for relief, and (3) for the ordinary unemployed ... 'the hope for the first two being that they will eventually work their way into the third, and the hope for those in the third being that one day they will work their way on to the land of England or in the Colonies.[24]

The scheme itemises a similar progression to the one that Booth's Darkest England Scheme had contained. In Marxist terminology the schemes were seeking to equip the lumpenproletariat to enter the reserve army of labour and then to provide ways for the reserve army of labour to become part of the working proletariat.

Mallock was certainly not opposed to labourers remaining on or returning to the land. His scheme for preventing wages sinking to below a minimum standard of humane living involved the assumption that all land should be cultivated and that the annual value of the gross agricultural product was sufficient to support the population. Therefore, the minimum humane standard of living cannot be higher than the value of the entire products which agriculture yields the agriculturalist who works his own soil, or a soil for which he pays no rent, and this can be calculated independently of sentimental opinion or class feeling.[25]

George Bernard Shaw's pamphlet, *Socialism and Superior Brains,* was the result of a letter written by Mallock rather than his books. In January 1909 Keir Hardie, founder of the Independent Labour Party, had delivered a speech attacking the fact that the huge increase in national income had not been shared by the working classes.

In response Mallock had written to *The Times* 'accusing Mr. Keir Hardie of ignorance of political economy, on the ground that an educated man would have known that as the increase had been produced by the exceptional ability of the employers and inventors, there was no reason to claim any share of it for the employee class.'[26]

Here is the gulf between Mallock and the socialists, the contribution of labour to wealth creation, and Shaw wrote a long rebuttal of the idea that the allocation of wealth at that time could be rationally defended:

---

24 McBriar, 1987, p. 220.
25 Mallock, 1886(a), pp. 34-6.
26 Shaw, 1909, Preface note.

Mr. Mallock has jumped at the conclusion that because ability can produce wealth, and is rare, and men who are rich are also rare, these rich and rare ones must also be the able ones ... The Fabian essayists have done their best to convince Mr. Mallock that if the Duke of Westminster makes 500 times as a landlord as Mr. Mallock does as an author, it is not because the Duke is 500 times as clever as Mr. Mallock. But Mr. Mallock is modest, and will have it so; and I will worry him no further about it ... Mr. Mallock is right in saying that Socialism, if it wants ability, will have to pay for it, but quite wrong in supposing that the price will be eight thirteenths of the national product.[27]

Despite his strong opposition to socialism, and the extreme nature of some of his arguments, with the dismissive tone about the residuum, Mallock was not without understanding of the effects of poverty on the individuals suffering from it. He used terminology reminiscent of Booth's about their struggle for existence hindering the poor from accepting the Christian gospel when he wrote:

Large and ennobling sentiments are all of them dependent on the welfare of the home in this way: they are hardly possible for those whose home conditions are miserable. Give a man comfort in even the humblest cottage, and the glow of patriotism may, and probably will, give an added warmth to that which shines on him from his fireside. But if his children are crying for food, and he is shivering by a cold chimney, he will not find much to excite him in the knowledge that we govern India.[28]

Mallock described the power and danger of socialism as resting on two falsehoods:

[O]ne a falsehood of the imagination, which represents wealth to the poor as a condition of extraordinary happiness; the other the falsehood of an intellectual theory which represents it as a possibility to make this condition general.[29]

Booth made a similar point in his lecture, but in a way that underlined why he would never take an extreme position on socialism, but would pick out those aims that he agreed with, disagree with what he felt to be untrue, while always underlining that any scheme or programme that left out the life-changing element that Christianity brought to the equation would be bound to fail:

Remember that many Socialists claim and obtain a large amount of sympathy by their professed compassion for the poor and suffering classes of society. They say, 'Look at the rich in their mansions and luxury and then look at the poor in their slums and starvation. This disparity ought not to be.' But the Salvationists say this as loudly as the Socialists and more loudly still, but at the same time we say if you get a man away from the public house, if you get him away from those vices which drag him down, and curse him and his family, he will rise spontaneously out of his poverty but if you don't emancipate him from this bondage no matter what laws and regulations you make for him or how well off he may become, you will not make him either a happy man or a useful member of society in this world or a fit citizen for the world to come.[30]

---

27 Shaw, 1909, pp. 17, 19.
28 Mallock, 1896(b), p. 11.
29 Mallock, 1882, p. 269.
30 Booth, 1904, p. S41.

Flint

Robert Flint's work on *Socialism* was first a series of lectures given in Edinburgh dating from January 1887.[31] The Marxist economic historian, E. J. Hobsbawm describes the book as 'the most extended and hostile British critique of [Marx's] thought'[32] of the time.

Flint's book shared many economic stances with Mallock although its tone was more conciliatory and the conclusions more central. Like Mallock, Flint emphasised that the proportion of paupers to the population had decreased in the previous seventy years, stating that it is possible to have both universal competition and universal improvement. Even those who 'lose' the competition may be better off than with no competition.[33] He was emphasising the other side of Charles Booth's arithmetic of woe, the actual level of poverty rather than relative values.

Flint opposed socialism on the grounds that it sacrificed the legitimate liberties of individuals to the will and interest of the community. Booth was to define socialism to his officers as the absolute supremacy of the state with regard to the fundamental liberty of the individuals composing the community. He criticised the idea strongly:

> Indeed this system would imply the complete mastery and control of every individual in the State and of everything possessed by him. If you had such a social state of things existing here as I have described, it could be illustrated by a great commercial enterprise of which one individual or company of individuals would be masters and proprietors, allowing no interference from without and no opposition from within. [34]

There is real irony in the final sentence of Booth's criticism for the illustration he uses is identical to the description his detractors made of the way he ran the Salvation Army.

Flint argued that it was necessary to balance the rights of individuals with those of the community. As a former lecturer in political economy, Flint judged that the radicals had over-emphasised the role of the individual 30 years before and now the socialists were seeking to over-emphasise the role of the state. He saw socialism as necessarily involving coercion, arguing that persecution does not lose its wickedness when it ceases to refer to religion.[35] Booth was to echo Flint's emphasis when he told his officers: 'Socialism is not mere co-operation. You can have co-operation without compulsion, but you cannot have Socialism without compulsion.'[36]

However, Booth cannot simply be slotted into an anti-socialist grouping. He may well have spoken in these terms to his officers but the scheme he introduced

---

31 MacMillan, 1914, p. 430.
32 Hobsbawm, 1979, p. 244.
33 Flint, 1894, p. 112.
34 Booth, 1904, p. S12.
35 Flint, 1894, p. 81.
36 Booth, 1904, p. S9.

and the work of his organisation showed the reality was more complex, because in practical terms he shared many of the aspirations of the socialists. Indeed Thomas Huxley claimed that Booth's Darkest England Scheme was a socialist reality under a religious skin.[37]

The Reverend Thomas Hancock, another contemporary critic of Booth, also viewed Booth's Darkest England Scheme as socialist and felt that it had been deliberately couched in socialist terms to ensure success:

> [Booth] has been forced to see that he can only ask the rich richly to endow his sect - or rather endow himself - by devoting its supreme attention to earthly things, by dressing it in a garment of socialism, by finding some wholesome and thriving social work for his officers to do. An 'army' of expensive officers cannot go on for a whole age beating drums, blowing trumpets, enlisting recruits, and causing its voice to be heard in the street. So deeply has the necessity of immediate social reform, and the fearful looking for judgement in the shape of a social catastrophe, seized upon the mind of our age, that a sect is now bound to be socialist, or to be a failure.[38]

Even H. M. Hyndman, an outspoken critic of Booth and his scheme, recognised it as containing some good socialist elements:

> We would even admit that General Booth may be able to reach certain portions of the population with his strange admixture of fanaticism and funniment, which we should be unable to touch. But it is some satisfaction to find that he and those perfervid religionists who act with him have at last been compelled to accept the fundamental principle of modern scientific Socialism: that, in order to produce any permanent improvement in the condition of a large number of the people, it is absolutely necessary that their social surroundings should be changed. That in a work of this kind the views should be accepted that character, disposition, and intelligence are dependent upon begettings and surroundings from birth, is indeed a triumph for the theory of material evolution.[39]

The age in which Booth published his book, *Darkest England,* and Mallock and Flint were writing theirs, was one in which the whole question of religious faith and social responsibility was being discussed from many angles. Within a generation, the two topics would be considered independently but at this point many of those fighting for social change still spoke from their church background and were therefore more intense in their criticism of the churches. Keir Hardie wrote an open letter to the clergy in 1905 in which he said:

> The Archbishop of Canterbury, writing the other day, said he had to devote seventeen hours a day to his work, and had no time left in which to form opinions on how to solve the unemployed question. The religion which demands seventeen hours a day for

---

37 Huxley, 1891, p. 7.
38 Hancock, 1891, p. 16.
39 Hyndman, 1890, p. 4.

organisation, and leaves no time for a single thought about starving and despairing men, women and children, has no message for this age.[40]

There is an enigma about Booth stating his opinion on socialism, claiming to be influenced by Mallock and Flint, and yet acting to find his own solution to 'the unemployed question' and, on occasions, apparently placing his organisation firmly on the side of labour, even prior to the commencement of the Darkest England Scheme. For example, the following is part of an article printed in the *Christian Mission Magazine* in 1874:

> The question of the relationship of labour and capital seems at last to be coming to that decisive struggle which has been foreseen in our country ... The price of labour, like the price of everything else, seems capable of endless change; but there can be no mistake about the marvellous awakening of mind, evidenced by the fact that the working classes, accustomed for centuries to take whatever was offered them and be thankful, or, at any rate, only to complain in whispers to one another, are almost universally beginning to talk about their rights, and to treat with other classes as equals.[41]

Flint argued that Christianity was not bound to the existing order and could accommodate itself to any merely economic or political change, saying that while socialism confined itself to proposals of an exclusively economic or political nature then, while the individual Christian may oppose them on economic or political grounds, Christianity had no direct argument with them.[42] Had the overseas colony in Booth's Darkest England Scheme proved successful, it may well have led to the identification of the Salvation Army with social imperialism which could have proved detrimental to its work in other areas and other eras. Booth seemed to recognise the possibility of the result when he said:

> I have resolved that neither The Army nor any of its Agencies shall be employed in political warfare either on one side or the other. I want Officers and Soldiers to be free to unite under one Flag for far greater ends than those involved in political strife, however important the questions involved may be.[43]

The idea that Christianity should be seen to transcend political allegiance was not accepted by all Christians. The Christian Socialists believed that their Christianity led them to become socialists. Booth on the other hand saw the majority of socialist authorities as avowedly anti-Christian and quoted what he termed 'one of the leading people of the Socialist system with a world wide reputation', whom he did not identify, as saying: 'We aim in politics at Republicanism, we aim in economics at Socialism, and in the domain of what is

---

40 Quoted in Haw, 1906, pp. 4-5.
41 *Christian Mission Magazine*, May 1974, p. 124.
42 Flint, 1894, p. 453.
43 Booth, 1904, p. S3.

called Religion we aim at Atheism'.[44] This quotation suggests that Booth's avowed opposition to socialism was coloured by its close connection with atheism. He opposed socialism on religious grounds but was in much closer accord with its economic and political aims.

William and Catherine Booth had a strongly conservative strand to their thinking which did not prevent them from following the road that they eventually took in practice with the social involvement of the Salvation Army. Catherine appealed for support for the Salvation Army on the grounds that it was on the side of law and order. For example she wrote to the Queen in 1882:

> It will, I feel sure, interest your majesty to know that many thousands of the lower and dangerous classes have already been won to temperance, virtue, and religion by the methods and spirit of this Army, to which fact many of your majesty's officers of justice in different parts of the kingdom would gladly bear witness.[45]

Salvationism and Socialism

However, there were many links between Salvationism and socialism during the period, which were recognised by socialists themselves and their opponents, if rarely articulated by the Salvationists. It was mainly a practical link rather than a philosophical one, yet it could only have occurred if the Salvationists and socialists were working for similar social aims. E. P. Thompson has described the mid-1880s to the beginning of the next century as 'a profoundly ambiguous moment when Salvationism ran in double harness with London Radicalism'.[46]

Salvationists and socialists were trying to reach the same people by using similar methods. They both used street meetings and processions. They joined forces at one point to fight the London authorities for the right to continue these street activities, leading Engels to write to Lafargue: 'You should also stand up for the *Salvation Army*, for without it the right to hold processions and discussions in the street would have been more decayed in England than it is'.[47] Socialists and Salvationists also joined forces during the London dock strike of 1889 when the Salvation Army became involved in supplying cheap provisions to the striking dockers and their families.[48] Bailey argued:

> Both movements, furthermore, drew from and invigorated an emerging working-class consciousness. It is a comparison which confirms that the Salvation Army was a movement both of the working class and in intimate relationship with the submerged, and which suggests that it warps historical reality to bracket the Army with organizations bent simply on imposing middle-class values on the uncultured poor.[49]

---

44 Booth, 1904, p. S44.
45 Booth Tucker, 1912, Vol. II, p. 227.
46 Quoted in Bailey, 1984, p. 135.
47 Quoted in Bailey, 1984, p. 137.
48 Bailey, 1984, p. 145.
49 Bailey, 1984, p. 137.

Ensor also saw similarities between the work that Booth was doing and the work of trade union officials, suggesting that the two careers required similar qualities and aims. The main difference between them seemed to be the period at which they began social work: 'In the eighties and the nineties a great many men became trade union officials or socialist agitators who, had they been born twenty years earlier, would have made careers like Spurgeon's or General Booth's'.[50]

In speaking of Mallock and Flint as influences on him in the field of political economy, Booth was placing himself in the conservative wing, as his natural inclination could well have been. At the same time, the work which Booth carried out in practice allied him much more closely to the socialist activists. He finally recognised this in an interview he gave to W. T. Stead in 1908:

> I am a Socialist, a Salvation Socialist, and always have been. A Salvation Socialist differs from a Fabian Socialist, for we begin at the other end. I am working at the tunnel on one side of the mountain, your political parties or Governments with all their schemes of social reform are working at the other end. God bless them, say I; I have nothing against them. But my way is not their way. My side of the mountain is not their side of the mountain, but if we both keep on at our own ends perhaps we may meet in the middle.[51]

Hattersley described these remarks as 'gibberish' and 'vacuous', stating that Booth 'was not a socialist, or anything else with a philosophical base, for his mind did not run to philosophy'.[52] True as this assessment undoubtedly is from the viewpoint of a political purist, Booth's words need to be placed in the context of the time in which they were spoken. The term 'socialism' was used rather loosely at the time, for example it was reported in 1888: 'Socialism is identified with any enlargement and Individualism with any contraction, of the functions of Government.'[53] At other times socialism could be used as a term almost synonymous with atheism, as Booth's lecture suggests, or as a description of any effort to mitigate the injustices suffered by the poor; the term was remarkably fluid in some circles.

As so often happens, the impact of Booth's work was not the one he would necessarily have foreseen. Engels saw in the work of the Salvation Army something far removed from what the ideas of Mallock and Flint could have been expected to produce:

> [T]he Salvation Army ... revives the propaganda of early Christianity, appeals to the poor as the elect, fights capitalism in a religious way, and thus fosters an element of early Christian class antagonism, which one day may become troublesome to the well-to-do people who now find the ready money for it.[54]

---

50 Ensor, 1992, p. 306.
51 *The War Cry*, 18 April 1908.
52 Hattersley, 1999, p. 355.
53 Collini, 1983, p. 17.
54 Engels, 1978, p. 27.

A Man with a Mind of his Own

Even with those people whose ideas he claimed had most influenced him, Mallock and Flint, Booth simply used what could be accommodated into his core beliefs to further his aims. The fact that he did so supports Hattersley's thesis that he had no pure philosophical stance. It also strengthens the argument that he needs to be viewed in the light of the leading popular thinkers of the day and the changing emphases, because his pragmatism and eclecticism were such that he was comfortable with using parts of their theories, yet not embracing the total philosophy.

Begbie spoke of Booth being influenced by both Mallock and Flint, joining their names in the same sentence, although they were not necessarily viewed as belonging to the identical school of thought. There is one link however that is telling in relation to Booth. They each made a similar statement in their books. Mallock wrote: 'There are always social questions; but there neither is, nor ever can be, any social question'.[55] Flint credited his quotation to Giambetta as: 'There is no social problem; there are only social problems'.[56]

Booth's scheme was large and one of social salvation. The question is whether it was a socialist scheme. For the Marxist, to address individual problems could be a hindrance to the only real social redemption through the overthrow of capitalism. For Booth, however, the individual could never be overlooked because Christian redemption was offered to the individual. Such a belief prevented him from fully accepting the ideas of Mallock that seemed to suggest 3,000,000 people living in poverty was somehow positive because it was a lower percentage of the total population than in previous centuries. Neither did he accept that the only solution was to overthrow the existing system. In Hattersley's words: *'In Darkest England*, like every other aspect of William Booth's social policy, was intended to ameliorate the worst features of the existing order rather than to change it'.[57]

Although Booth criticised the effects of capitalism, his scheme was not so broad that it encompassed the overthrow of capitalism. Large as the scheme was, it was firmly placed within many of the existing parameters of capitalist society. That is why, while the socialists acclaimed some of its aims, the Darkest England Scheme could also be seen as an instrument of social control. The scheme in its realisation was less broad than its conception and it only ever addressed social questions and social problems. This it did successfully but it never addressed *the* social question or *the* social problem.

Conclusion

The social scheme was only one of the two foci within the ellipse that was the Salvation Army, and in Booth's eyes the spiritual help he offered, the evangelical

---

55 Mallock, 1896, p. 139.
56 Flint, 1894, p. 273.
57 Hattersley, 1999, p. 373.

redemption was the solution to *the* social problem:

> The fact is that if you make a man truthful and honest, and benevolently disposed towards his fellows, you do far more towards the creation of that spirit which takes the well-being of society in general, than you would by making him support some Act of parliament.[58]

His faith did not mean that he lessened his attempts to address social problems but it did mean social issues and the political issues they raised were seen in a post-millennial paradigm. 'The dual mission of The Salvation Army, undergirded by Booth's full understanding of redemption as both personal and social, was preparatory to the establishment of the millennial kingdom on earth.'[59]

---

58 Booth, 1904, p. S7.
59 Green, 1989, p. 68.

Chapter 8

The General in Command

Introduction

There were two changes that took place in the Salvation Army in the period after the publication of *Darkest England*. They both combined to render the organisation more 'establishment'. One was the growth of the organisation itself which meant that more time and attention was now spent looking at the running of its own systems. The other was that its higher public profile now came from the social work it did rather than its aggressive evangelicalism. The Army had always been more in tune with the age on social rather than theological issues and with the changing attitude to religion within society at large its religious activities began to be viewed by many as eccentric rather than threatening.

By 1890, by virtue of its size, the Salvation Army could no longer function as the small activist organisation it had been in the 1860s and 1870s. Its size affected both the work it could do and the ethos of the organisation itself.

Due to its size and the scope of its social work it was being brought into a new arena where it would be compared with organisations other than churches, where its work would be judged by different criteria and rejected and accepted for reasons that were non-theological.

Organisational Size

Joseph Schumpeter, in his study of the development of capitalist society, has examined the change of the position of the entrepreneur in developing capitalism and how 'economic progress tends to become depersonalized and automatized. Bureau and committee work tends to replace individual action'.[1] To describe the change he used a military analogy which is of particular pertinence in discussing the Salvation Army:

> Of old, roughly up to and including the Napoleonic Wars, generalship meant leadership and success meant the personal success of the man in command who earned corresponding 'profits' in terms of social prestige. The technique of warfare and the structure of armies being what they were, the individual decision and driving power of the leading man - even his actual presence on a showy horse - were essential elements in the strategical and tactical situations. Napoleon's presence was, and had to be,

---

1 Schumpeter, 1996, p. 133.

actually felt on his battlefields. This is no longer so. Rationalized and specialized office work will eventually blot out personality, the calculable result, the 'vision'. The leading man no longer has the opportunity to fling himself into the fray. He is becoming just another office worker - and one who is not always difficult to replace.[2]

William Booth was a General of the Napoleonic school; he flung himself into the fray and led from the front. By the time he died, the Army had a detailed infrastructure and administration to be run and William's son, Bramwell, who succeeded him, was a General along the more modern lines. However it was William himself who put the administrative parameters in place and then handed over the administration to Bramwell. It was therefore the increasing size of the Army that led to the change and the change was gradual, although it became more apparent at the end of the century.

Norman Murdoch pinpoints the first shift in emphasis as occurring in 1869 when the Christian Mission purchased the People's Market in Whitechapel, to use as a meeting hall:

> Where before he had rented buildings, now he was an owner. Owners are stable and liable for long-term obligations. He had gone from secular halls to a building employed for mission purposes alone. Such permanency has a settling effect; mortgages cause missioners to be more concerned with upkeep than outreach.[3]

Murdoch's assessment of the missioners is reminiscent of words of Chadwick about the Primitive Methodists: 'The more property the less corybantic [frenzied]. The more they met in chapels the less they shouted in streets.'[4] Murdoch placed the change too early. The very fact of owning a building would have affected the administration and almost certainly increased the time spent on administration, if only marginally. However the People's Market was bought before the most aggressive and successful years of growth of the mission, which suggests that he misjudged the relative concern the missioners had with upkeep as against outreach. Nevertheless. as the work increased, it was William Booth himself who turned his attention to its continuation as an organisation. Bramwell described his father as a legislator rather than an organiser: 'He laid down the law in every detail, thinking of everything, and left others to organise the machine'.[5] Bramwell estimated that William gave more attention to writing the *Orders and Regulations for Field Officers,* published in 1886, than to anything else he wrote. The following sentence is a direct quote from Bramwell about his father:

> His anxiety was to compile in that book a set of regulations which would *perpetuate the Salvation Army,* and preserve it from the mistakes and confusions which had befallen so many other societies in the religious sphere.[6] (Italics added)

---

2 Schumpeter, 1996, p. 133.
3 Murdoch, 1996, p. 61.
4 Chadwick, 1992, Vol. 1, p. 389.
5 Quoted in Horridge, 1993, p. 55.
6 Quoted in Horridge, 1993, p. 55.

Booth had changed from the missioner in the East End just twenty years before who had not wanted to start his own organisation. Murdoch argued that by 1888 there was a virtual civil service system organised at the headquarters with an examination system for staff officers.[7] In his opinion by this time 'getting ahead' within the Army system had become the aim for some officers.[8] Such internal dynamics were bound to put pressure on the organisation to move away from its activist roots. A truly activist organisation is almost invariably small: 'Radical and reform movements by their very nature tend to attract certain types of personality and activists are always in a minority.'[9] A larger organisation would not necessarily need or even easily accommodate those same personalities. It was a paradox that was not confined to the Salvation Army but could also be seen, for example, in the Tractarian Movement of the Church of England:

> As public men, guiding controversy, facing the practicable, commanding a party, conciliating opinion, Newman, Pusey and Keble were sad incompetents. As moral guides, representing in their persons the ideals of sacramental and ascetic life which they commended, they sent out to the English religious conscience a call which sounded through the century.[10]

By the end of the nineteenth century there was much to perpetuate and administer. By 1888 the Salvation Army was working in 24 countries; by 1898 it was working in 39 countries. With the introduction of institutional social work there was even more administration required. After reaching this size there is a danger of organisational inertia, just to continue can become an aim in itself, and because of its size and the strength of the organisational ethos those who work within it can judge their achievement by comparison with others within the organisation rather than in relation to the realisation of the 'external' mission goals.

Furthermore the decision-making process tended to become slower and more tentative. In the *Christian Mission Magazine* of March 1874 there was an appeal for halls for the working classes, including the possible purchase of an area under the railway arch at Bethnal Green, for which it was necessary to raise £200. The same March issue contained an article, written by Catherine Booth, in which she spoke of her wish to commence a drunkards' rescue society.[11] A month later, there were a further two articles. The first was a report of the opening of a new hall in Bethnal Green, under the railway arch. The second was the first report of the work of the drunkards' rescue society.[12] While this evidence indicated the speed with which projects were carried out during the 1870s, by less than two decades later, the implementation of planning had slowed down. In addition, once there was an organisation to perpetuate and protect, the question of risk-assessment would enter the decision-making process.

---

7 Murdoch, 1996, p. 133.
8 Murdoch, 1996, p. 133.
9 Harrison, 1990, p. 155.
10 Chadwick, 1992, Vol. 1, p. 231.
11 *Christian Mission Magazine*, March 1874.
12 *Christian Mission Magazine*, April 1874.

Catherine Booth was determined in her defence of the use of organisational skills and techniques to carry forward the main work of the Salvation Army:

> Does anyone object that this is reducing religion to mere machinery? I answer, No! It is but providing a machinery through which the Spirit of Christ can operate. It is only reducing *sentiment to practice* ... We must give up sentimentalizing. Sentimentalizing is of no more use in religion than in business, and we must set to real practical common-sense scheming and downright hard work. If ever the Gospel is to make headway against the rush of evil passions, worldly ambition, and devilish animosity, it must be by determined, deadly warfare, conducted with at least as much care, sagacity, and persistency as men bestow on earthly enterprises for gain or glory.[13]

William Booth, however, lived longer than his wife and in his old age there were signs that he was prepared to hand over the administrative side of the Salvation Army and return to a more activist role for himself: 'He was God's salesman not His chief executive. And it was to that role which he more and more reverted during the last ten years of his life.'[14] His organisation did not revert with him.

Even in its move towards administrative efficiency, the Salvation Army was part of a more general movement. For example, Beatrice and Sidney Webb of the Fabian Society were arguing that the most effective way of introducing socialism was to devise the administrative machinery necessary to cope with social problems, thus easing the transition towards a socialist society:

> The direction in which the [Fabian] Society was developing, so it seemed to many of its erstwhile adherents, was away from the moral and humanitarian impulses which had initially inspired its 'Socialism', and towards 'Efficiency'. Increasingly dominated by the Webbs and Shaw, the Society came more and more to be identified with the idea of bureaucratic rule by the specially trained expert.[15]

The changes in the Salvation Army can also be seen as a normal result of the growth in numbers. Ian Ker has said of the change in status of the Roman Catholic Church in England during the nineteenth century what could equally easily be applied as a description of the Army: 'But the phenomenal growth of a tiny, despised sect into a major religious body brought with it new strains and tensions.'[16] Cardinal John Henry Newman was to pinpoint the causes of these tensions in 1877 when he wrote an essay 'on the conflicting interests, and therefore difficulties of the Catholic Church, because she is at once, first a devotion, secondly a philosophy, thirdly a polity.'[17] The three functions are based on different principles, use different means and are liable to different corruptions. By

---

13 Booth Tucker, 1912, Vol. II, pp. 51-3.
14 Hattersley, 1999, p. 430.
15 Collini, 1983, p. 77.
16 Ker, 1990, p. 463.
17 Ker, 1990, p. 701.

1890, as the Salvation Army grew in size, it faced many of the same tendencies to internal tensions that Newman diagnosed for his own church:

> Truth is the guiding principle of theology and theological enquiries; devotion and edification of worship; and of government, expedience. The instrument of theology is reasoning; of worship, our emotional nature; of rule, command and coercion. Further, in man as he is, reasoning tends to rationalism; devotion to superstition and enthusiasm; and power to ambition and tyranny.[18]

Pamela Walker has argued that the real turning point for the Salvation Army came with the publication of the *Darkest England* book. With the institutionalisation of its social work an element of professionalism entered in and it was no longer simply a spontaneous expression of its Christianity. Walker's conclusion was that it was this change that brought the Army into the main stream of religious and social activity at the end of the century:

> [The Salvation Army] was no longer pulling the devil's kingdom down with brass bands playing music hall tunes, fiery preachers and processions through working-class neighbourhoods. Instead it became a religious sect with a social service wing that was often the more vibrant and prominent half, creating strong ties to other Christian and state-run agencies.[19]

The increasing professionalisation of the Salvation Army's social wing was a variant of what was happening in charity work generally. Peter Mandler has argued that while professionalisation gave social workers more authority it could also mean less genuine contact between them and the poor, with the social workers becoming more *dirigiste*. 'The professionalisation of giving led inevitably to more bureaucratic and less personalised mechanisms.'[20]

By the end of the century, further changes were occurring within the relationship between the work of the Salvation Army and its environment. It had become a working man's church not a church of the residuum. Bramwell Booth wrote in the late 1890s that only a small proportion of its members were converted drunkards and thieves, the vast majority of its members were working people.[21]

Such a fact already made the organisation less threatening but, in addition, the working population in general and the residuum itself were both less threatening to society at large by the end of the century. Stedman Jones argued that although the working classes still remained virtually impermeable from the classes above, labour no longer reflected class combativity; it was not threatening and subversive but conservative and defensive.[22] Robert Roberts described the lack of combativity from the point of view of those who lived in the slums at the turn of the century:

---

18 Ker, 1990, p. 703.
19 Walker, 1992, p. 264.
20 Mandler, 1990, p. 28.
21 Booth, Bramwell, in Haw, 1906, p. 152.
22 Stedman Jones, 1996, p. 215.

The class struggle, as manual workers in general knew it, was apolitical and had its place entirely within their own society. They looked upon it not in any way as a war against the employers but as a perpetual series of engagements in the battle of life itself ... Hyndman Hall, home of the Social Democratic Federation, remained for us mysteriously aloof and through the years had, in fact, about as much political impact in the neighbourhood as the nearby gasworks.[23]

In addition, the residuum was being seen more and more as separate from the rest of the working classes. It did not therefore seem either so large or so threatening a group, 'but a small and hopeless remnant, a nuisance to administrators rather than a threat to civilization ... no longer a political threat - only a social problem'.[24]

At the same time there was a reduction of confrontational intensity over religion. The final decade of the century was noted for a spirit of cynicism and ennui, as epitomised by Oscar Wilde, and this spirit extended to the way in which religion was regarded:

The atmosphere of the nineties was mellower. As the scientist achieved his freedom and did not need to be aggressive like Tyndall, the atheist and agnostic achieved their freedom. They ceased to be so impassioned. They went their way, neglecting religion, critical of the churches, but without expressing the fury and ardour which sometimes marked the mid-Victorian agnostic.[25]

Not everyone saw the Salvation Army as increasing in respectability during the nineties. In the introduction to *Socialism, Utopian and Scientific*, Engels used the Army to epitomise lack of respectability: '[A]gnosticism, though not yet considered "the thing" quite as much as the Church of England, is yet very nearly on a par, as far as respectability goes, with Baptism, and decidedly ranks above the Salvation Army.' [26]

Yet, the tide of opinion was turning and more people were beginning to see the Army as on the side of the establishment. George Bernard Shaw, in his play *Major Barbara,* has Undershaft, the arms manufacturer, reply to a statement that he does not understand what the Army did for the poor: 'Oh yes I do. It draws their teeth: that is enough for me as a man of business.'[27] Such a view of the Army

---

23 Roberts, 1971, pp. 4, 14.
24 Stedman Jones, 1992, pp. 320-1.
25 Chadwick, 1992(b), p. 114.
26 Engels, 1978, p.14. The Russian editor of the 1978 edition had no doubts about the political stance of the Salvation Army, adding the following footnote: 'The *Salvation Army* - a reactionary religious and philanthropic organisation founded by the evangelist William Booth in England in 1865; subsequently it spread its activities to other countries. It was in 1880 named Salvation Army and reorganised on military lines. Largely supported by the bourgeoisie, this organisation launched a broad religious propaganda and set up a network of charitable institutions for the purpose of diverting the working people from the struggle against the exploiters. Some of its preachers resorted to social demagogy and sham condemnation of the selfishness of the rich.'
27 Shaw, 2000, p. 98.

seems far removed from the beginnings of Booth's mission in the East End, and yet it was the claim that Catherine Booth had already made on behalf of the Army in her letter to Queen Victoria.[28] E. H. Thornberg's study underlined the paradox of the way in which the Salvation Army can be seen as both breaking and then reimposing social control:

> By its activities, the Salvation Army has disturbed, and still disturbs in some ways, social control. It has broken and still breaks individual habits and collective customs. It introduced new ways and new practices in worship and street life. But at the same time, salvationism has been an extraordinary factor in leading people back to social control.[29]

The Salvation Army was rather like the Methodists in being led by its own internal organisational dynamic away from its earliest roots. It was fulfilling the progression identified by Octavia Hill, when she learnt with some dismay that the entrance fee to the Working Men's Club at Barrett's Court was being increased from 1d to 2d per week:

> [B]ut perhaps all good things must rise with their original elements and other new organisations meet the wants of the lowest, beginning again and again till the whole is raised.[30]

The difference from the Methodists was that the Army had two foci and in the interaction between the two the residuum continued to have its part in the ongoing organisational dynamic. The residuum was to continue to loom large in the public perception of the Salvation Army and in its members' own understanding of their role.

Booth's work, stemming from *Darkest England,* led to the Army being compared with, and measured against, some of the most influential groups of thinkers and doers of his time, namely the Charity Organisation Society, the Social Darwinists and the Social Imperialists. In different ways the Darkest England Scheme brought Booth and the Salvation Army into the company of these organisations and schools of thought.

The Charity Organisation Society

The Charity Organisation Society (COS) and Booth were to some extent working in parallel but there were fundamental differences in their views of poverty and charity and consequently in their methods.

Like the Salvation Army, the COS was founded in London in the 1860s and grew out of the circumstances of that time. Its idea of charity was to reconcile class differences through friendship between the classes, relying in part on the middle

---

28 Booth Tucker, 1912, Vol. II, p. 227.
29 Thornburg, c. 1930, p. 11.
30 Quoted in Darley, 1990, p. 138.

classes having enough leisure time and guilt to do this work. The COS aimed to end poverty and produce a self-reliant community among those it was helping. It was based on the work and thought of Thomas Chalmers, a leading Evangelical, and built on the experience of the Metropolitan Visiting and Relief Association (MVRA) and of Octavia Hill, a pioneer in the ideas of model housing, who used the occasions when she collected the rent to get to know the families and give advice.[31] The MVRA was among the first to use some form of case papers, a practice continued by the COS and that was to become an important part of their methods.[32]

The two ideas that were prevalent in the 1860s were that people should be helped to help themselves and that the use of scientific method and fact-finding could help solve most problems, even social ones. The COS was to preach the importance of inculcating thrift and hard work in the poor and also to introduce the idea of case studies of those it was seeking to help. The latter is seen as one of its major contributions to welfare, as it is still the basis of modern social work.

The principles of the COS upon which it hoped to base its attack on poverty were listed in its 1875 report:

(1) systematic co-operation with Poor Law authorities, charitable agencies, and individuals;
(2) careful investigation of applications for charitable aid, by competent officers;
(3) judicious and effectual assistance in all deserving cases;
(4) the promotion of habits of providence and self-reliance; and
(5) the repression of mendicity and imposture, and the correction of maladministration of charity.[33]

It can be seen from the above list where differences with the ethos of the Salvation Army might arise, and they are numbered to correspond to the COS principles:

(1) The Salvation Army was not always good at co-operating with other agencies. It had particular problems with the COS, in part due to differences in emphasis but in part also because Booth saw in the COS an attempt to interfere with, if not take over, his social efforts, something that did not suit his personality.
(2) Booth would have been less likely to insist on careful investigation than the COS, particularly at the start of his scheme when he was optimistic about the numbers of people he could help.
(3) One of the major contrasts between the COS and the Salvation Army was the former's insistence on the differentiation between the deserving and the undeserving poor.
(4) The principle of promoting habits of providence and self-reliance would carry the Salvation Army's full endorsement.
(5) The Salvation Army was not involved in anything that equated with the COS's fifth principle.

---

31 Mowat, 1960, pp. 10-3.
32 Mowat, 1960, p. 32.
33 Mowat, 1960, pp. 25-6.

The COS's emphasis on helping the deserving poor fitted in with its case-study stance because such a method is time consuming and so relatively fewer people could be helped. These two factors together placed a limitation on the scope of the COS's work. Booth, by contrast, when he launched his scheme, placed no limit on those he saw being helped by it, because, having rejected the doctrine of election years before, he thereby embraced the concept of the possibility of redemption for everyone.

There was open disagreement between the COS and Booth over the social activity of the Salvation Army. According to McBriar 'opponents of the COS had the temerity to argue that the effects of its strict policy were wholly offset by the Army's generosity'.[34] Certainly at one point Booth responded to the controversy by saying: 'the Charity organisation believes in the survival of the fit ... We believe in the survival of the unfit.'[35] Octavia Hill was a staunch advocate of the views of the COS, causing a relative of hers to describe as follows her enthusiasm for their theories: 'Her sympathies with the enquiry traditions of the Society, and with the restrictions on reckless relief, often startled and repelled some of the more impulsive philanthropists.'[36]

There was a tension within the COS organisation between the theory of the committee's rules concerning the refusal of immediate help in order to give the more permanent help of inculcating self-help and individual effort, and the feelings of the COS visitor when faced with someone's seemingly desperate situation.[37] This was a tension that also existed between the COS and the Salvation Army together with many other charities. The tension was between those who firmly believed in considering the long-term implications of charity, as they saw it, and those who when faced with suffering considered the immediate benefit they felt their good works could do.

Social Darwinists

Booth was unwilling to allow Darwin's findings on evolution and natural selection to change his theology in any way. It is therefore surprising to find in his social writings a suggestion that he had accepted the implications of Social Darwinism. Fishman pointed this out when he quoted from Booth: 'In the struggle of life the weakest will go to the wall ... All we can do is to soften the lot of the fit.'[38] However a reading of the full paragraph from which this quotation is taken suggests that Fishman may be reading too much into it. The paragraph goes on to refer to the difficulty of inculcating moral strength and is more like the classic Booth: 'No amount of assistance will give a jellyfish a backbone. No outside

---

34 McBriar, 1987, p. 60.
35 Quoted in Coutts, 1978, p. 37.
36 Maurice, Edmund, quoted in Darley, 1990, p. 119.
37 Darley, 1990, p. 127.
38 Fishman, 1988, p. 262.

propping will make some men stand erect. All material help from without is useful only in so far as it develops moral strength within.' [39]

It seems more likely, therefore, that Booth was using the common expressions of the time to explain what he saw around him. He could see the weakest going to the wall in the East End every day, with or without the theory of the survival of the fittest. What is more indicative of Booth's acquaintance with the social implications of Darwin's theory is his decision to subtitle his *Darkest England* programme: 'The Scheme of Social Selection and Salvation'. [40]

In order to judge the significance of this it will be necessary to consider the various strands of social Darwinism that were developing at this time. Darwin was not the founder of evolutionary thought, which pre-dated him. He and A. R. Wallace discovered the principle of natural selection at almost the same time, although it would come to be associated with Darwin's name rather than Wallace's. The theory of natural selection was a finding in biological science, although both Wallace and Darwin came to their conclusions with the help of Malthus's theory of population. [41] Darwin's biographers claim that Darwin was always aware of the social implications of his theory:

> 'Social Darwinism' is often taken to be something extraneous, an ugly concretion added to the pure Darwinian corpus after the event, tarnishing Darwin's image. But his notebooks make plain that competition, free trade, imperialism, racial extermination, and sexual inequality were written into the equation from the start - 'Darwinism' was always intended to explain human society. [42]

Greta Jones has argued that at the time Darwin published his work, thinkers such as Mill, Comte and Spencer were searching for a scientific framework for social investigation. They would have found one without Darwin, but Darwin's book, *The Origin of Species,* provided a framework. His influence was enormous although, according to Jones, reformers such as W. H. Mallock overestimated his input on social thought. [43] Herbert Spencer was already a social-evolutionist before the publication of *The Origin of Species*. He added the idea of natural selection to his formerly wholly Lamarckian view of evolution, the idea that mankind is progressing to a perfect or ideal state, and it was Spencer who introduced the term 'survival of the fittest'. [44] Darwin never accepted the idea of evolution as simply the realisation of an archetype. He stated that in his theory there was no absolute tendency to progress, that it was possible for species, including man, to remain stable or even degenerate. [45] Darwin even referred to Lamarck's view of a tendency to progression as nonsense. [46]

---

39 Booth, 1970, p. 44.
40 Booth, 1970, preface.
41 Hewetson, 1946, pp. 5-6.
42 Desmond & Moore, 1991, p. xix.
43 Jones, 1980, p. 4.
44 Semmel, 1960, p. 42.
45 Desmond & Moore, 1991, p. 275.
46 Desmond & Moore, 1991, p. 315.

The debate over progression was only one of the disagreements in what was to continue to wear the umbrella title of Social Darwinism. By the 1880s a debate was in progress on state intervention in social welfare and self-called Social Darwinists were lined up on both sides of the argument.[47]

One of the more extreme routes that Social Darwinism was to take was via imperialism to eugenics and thence to Nazism. Imperialism was a way of transporting the fight for the survival of the fittest from an intra-national to the international stage. However in order for a nation to win that struggle, according to the Social Darwinists, it was necessary to ensure that the working classes were healthy, fit and well-trained. Francis Galton believed that the way to ensure healthy working classes was by eugenics, which would involve taking action to encourage procreation on the part of fitter stocks and discourage the procreation of the unfit, which would be monitored in part by the compilation of a 'golden-book' of the eugenically fit and the issuance of eugenic certificates.[48] It is not hard to see how such ideas would issue eventually in a Nazi state. What is more surprising is that at the beginning of the twentieth century eugenics as a 'religion' was supported by many of the Fabians, including George Bernard Shaw, and Sidney and Beatrice Webb, who were at the same time backing the efforts of Booth's organisation to run government-funded colonies for the residuum.[49]

Social Darwinism was used as a basis for other arguments. Huxley interpreted it as a defence of the economics of laissez-faire. Kropotkin, the anarchist, claimed in his book, *Mutual Aid*, that having read *The Origin of Species*, he studied the animal kingdom and found that the most successful animals in the fight for survival were not those with the sharpest claws and the longest teeth but those that cease competition between individuals and instead combine together to secure food, safeguard their young and defend themselves against their enemies. He claimed Darwinian support for this viewpoint by referring to *The Descent of Man*:

> The small strength and speed of man, (he wrote,) his want of natural weapons, etc., are more than counterbalanced, firstly, by his intellectual faculties (which, he remarked on another page, have been chiefly or even exclusively gained for the benefit of the community); and secondly, *by his social qualities*, which led him to give and receive aid from his fellow men.[50]

Booth would have felt at ease with the idea that mutual aid and social help were positive and constructive, although he would have been less happy with Kropotkin's other conclusion that mutual aid was only successful where there was no form of government or central control. Of the other strands of Social Darwinism he would probably have felt most comfortable with Spencer's idea of progression. The idea of perfectibility is present within the evangelical Christian religion, although coming from a transcendent God rather than immanent in nature, and

---

47 Jones, 1980, p. 55.
48 Semmel, 1960, p. 46.
49 Semmel, 1960, p. 51.
50 Hewetson, 1946, p. 18.

there is a faint suggestion of generational improvement in Booth's scheme when he speaks of it enabling the children of those helped to be saved, even if the fathers are not.[51]

However there is strong evidence to suggest that Booth called his Darkest England Scheme one of social selection because he saw it as opposing and seeking to mitigate the effects of the other two strands of Social Darwinism. He attacked pure laissez-faire economics as the 'let things alone' laws of supply and demand that are excuses used to salve the consciences of those who do nothing to help those who are in trouble.[52]

There is an even more explicit attack on the ideas that led to eugenics when he says that his scheme will be acceptable to most schools of thought in social economics:

> [e]xcepting only those anti-Christian economists who hold that it is an offence against the doctrine of the survival of the fittest to try to save the weakest from going to the wall, and who believe that when once a man is down the supreme duty of a self-regarding Society is to jump upon him.[53]

The core of Booth's belief and motivation was opposed to what the most vocal of the Social Darwinists were hoping to achieve. He could never adopt their policies but only work against them. However, because his ideas were not developed in a vacuum and he was responding to the events of his day, Booth did borrow some of their ideas and terminology to communicate his own scheme. If the social salvation of his scheme was a broadening of his earlier work for individual salvation, the social selection was his response to Social Darwinism. The people who were being thrown to the wall by the process of the survival of the fittest, namely those who were rejected in the implementation of natural selection, were exactly the people whom Booth would select for the implementation of his scheme of social selection.

Social Imperialism

In his study of the nineteenth century, E. J. Hobsbawm labels the period 1875-1914 the Age of Empire. Booth launched his Darkest England Scheme at a time when there was a strong mood of imperialism and belief in the power of the empire. Booth has been described as both an imperialist and a social imperialist. One of the strongest advocates of Booth as imperialist was Norman Murdoch who attributed the success of the Salvation Army in part to Booth's creation of a 'Christian imperium'.[54] Glenn Horridge argued that in changing the name from the Christian Mission to the Salvation Army at a time when people were very aware of military

---

51 Booth, 1970, preface.
52 Booth, 1970, p. 43.
53 Booth, 1970, p. 18.
54 Murdoch, 1996, p. 115.

might and 'the British Army and Navy were considered invincible and omnipotent' Booth caused his Army to appear a 'very powerful physical force'.[55]

Booth's adoption by the Social Imperialists sprang from his connection with Stead and his plan for an overseas colony within the Darkest England scheme. Booth was a product of his times and he was English but never fiercely partisan. He was aware of the dangers to the British Empire from a lack of moral strength. He used the language of his time; just as he used the terms of Social Darwinism so he would use the terms of empire, but not always uncritically. The language of imperialism could be used merely as the springboard for a sermon. In the May 1878 edition of the *Christian Mission Magazine* the leading article made mention of the fact that England was expected to go to war imminently. Headed 'Rushing into War' the article included these lines:

> Let every one who values the favour of God do what in them lies to prevent such war. But whatever the Godless governments of our own or any other country do, thank God we are more than ever determined to fight only for Him.
>
> Yes, the empire is in danger, and no mistake. It is in danger of perishing through the disregard of God, the profanity, the open iniquity, the drunkenness, and debauchery, and profligacy of every kind which becomes more manifest every day.
>
> Oh, we entreat you, awake to the awful reality! All that every power in Europe could do against our country is as nothing compared with the fearful desolation that sin is bringing upon us.[56]

There is no belief in the impregnable might of empire here. Booth did not lose all the conditioning of living in London as England was at the zenith of imperial power. There were still suggestions that London was the centre of the earth. However this was more as the New Jerusalem in the millennium than a focus of military and industrial power.[57]

Another sense in which Booth was imperial was a by-product of the fact that he commanded, from London, an organisation that operated in most areas of the world. To this extent, he was paralleling the Empire and this impression would be heightened by his penchant for using the language of the moment. When William Booth died a book of memorial essays was produced. W. H. Fitchett plainly saw Booth's work in imperial terms, providing a chapter that was entitled 'The Imperial Side of a Religious Movement'. The essay was based on *The Salvation Army Year Book* for 1908 which gave details of the Salvation Army's work around the world. The argument for the Salvation Army having an imperial side seems to be based on the fact that details of its work around the world appeared under the heading, 'Countries and Colonies Occupied'. The writer then continued: 'The list begins with 'Continents'. So Alexander might have written, or Caesar; so Napoleon dreamed.'[58]

55 Horridge, 1993, p. 96.
56 *Christian Mission Magazine*, May 1878, pp. 113-4.
57 Green, 1989, p. 73.
58 Fitchett, n.d., p. 243.

There is a clear suggestion here of seeking to superimpose a school of thought on the premise that the use of imperial language presupposes imperial ideals. Reference is made to the subject of emigration-colonisation that fills a complete section of the year book. Making assumptions about his ability to read Booth's mind, the writer resolves:

> General Booth was thinking, not of the sect, but of the Empire, and he undertook his emigration schemes not to serve the interests of his Army, but to advance the welfare of humanity in general and of the British Empire in particular.[59]

No evidence is presented to back up the conclusion that Booth's scheme was implemented for the good of the British Empire. The problem is that there were two main motivations for people becoming social imperialists. One was to take control of the colonies more firmly by peopling them with labourers from England and, by the rewards offered by emigration, to reduce the risk of trouble at home and incorporate the working classes into the imperialistic system.[60] The other was the belief that the best way to solve the problem of poverty in the city was to give the poor the opportunity to emigrate to where there was land for them to grow the food to feed themselves. The results of both these aims were in, practical terms, the same, and motivation is not easy to determine.

Booth's emigration scheme turned him, in a practical sense, into a social imperialist. From his writings it would be possible to make a strong argument that Booth became such because he saw it as a virtuous way to ease the problems of poverty in the East End. However in seeking to implement his plans, he became involved with others, of whom two in particular who were quite definitely imperialists, namely W.T. Stead and Cecil Rhodes. Stead was involved in the writing of the *Darkest England* book and Rhodes was involved in lengthy discussions about the possibility of providing land in Africa for the Army's proposed overseas colony.

The question of the degree to which Stead was responsible for the writing of *Darkest England* has always been disputed. Stead has contradicted himself in correspondence, details of which are given in Whyte's biography of Stead.[61] The first letter quoted from is dated November 1890 and Stead refers to himself in it as offering to do the 'hack' work to get Booth's material into shape. In another letter he denies the rumour he was paid £5,000 for the book, saying it was not his book and he did not receive a penny-piece for any of the help he had been glad to give Booth. However, in a third letter, written to Milner on 23 October 1890, there is evidence of rather more influence. He wrote of taking care to include a large part of his leader on the *Bitter Cry of Outcast London*. Inglis has shown that the end of the first chapter of *Darkest England* was taken almost verbatim from the leader in the *Pall Mall Gazette* of 16 October 1883.[62] Perhaps even more significantly Stead went on to say: 'You will be delighted to see that we have got the Salvation Army

59 Fitchett, n.d., p. 251.
60 Semmel, 1960, p. 13.
61 Whyte, 1927, Vol. II, pp. 12-3.
62 Inglis, 1963, p. 203.

solid not only for Social Reform but also for Imperial Unity. I have written to Rhodes about it and we stand on the eve of great things.'[63]

Rhodes was one of the most high-profile of social imperialists and Semmel quotes him as saying that the only way to avert a bloody civil war in the United Kingdom is for colonial statesmen to acquire new lands to settle the surplus population.[64] Hobsbawm has assessed Rhodes's success as a social imperialist as follows:

> Probably Cecil Rhodes' version of social imperialism, which thought primarily of the economic benefits that empire might bring, directly or indirectly, to the discontented masses, was the least relevant. There is no good evidence that colonial conquest as such had much bearing on the employment or real incomes of most workers in the metropolitan countries, and the idea that emigration to colonies would provide a safety-valve for overpopulated countries was little more than a demagogic fantasy.[65]

Hobsbawm went on to say that because emigration was so easy to arrange during the period 1880-1914, very few of the emigrants went to organised colonies. Booth's scheme for an overseas colony never came to fruition. Suitable land was never negotiated. Apart from a few small schemes in the United States the main result of this part of the scheme was an Emigration Department to help arrange assisted passages.

Booth is still described in social history textbooks as a social imperialist. Stedman Jones described *Darkest England* as the 'first popular success' of the social imperialists.[66] However he was not a successful social imperialist, so that his organisation is less likely to be associated with imperialism than if he had founded a successful colony. Booth would not have known at the time that this seeming failure would in time be more an advantage to his organisation. During the twentieth century identification with imperialism could well have been a drawback.

It is easy to see social imperialism as a theory that Booth could adopt because it could work to his central goal. From the evidence it is not clear if Booth was using the social imperialists or if they were using him. It is possible they both saw advantage in the co-operation. In the end it worked for neither on the scale and in the format hoped for.

Darkest England Scheme Results

There are several ways of attempting to measure the results of the Darkest England Scheme. It is possible, like Frederick Coutts, to give quantitative details of parts of the scheme four years after its launch:

---

63 Whyte, 1927, Vol. II, p. 13.
64 Semmel, 1960, p. 16.
65 Hobsbawm, 1995(b), p. 69.
66 Stedman Jones, 1992, p. 311.

By Christmas 1894 ... there were 3,500 beds available for men at a charge of twopence per night, and five hundred priced at one penny. There was also cubicle accommodation for another hundred men at threepence per night, with two further shelters offering more than thirteen hundred men feeding, sleeping, reading and smoke room facilities from fourpence to sixpence per night ... Any man who was literally penniless could earn his overnight stay in one of the cheaper shelters by chopping firewood, but anyone in search of more regular employment could enter one of the four elevators - or 'sheltered workshops' - or be taken on at the Salvage Wharf at Battersea. This last could employ up to three hundred men, most of whom stayed between two and three months.[67]

[At Hadleigh] the farm, dairy, market garden, nursery, poultry and industrial sections were all in operation. Wheat, oats, barley and rye were being raised, together with roots for consumption and seed. The stock included five hundred head of cattle, two hundred sheep and over five hundred pigs. The dairy contained some eighty cows and heifers and the total milk yield was being sold at prevailing prices. Seventy-five men were employed on over two hundred acres of fruit and market gardening. Seventy acres of fruit trees had been planted by the colonists themselves, and a small nursery had been established....In the same year some three million bricks were produced by the brickfields, and a small steam joinery helped to meet the domestic necessities of the colony.[68]

Jenty Fairbank has collated a list of the elements of the Darkest England Scheme, marking with an asterisk all those elements that were in operation by 1906 (reproduced in Table 7.1).

Table 8.1 Elements of the Darkest England Scheme

Food depots*
Night shelters*
Workshops and labour yards*
Labour bureaux*
The Household Salvage brigade
The farm colony*
The industrial village
Agricultural villages*
The overseas colony
Universal emigration*
The salvation ship*
Slum visitation and nursing*
Prison-gate brigade and ex-criminals homes*
Whitechapel-by-the-Sea

Travelling hospital
Inebriate homes*
Rescue homes*
Preventive homes*
Inquiry office*
Refuges for street children
Industrial schools*
Asylums for moral lunatics
Improved lodgings*
Workmen's cottages
The poor man's bank*
The poor man's lawyer*
The intelligence department*
Matrimonial bureau

*Elements that were in operation by 1906

Source: Fairbank, 1987, p.149

---

67 Coutts, 1978, p. 119.
68 Coutts, 1978, p. 128.

In addition the work listed in Table 7.2, not originally proposed in the Darkest England scheme, was being undertaken by the Army by 1906:

Table 8.2 Additional Social Work by 1906

Wood yards	Midnight soup kitchens
Shoe blacking brigades	Midnight work amongst women
Street cleaning brigades	Special training home for social officers
Express brigades	Maternity homes
Knitting and needle workrooms	Farthing breakfasts for children
Laundries	Hospitals
Police-court visitation	Servants' homes

Source: Fairbank, 1987, p.149

Tables 7.1 and 7.2 show the impact on the Salvation Army of the later 'reactive exchange' between the residuum and Booth. While a separate Social Trust was created for the money for the social work, it was still a pull on resources of both time and personnel.

It was also to fundamentally alter the perception of the Army in the eyes of the public. The Darkest England Scheme raised the profile of Booth and his Army and, as with the Maiden Tribute, caused him to be applauded and vilified for reasons other than his style of Christianity.

Some critics objected to Booth's scheme on political and economic grounds. Examples of these critics were C. S. Loch[69] and W. Hazlitt Brown.[70] They both disputed Booth's calculation of a residuum that numbered three million. It was true, almost without exception, that those who had a new scheme calculated the 'submerged' as numbering around three million while those who were already at work in this field put the figure at much closer to one million.[71]

Once Booth launched his Darkest England Scheme his work came much more into the public domain. He was asking for a total of one million pounds to run the scheme, a large sum for those days, and one to give apoplexy to his detractors. The very size of what he was proposing caused grave concern, for he wanted a scheme of social salvation that was 'as wide as the scheme of eternal salvation'.[72] So Thomas Huxley, his most virulent opponent, wrote of the great danger of giving money and therefore power to someone of fanatical religious persuasion.[73] It is easy to see the reasoning behind Huxley's original criticisms, especially in view of the amount of power that was in Booth's hands due to the autocracy of the organisation. However, as the correspondence in *The Times* continued, Huxley's attacks descended into personal vitriol which greatly undermined his case.[74] Part

---

69 Loch, 1890.
70 Hazlitt Brown, 1891.
71 Booth, 1970, p. 23.
72 Booth, 1970, p. 36.
73 Huxley, 1891.
74 Huxley, 1891.

of Huxley's strong objection to Booth's scheme lay in his own background. His own 'meeting' with the poor of London had led him to look for a new solution for their plight and he doubtless considered that Booth was moving backwards to an older, failed salvation, as Huxley saw it.

> Night-time found [Huxley] in his tiny dockside surgery, venting his anger. The wide-eyed boy who loved metaphysics and religion and dreamed his way into the immensity of geological time asked himself: how could a 'solitary Philosopher' be 'happy in the midst of poverty'? The pleading faces were to haunt him for life. They put the moral fire into his drive for a New Reformation. Christianity had failed the starving. Politics had failed them. The young evangelical would look for a new sort of salvation.[75]

Booth and Huxley had seen the same problem and been similarly affected but their search for solutions had taken very different routes. Thus, in Huxley's eyes, Booth was an obstacle to the move to the new salvation; which was, perhaps, a parallel of the way Marx would have viewed Booth's scheme. For Booth was seeking to make the present system bearable which, while not the opium of purely religious comfort, was an opiate nonetheless in that it could help to put back the overthrow of capitalism.

Huxley's questions led to a Commission of Enquiry being set up into the use of Army funds, particularly in relation to social funds, in which Booth was exonerated. However, not everyone was convinced:

> As to Booth, he wanted money for the Salvation Army - and he has got it. The quarrel with Frank Smith shows this clearly enough. Smith wanted the money subscribed for the Social reform scheme, and to be applied strictly for that purpose; Booth wanted it to be placed in the general fund of the Salvation Army, an institution in which the fat salaries and good places are all enjoyed by members of the Booth family. By this time the middle-class fools who subscribed the cash must feel uneasy in their minds concerning the destination of the funds. Booth can chuckle, however; the bubble may burst as soon as it likes, his object is attained; 'he is all right, for he has got the £ s. d.,' and we may depend upon it he will keep it. The Booth Confidence Trick has been a complete success - for Booth.[76]

The level of reaction and publicity, good and bad, would have been unthinkable for an organisation that had remained as purely an evangelical sect, however successful its methods.

Among many who preached sermons based on Booth's books were the Rev. Thomas Hancock and R. W. Dale. Hancock was very scathing of the scheme and implicitly accused it of not being truly Christian. For example, he wrote:

> [W]hat [Jesus] did amongst the hungry by the power of His Word and by the simple obedience of His twelve chosen apostles, Mr Booth promises to do by the power of

---

75 Desmond, 1994, pp. 3-4.
76 *The Commonweal*, January 1891, p. 5.

money ... The contrasts between the Lord's salvation and Mr Booth's 'scheme' of social salvation, I need not say, are endless.[77]

In a sense these arguments were not new. They had been part of the debate on Christian Socialism for years. What was different was that Booth, by the publication of his book, became the focus for these arguments. The additional element in Hancock's criticism of Booth is once again the fact that Booth was asking for money, which to Hancock made it an 'earthly scheme and therefore perforce not of God.'[78] In the middle of his second sermon, aimed purely at persuading people not to give any money to the scheme, he admitted he had not read its details, but felt obliged to speak out against those who rushed to support it.[79]

Dale's sermon was in favour of the scheme, for two reasons. First, although not all parts of the scheme were new, he felt that 'by placing these separate methods in close relation with each other it enormously increases their efficiency'.[80] His second reason for supporting the scheme was that it was to be run by the Salvation Army, many of whose members had been saved from the kind of lives they were now trying to change for others In addition the Salvationists had a habit of obedience to authority and a 'boisterous and rollicking' religion.[81]

In fact, both critics and supporters of *Darkest England,* apart from those who had not read it, were agreed upon the elements that made this scheme different. These were the size and scope of the scheme and the fact that it was so completely allied to evangelical religion. As Hattersley has pointed out, Booth was original in neither his evangelicalism nor his social scheme, but he did have a particular gift for communicating with the poor and working classes: 'William Booth spread the idea of constructive compassion, as he spread the idea of redemption, in places where the good news had previously not been heard.'[82]

Such debate on its merits and demerits in the press and in the pulpits greatly increased the scheme's impact. The rate of sale of the book was described as 'phenomenal'. The first edition of 10,000 was exhausted in the day it first appeared. Within a month a second edition of 40,000 had been printed and a third edition of another 40,000 copies was being printed.[83] By February 1891 nearly 175,000 copies had been issued.[84] One year after its first appearance a fifth edition of 200,000 copies was advertised.[85]

Booth never received the £900,000, or the promise of £30,000 per annum, he said he needed to run the complete Darkest England Scheme. What he did receive

---

77 Hancock, 1891, p. 1.
78 Hancock, 1891, p. 17.
79 Hancock, 1891, p. 17.
80 Dale, 1890, p. 7.
81 Dale, 1890, pp. 10-3.
82 Hattersley, 1999, p. 440.
83 Sandall, 1979, Vol. III, p. 79.
84 *The War Cry,* 7 February 1891, p. 7.
85 Sandall, 1979, Vol. III, p. 79.

was the £100,000 he had required as a sign that he should start the scheme. As the details above show, this was enough to launch the Salvation Army into the realm of institutionalised social work. It was not simply that institutions grew out of its work, but that now the work was focused on tackling some of the wrongs created by the system. Booth and his Army were seen as tackling issues that did not relate solely to the religious sphere. It brought them greater publicity although Walker argued that the Army was rather capitalising on a public prominence which it already enjoyed.[86] It also brought Booth into the realm of politics and economics. His work would be judged now not only by its spiritual efficacy and his own personal motivation, but also within the parameters of the disciplines of politics and economics.

There were economic results that Booth would not have foreseen, such as that described in an article in *The Commonweal*:

> Meanwhile, General Booth's scheme, which was to save the 'submerged tenth,' has had one effect, for which probably his middle-class patrons will have little cause to thank him. Tramps, outcasts, and unemployed workmen are all drifting to London. Didn't a Warwickshire police-superintendent declare the other day that the Warwickshire roads were filled with tramps marching to London, under the impression that General Booth will be able to provide them all with work, food and shelter?[87]

There were several complaints to *The Times* that the Salvation Army was using sweated labour.[88] There was very little difference to be seen between the Army making men chop wood before they stayed overnight in one of its shelters and the workhouse exacting a day's work the next day for a night's lodging. The unions objected that the Army was not paying union rates and the employers who were its competitors in the market complained that the Army was undercutting their prices. The Army denied the charges and Rider Haggard printed the denials from the officer in charge of the Spa Road Institution about what happened there:

> [The Salvation Army] neither sweated nor undersold. The men whom they picked up had no value in the labour market, and could get no value in the labour market and could get nothing to do because no one could employ them, many of them being the victims of drink and entirely unskilled. Such people they over-looked, housed, fed and instructed, whether they did or did not earn their food and lodging, and after the first week paid them upon a rising scale. The results were eminently satisfactory, as even allowing for the drunkards they found that but few cases, not more than ten per cent, were hopeless. Did they not rescue these men, most of them would sink utterly; indeed, according to their own testimony many of such wastrels were snatched from suicide. As a matter of fact, also, they employed more men per ton of paper than any other dealers in the trades.[89]

86 Walker, 1992, p. 262.
87 *The Commonweal*, January 1891, p. 1.
88 E.g. *The Times*, 4,6,10 January 1893.
89 Haggard, 1910, pp. 28-9.

The Salvation Army was merely finding the same problems that others who had tried similar schemes had already come up against. For example the Charity Bureau in Antwerp 'tried deliberately to increase the proceeds of pauper industry, but such efforts had to be dropped because of the resistance of local entrepreneurs and because most paupers were unskilled labourers, whose low-quality work was difficult to market'.[90]

The Army felt able to defend itself and was often called upon to do so. Nevertheless the Army had new and different issues to resolve in introducing a social programme and thereby entering the realm of politics and economics. In the realm of religion the motivation for one's actions was crucial, in economics the results, both direct and indirect, were really all that mattered. Whereas theology outlined a reliable progression, for example salvation followed repentance, economics and politics offered no such guarantees and the outcome of actions in these spheres could be very different from what was intended.

In addition, while in the realm of theology Booth was dealing with what he believed to be eternal truths, the social, economic and political arena in which he launched his social scheme was constantly changing so that solutions might not stay solutions for long. Such was Stedman Jones's appraisal of Booth's scheme:

> [With the end of the Dock Strike] the residuum was no longer a vast horde capable of holding the capital to ransom, but a small and hopeless remnant, a nuisance to administrators rather than a threat to civilization ... Once disentangled from the respectable working class, the residuum could not on its own overturn London. Once detailed social investigation and the activity of the strikers themselves had established a clear distinction between the 'legitimate' claims of labour and the ugly symptoms of 'social disease', fears of revolution could be turned aside ... The rapid fading away of general Booth's scheme to save the outcast spoke as eloquently as the dock strike of the changed middle-class attitude towards the casual poor.[91]

Although Booth's scheme was in tune with the times at its launch, there is a sense in which the success in terms of numbers was tempered by the changes taking place in the social and political climate within which the scheme operated.

Bernard Bosanquet of the COS stated that Booth had no understanding of economics and that his good intentions would therefore have bad results. First Bosanquet disagreed that pauperism was increasing, and secondly he stated that the residuum was not a stagnant pool that could be 'drained like sludge', but was constantly being renewed. Bosanquet was right on both of these points although not necessarily correct in the conclusions he drew about the best way of dealing with the residuum. Bosanquet's criticism shows that by the introduction of Booth's Darkest England Scheme his organisation and its work could now be criticised and praised, while totally ignoring its religious motivation, according to the criteria of a different paradigm.[92]

---

90 Mandler, 1990, p. 53.
91 Stedman Jones, 1992, pp. 320-1, 327.
92 McBriar, 1987, pp. 60-1.

On the subject of the deserving poor, public opinion was moving in the direction of the state intervening to deal with the worst conditions of poverty. In 1898, Booth's son, Bramwell, wrote in *The War Cry* about the section of the population that some described as worthless:

> But how did they become worthless? Is it not a fact that, with regard to the majority of them, they were born in dens unfit for beasts to dwell in; that if the community did not escape the burden of giving them any sort of training or education, it contrived to bestow a minimum of anything likely to produce any moral enlightenment; that they were left to the drink snare, and permitted unrestrained to drink themselves into degradation, brutality and crime? It is notorious. Even the Charity Organisation admits it. If they are 'worthless' it is because Society has wrecked them, or allowed them to be wrecked.[93]

In addition to William Booth being part of the charity world, he was part of a larger field of people who were addressing the problem of unemployment. Booth's lack of understanding of economic policy meant that he was not able to judge the economic implications of his proposals. In this he was not alone at the time. Harris states that although unemployment began to be seen as an economic problem, economic theory was not applied to the search for a solution before World War 1. In 1892 the minister most closely associated with unemployment was the Home Secretary, because it was seen mainly as a threat to public order.[94]

Not everyone was agreed that unemployment was all bad. Not all shared Booth's view that the suffering it caused needed to be addressed. For those with different priorities, maximum profit needed to be considered as well as maximum welfare. A pool of casual labour could be important in allowing wages to fall in a recession and then permitting rapid expansion in a boom. However, casual labour was more likely to be inefficient, with lower levels of fitness, skill and concentration. For Harris, Booth was among the first to see unemployment in terms that were later to be part of the national argument:

> Booth was one of the first writers to suggest that unemployment might be a cause as well as a result of sickness and physical degeneracy; and he drew attention to a factor subsequently emphasized by Hobson and the Webbs, that unemployment was not a prerequisite of industrial efficiency, but a form of chronic personal and social waste.[95]

Booth's scheme of factories, labour and overseas colonies was part of a series of schemes to create work for the unemployed. Some of these colonies were seen as Utopian and others were intended to be punitive. The characteristic they all shared was that they failed to reach more than a minute portion of the unemployed.

By the beginning of the twentieth century, Booth's organisation was finding there were disadvantages to the policy of not discriminating between the deserving and undeserving poor. The Salvationists found that their social work was being

---

93 *The War Cry*, 17 December 1898, p. 4.
94 Harris, 1972, p. 81.
95 Harris, 1972, p. 125.

hampered by a class of vagrant that was not susceptible to being helped by their programme. A form of penal colony was, therefore, proposed. For this and also for the establishment of an overseas colony (still a dream), the Salvation Army was seeking financial aid from the Government, for by now the Government was becoming more involved in welfare. Serious consideration was given to the possibility of the Salvation Army becoming part of a Government solution to the problem of unemployment.[96]

Harris listed the four main objections that were raised to the Army being used in this way:

(1) The fact that despite Booth having been cleared of misuse of funds by a Committee of Inquiry into the Darkest England funds there was still disagreement about just how funds had been used and a feeling that the Army should not be entrusted with Imperial funds.

(2) There had been a failure on the part of the Army to keep accurate statistical records of those who had found employment through its factory and farm schemes. It was claimed that the majority of those who were listed as having been found work had only been given temporary work or had been placed in the Army's own 'elevators'. The Army did not differentiate between these in its figures nor did it follow up on those who left its homes or colonies. In other words there was no record of the permanence of its 'successes'.

(3) There was opposition to the Army from trade unionists and others because it was claimed the produce of the farms and workshops was being sold at a price that undercut the market rate.

(4) The Salvation Army was a sect that made no secret of its religious motives or aims in its social work. There was a strong feeling that Government money should not be used to fund such a programme.[97]

However the Army was not so far from being granted Government funds to proceed with its plans. Rider Haggard had investigated Army agricultural projects, as well as the elevators, and reported positively, supporting a request for funds.[98] It seems incredible that the organisation could consider being part of a plan for *punitive* camps and could be willing to be seen to be acting for the Government in running them. Yet such was the Army's position, as is clear from a booklet published by the Salvation Army in 1909 and entitled: *The Vagrant and The Unemployable: A Plea for the Compulsory Restraint of Vagrants and their Employment in Labour Colonies*. Despite a condition being placed in the plan, by the Army, about the possibility of redemption for those in the camps, it must be admitted that the camps can only be seen as a huge compromise of the original plans and goals for the farm colony.

The Army's views on unemployment were much closer to the minority report of the Poor Law Commission than to Beveridge's majority report and had the minority proposals been adopted Booth's scheme might have moved further ahead.

---

96 Harris, 1972, pp. 129-30.
97 Harris, 1972, pp. 131-4.
98 Haggard, 1910, pp. 12, 234.

The majority report, in the preparation of which Helen Bosanquet, wife of Bernard, played a significant role, was written from the COS view of poverty. The minority report was in large part the work of Beatrice Webb of the Fabian Society.[99] They each started from a different view of poverty and were therefore unlikely to agree on the solutions.

Helen Bosanquet had previously written a chapter on 'The Industrial Residuum' in *Aspects of the Social Problem* in which she had focused on the defects of character of the members of the residuum and the majority report emphasised the moral causes of pauperism, drink, gambling and thriftlessness, for example.[100] The minority report, in contrast, emphasised the social causes of pauperism.

It was at this point that the Salvation Army came as close as it would during Booth's lifetime to leaving behind its roots as an activist movement and pressure group by becoming an establishment organisation. Harris makes the following assessment:

> In view of [the] manifold objections, what is perhaps most surprising about proposals for making the Army an organ of public administration is not that they were ultimately rejected but that they should ever have been considered at all. Yet Lord Rosebery in 1905 suggested that General Booth should be given a government contract to deal with the 'residuum'; and the Westminster Review proposed that the Army should be made part of a newly constituted department of 'National Health'. [101]

In terms of quantitative results, the Darkest England Scheme, though impressive in what it achieved, did not fulfil the goals that Booth enumerated. He himself would later state that, by including all the social work in which the Army was involved around the world by the end of his life, it had exceeded expectations. This does not alter the fact, however, that in terms of its original goals, the Darkest England Scheme did not succeed as a whole.

The question is again one of quantitative versus qualitative achievement. It has already been argued that the organisation's size inevitably changed it. The success of the Darkest England Scheme would have had an enormous quantitative impact on the Salvation Army at the time, in terms of the money it handled and the poor who came within its social programme.

It is likely however that to succeed it would have been necessary to have been publicly perceived as aligned with the Government in its social control programme for the farm colony portion of the scheme, and with the Social Imperialists for the overseas colony portion of the scheme. For an organisation that still saw itself as identifying with the poor, such 'successes' could only have brought long-term negative results.

---

99 Harris, 1972, pp. 134-5.
100 McBriar, 1987, pp. 124-5.
101 Harris, 1972, pp. 134-5.

Atmosphere of the Times

The last decade of the nineteenth century saw a continuation of the diffusiveness in religion and between disciplines that had begun in mid-century. The first edition of Alfred Marshall's *Principles of Economics* was published in 1890, the year in which Booth's *Darkest England* was published. Booth and Marshall would have been in agreement on the kind of human characteristics, such as honesty and social care that attracted their approval. Writing to *The Times* in February 1891, J. T. Cunningham wrote that 'philanthropists like Mr Booth and economists like Alfred Marshall are approaching nearer and nearer to harmony'.[102]

Tristram Hunt has described Marshall and Booth as both being part of the 'intellectual retreat from London'. He likens Booth's plans for the various colonies of the Darkest England scheme to Marshall's proposal for:

> the removal of large sections of the working population into industrial colonies outside the degenerative filth of the capital. Manufacturers would gain from low rents and the workers would thrive in a healthy environment. There was no longer any point in trying to reform London. It was beyond saving.

Marshall did not place economic welfare as the highest aim of society, he sought instead to maximise human well-being. The idea of progress was crucial to Marshall. Despite much of his economic work being concerned with comparative statics the dynamic of evolutionary growth was vital to his economic and social ideas.[103]

For Marshall, progress was purposive and economic growth and human betterment had a symbiotic relationship. Believing in this made him very selective in the economic illustrations that he used. He saw man on the economically driven evolutionary growth path from alcohol to tea and not tea to alcohol. He was totally persuaded that higher wages would be spent on better food and a purer lifestyle, not opium and pornography. He believed that it was the hard manual work of the day that meant men were only willing to spend the evenings in the pubs. Booth shared Marshall's belief that economic conditions could be of crucial importance in determining a man's capacity for improvement. He did not believe progress was inevitable, immanent in the system, but he did believe it was possible.

As a result of Marshall's belief in the civilising power of evolution, he accepted that there would come a day when there were no more reasons for people not to have the 'characteristics of gentlemen'.[104] At this point they would no longer be able to blame their circumstances but only be able to blame themselves. Marshall appeared quite prepared to write off the residuum. He did not share Booth's evangelical imperative that everyone can be saved, while they still live.

Marshall's economic philosophy, rather than his economic theory, is summarised by David Reisman:

---

102 Hattersley, 1999, p. 390.
103 Reisman, 1987, pp. 343-4.
104 Quoted in Stedman Jones, 1992, p. 5.

Market mechanism and State intervention, Marshall believed, are but instruments, to be selected or rejected on grounds of expediency rather then dogma. What matters most of all is attainment of the end. And that end is the uplifting and upgrading of the tone of life.[105]

Booth's Christian beliefs were held with absolute conviction but in the realm of economics and politics he was a pragmatist and the words about Marshall could equally apply to him. The result was that he would use any 'ism' that did not oppose the Christian religion if it could help towards lifting the individual, increasing his sense of worth and aiding his own self-development.

For Marshall, the person was formed to a large extent by circumstances and he saw such virtues as honesty and deliberateness as evolutionary characteristics. It was his insistence on examples to back up his belief that evolutionary change led to greater social care, for example, that led to him being accused of complacency by Schumpeter.[106] In Marshall's view of the world there was less room for aggression and antagonism, a distance from the reality of the struggle for survival:

> In place of the calculating 'economic man' invented by nineteenth-century political economists, Marshall imagined a reasoning ethical man whose idealized attributes were drawn from the intellectual interests and economic standards of himself and his comfortable university friends. Thus, Marshall's earliest and most persistent remedy for poverty was the promotion among the less fortunate classes of education, opportunities and skills that would enable them to emulate the middle classes and compete with them successfully.[107]

> It was entirely consistent with contemporary faith in the efficacy of a moral person that socialism should be described as an attempt to teach the wealthy a new morality, rather than as a doctrine of class war or social revolution.[108]

As the Salvation Army grew in size and gained recognition, Booth, in old age, was to share in the complacency of the time and to view the beginnings of the social work in a 'glow' that was distanced from the reality of the struggle. Booth's own conclusion about the result of the Darkest England Scheme was made in 1911: 'Truly our future chroniclers will have to record the fact that our social operations ... imparted a divine dignity to the struggles of the early years of The Salvation Army's history.'[109]

However, despite the sense of what had already been achieved and because of his belief in immediate redemption for each individual, Booth continued to work for the salvation of still more. Because of how many had been saved, he was still positive into old age, with a sense of the redemptive work moving forward. By contrast, Marx's framework for societal redemption could only occur at one point in time, and in old age that time, for him, was passing.

---

105 Reisman, 1987, p. 2.
106 Reisman, 1987, pp. 3-4.
107 Soffer, 1978, p. 76.
108 Soffer, 1978, p. 74.
109 Quoted in Fairbank, 1987, p. 151.

Booth was quite old when Rudyard Kipling criticised what he termed the 'distasteful exhibition' of Salvationists playing timbrels, to which Booth replied that if he thought it would save one more soul for Christ, he would be prepared to stand on his hands and play his tambourine with his feet.[110]

By contrast Marx was to write to Engels in 1863:

Re-reading your book has made me regretfully aware of our increasing age. How freshly and passionately, with what bold anticipations and no learned and scientific doubts, the thing is still dealt with here! And the very illusion that the result will leap into the daylight of history tomorrow or the day after gives the whole thing a warmth and vivacious humour - compared with which the later 'gray in gray' makes a damned unpleasant contrast.[111]

If antagonism seemed to have been eradicated from much of the economic pronouncements during the final decade of the century, there was also less aggression in religion. There is doubt about the degree to which economic confidence had percolated down to the working classes but religious doubt and agnosticism were widespread by this time:

This is what everyone sees to constitute the special moral feature of our times: the *masses* are losing the Bible and its religion. At the Renascence, many cultivated wits lost it; but the great solid mass of the common people kept it, and brought the world back to it after a start seemed to be made in quite another direction. But now it is the *people* which is getting detached from the Bible.[112]

Agnosticism and atheism now had the confidence and calm of orthodoxy:

The closing decades of the nineteenth century were the true era of 'the death of God'. Almost more disturbing than the philosophy of Nietzsche with which the phrase is associated was the fact that 'the background of all the world was not merely atheism, but atheist orthodoxy, and even atheist respectability. That was quite as common in Belgravia as in Bohemia. That was above all normal in Suburbia.' This was the new state of things. This was the new world in which the ideas which had existed only in coteries in the 1840s, 50s and 60s were now commonplaces.[113]

Agnostics and atheists therefore felt strong enough to cope with the faith of those who still believed, they had no need to meet faith with the aggression of Thomas Huxley. The atmosphere was, in Chadwick's words, 'more mellow'.[114] In the evolutionary belief of the age some thinkers took over Cardinal Newman's idea

---

110 Barclay, 1975, p. 232.
111 Marx, Karl, letter to Friedrich Engels from London on 9 April 1863, reprinted in Marx & Engels, 1962, p.539
112 Wilson, 1999, p. 264.
113 Wilson, 1999, pp. 281-2.
114 Chadwick, 1992(b), p. 114.

of the development of doctrine and transformed it into the belief that the 'Church itself could evolve into a kind of universal religion of humanity'.[115]

Oscar Wilde personified the era of *fin-de-siècle;* his biographer claims that 'without Wilde the decade could not have found its character'.[116] Wilde himself recognised the falseness of the complacency and optimism. He mocked the attitude of the comfortable classes to the poor, for example in *The Picture of Dorian Gray:*

> Had he gone to his aunt's he would have been sure to have met Lord Goodbody there, and the whole conversation would have been about the feeding of the poor, and the necessity for model lodging-houses. Each class would have preached the importance of those virtues for whose exercise there was no necessity in their own lives. The rich would have spoken on the value of thrift, and the idle grown eloquent over the dignity of labour.[117]

It was an era in which to cultivate an appearance of nonchalance and languor, where style took precedence over substance. Linked with the optimistic view of the economists and the general loss of faith it did not seem the era for aggressive evangelicalism.

Conclusion

The Salvation Army's willingness to seek to solve what some now saw as the reduced problem of poverty that remained from earlier decades, and, in a way, to act as a buffer or a conduit between the classes, made the organisation acceptable in the more tolerant climate of the end of the century.

It is possible that it was at this point that the two foci, evangelism and social action, that were the result of William Booth's earlier engagement with the residuum in the East End were the most crucial in determining the continuing form of the Salvation Army.

The organisation had grown on an international scale and it had been in existence for three decades. There now existed a structure that required time and effort being expended on its internal workings in order to perpetuate it. If the organisation had remained an aggressively evangelical sect it is likely that it would have become marginalised in the era of Wildean nonchalance and agnostic orthodoxy.

However if its involvement in social work had led it to abandon its evangelical theological stance in favour of a more liberal incarnationalism there would have been a danger that in compromising its theological roots to adapt to the times it would also have lost its individual identity. Diane Winston has made a similar point about its conservative theology preventing the Salvation Army in the

---

115 Wilson, 1999, p. 350.
116 Ellmann, 1987, p. 288.
117 Wilde, 1997, p. 13.

United States from being swamped by the consumerism that it adopted to some degree.[118]

Despite its growth the Salvation Army had not become so successful in its social work that this wing grew out of proportion to its evangelical work nor that it became identified with success in a specific economic or political mould.

In a more mellow age the Salvation Army became accepted. However much the organisation viewed its own evangelicalism as aggressive, to the public it had mellowed by virtue of its social wing and was no longer seen as a threat. It was no longer a threat in terms of its social work, for the envisaged scale of William Booth's scheme had never materialised and its success was constrained within the parameters imposed on it by economics and politics. It worked within the existing system.

From the dynamics of the interaction between William Booth and the London residuum there had evolved a mix of atonement theology and incarnational social conscience that had crystallised and institutionalised into the Salvation Army. No longer seen as threatening by either the religious or secular authorities it had carved a niche for itself.

---

118 Winston, 1999, p. 49.

Chapter 9

Fifty Years On

Centrality and Dissemination

By the end of their lives both Booth and Marx could see their ideas and work developing beyond themselves and probably their own wishes. Kolakowski argued that such a development is inevitable.

> It is a well-known fact, to which the history of civilization records no exception, that all important ideas are subject to division and differentiation as the influence continues to spread.[1]

Lyon described the impact that Marx's ideas were having by the time of his death:

> Eventually during the last decade of his life (1873-83) Marx' ideas became widely known in Europe and parts of North America ...[A]ll kinds of vulgarizations of Marxism also emerged, characterizing Marx in roles to which he could never subscribe. And Engels' own writing, even though Marx approved of it at the time, gave rise to conceptions of Marxism quite incompatible with the central themes of the latter's work. Marx, irritated by these deviations from his understanding of the world, once hotly declared 'As for me, I am no Marxist'![2]

By the end of Booth's life the organisation he had founded had developed its own ethos, identity and dynamic. If the scheme Booth launched did not always produce the results he envisaged, so his organisation developed in its interaction with the life of the countries where it worked in ways he could not have predicted.

Booth may have been an autocrat, who could set out regulations for his organisation, but he could not control the dynamic reaction once his organisation moved into new cultures and spheres.

However, in the impact of the London residuum upon the core beliefs and ideas of Booth and Marx there has been found to be a homomorphism. This impact came from the level of poverty, the number of people in poverty and the durability of poverty. Clearly Marx and Booth did not reach the same conclusions, but they were both caused to broaden their ideas by the evidence before them, in Blue Books, in newspaper reports and in the human beings before their eyes.

---

1 Kolakowski, 1989, p. 3.
2 Lyon, 1988, p. 160.

Present and Future

Regarding the question of redemption, there were always important differences in its timing between Booth and Marx. Redemption would come at a future point in history, according to Marx. Redemption was available in the present, according to Booth. It gave Booth's work an urgency that continued into his old age. Yet, as has already been argued, in another sense the chronology of their redemptive schemata grew closer. Booth always maintained that the best hope for society was the redemption of the individual.

For Marx the starting point was a societal redemption that would enable each individual member of society, including the surplus population, to develop into a universal individual who would thereby enrich society.

When Booth launched his Darkest England Scheme he was implicitly accepting that the system that created a surplus population might need to be reformed in order for its members to be able to appreciate and accept individual redemption and thereby benefit society. A similar chronology to Marx's was tacitly accepted within the scheme.

The Darkest England Scheme and Marxist Terminology

Booth's scheme was, in Marxist terminology, aimed at the relative surplus population. A reading of the scheme shows that it was aimed at the lowest stratum of relative surplus population, the lumpenproletariat, those who were not equipped to function within the capitalist production system. By training in the 'elevators' they would learn skills that would enable them to become part of the reserve army of labour. They could then be drawn into the production system at the relevant point in the cycle. Those who could not find work in this way or chose otherwise could be trained in farming techniques. The question of whether they would thereby join the proletariat is a question of fact. In Marx's own words:

> [W]here the capitalist landlord has expropriated the peasant ... the real worker of the land is as much a proletarian wage labourer as the city worker, and thus has directly the same interests.[3]

Booth's total scheme, however, included the idea of those trained at the farm colony being enabled over time to purchase small-holdings, which would in effect return them to the peasantry. As Marx saw, in such a situation their relationship to the interests of the proletariat is more fluid:

> [E]ither the peasantry hinders every workers' revolution and causes it to fail, as it has done in France up till now; or the proletariat (for the landowning peasant does not belong to the proletariat and even when his own position causes him to belong to it, he does not think he belongs to it) must as a government inaugurate measures which

---

3 McLellan, 1992, p. 237.

directly improve the situation of the peasant, and which thus win him for the revolution.[4]

Although it may be possible to express Booth's scheme in Marxist terminology, it was not in any sense a Marxist scheme, for it sought to bring improvement within the parameters of the existing capitalist system. To the extent that it succeeded, it worked against the move towards the socialist revolution.

The Salvation Army and Marx's Criticisms of Religion

Marx had three main criticisms of religion: that it was an inversion, that it was an ideology and that it was an opiate.

By Marx's own criteria the Salvation Army's religion was an inversion. By its belief in a transcendent God, it ascribed to him all those virtues which Marx maintained came from man himself. Booth and Marx would always be fundamentally opposed on this point.

Booth's organisation began as a challenge to the establishment, since it did not accept the norms of church life. As has been shown, however, as it began to succeed it moved slowly towards the establishment. Hobsbawm described the problems common to millenarian movements:

> Some millenarians, like some revolutionaries, do indeed tacitly drop their revolutionism and turn into de facto acceptors of the status quo, which is all the easier if the status quo becomes more tolerable for people. Some may even turn into reformist ones, or perhaps discover, now that the ecstasy of the revolutionary period is over, and they are no longer swept away by it, that what they wanted really does not require quite so fundamental a transformation as they had imagined.[5]

By 1900 the Salvation Army, for a variety of reasons, was no longer a threat to the establishment. This it showed in the first decade of the new century by its willingness to work with the Government. It had not ceased totally to challenge, but in many areas it had become a de facto acceptor of the status quo. It could well therefore have earned Marx's opprobrium as an ideology in a way that would not have been true of the Christian Mission in 1865.

Lyon has added an extra dimension to Marx's criticism of religion as an ideology:

> For Marx suggested not only that religion is a means of self-awareness by which people make sense of the world but also that its character varies in different social and material circumstances.[6]

---

4 McLellan, 1992, p. 237
5 Hobsbawm, 1971, pp. 62-3.
6 Lyon, 1988, p. 18.

In this sense the Salvation Army fulfilled Marx's view, in that the form it took was largely determined by the social and material circumstances of the residuum of London's East End and the interaction between their circumstances and Booth's own religious and economic background.

Salvationists themselves would have disputed that their organisation was in any sense an opiate or that they were helping people to accept poverty and unfair conditions. In their eyes they were working against poverty and injustice. However, according to some Marxist critics, in particular Hyndman, they were making capitalism acceptable by offering 'half' solutions to the real problems caused by capitalist production, which could only really be solved by its overthrow. The Salvation Army was, therefore, according to these criteria, performing the function of an opiate.

Nature and Nurture

Marx was clear. Redemption for the individual came only through societal redemption. In the nature versus nurture debate he was firmly on the side of nurture, underlined by his identification of both the Moselle workers, in his earlier writing, and the relative surplus population, in his mature writing, as essentially passive victims of the system. There is little scope for them to change it by their own initiative; they have simply to fulfil a role determined for them in bringing about a future societal redemption.

When he launched his Darkest England Scheme, Booth was stating the importance of nurture, in that the system as it stood precluded the residuum from achieving their own economic redemption and, sometimes, from accepting spiritual salvation. However, he was still an evangelical revivalist who emphasised an individual redemption that transformed nature and transcended nurture. In addition he had a background culture from his Nottingham days of active resistance rather than passive victimhood. This history, allied with his theological position, led him to an interventionist approach at the micro-level, aimed at achieving an individual spiritual and material redemption.

Atonement and Incarnation

Booth was a complete pragmatist. He would try, and if necessary then discard, any plan or idea that would work towards his goal. But his goal never changed. He remained fundamentally committed to a faith in the Atonement and, thereby, in the possibility of salvation for everyone. Taken to its limit, such a belief should lead to the opinions that Samuel Barnett displayed when he was at St. Jude's, with his emphasis on the need for a life to be changed before material help could be given, lest the material help reduce the sense of need to seek salvation. Booth, however, came from a background in which he had experienced poverty, and this prevented him from applying the cold, unmodified logic of what he believed. Instead he showed the kind of Christian compassion that has been viewed as emphasising the

Incarnation at the expense of the Atonement, yet Booth did not compromise his emphasis on the Atonement.

The combination of the theology of the Atonement with the social involvement of the Incarnation held the extreme of each in check, but there was no bland, formulaic resolution of the two. It was this dialectic that caused Booth to move forward and adapt. It was a living dialectic that he never resolved but bequeathed to his organisation.

Marx - Youth and Age

Marx had first begun to consider economics through the suffering of the poor around him in the Moselle region of Germany. He saw their poverty as arising from the injustice of the political and judicial systems and the inequity of private property. He recognised the proceedings of the Rhenish parliament in relation to the thefts of wood and the situation of the Moselle wine-growers as the impetus for occupying himself with economic questions. Nevertheless he was drawn into more purely political polemics with his writing about Paris and was dismissive of the lumpenproletariat because of their tendency to be influenced into anti-revolutionary activity. However the time spent studying the economic system in England and especially the mass of the residuum in London, including the lumpen elements within it, caused him to depict the residuum in a more complex, sophisticated way, as created by the economic and political system, much more reminiscent of his earliest writings:

> But in fact it is capitalist accumulation itself that constantly produces, and produces indeed in direct relation with its own energy and extent, a relatively redundant working population, i.e. a population which is superfluous to capital's average requirements for its own validation, and is therefore a surplus population.[7]

> But if a surplus population of workers is a necessary product of accumulation or of the development of wealth on a capitalist basis, this surplus population also becomes, conversely, the lever of capitalist accumulation, indeed it becomes a condition for the existence of the capitalist mode of production. It forms a disposable industrial reserve army which belongs to capital just as absolutely as if the latter had bred it at its own cost.[8]

As a young man Marx wrote:

> The community of several thousand souls to which I belong is the owner of the most beautiful wooded areas, but I cannot recollect an occasion when members of the community derived direct advantage from their property by sharing in the distribution of wood.[9]

---

7 Marx, 1986, p. 782.
8 Marx, 1986, p. 784.
9 Marx, 'Justification of the Correspondent from the Mosel' reprinted in Marx/Engels. 1975-86, Vol. I, pp. 334-5.

He saw the poverty as caused by the unequal allocation of resources, with a few amassing at the expense of the many. He further saw the poverty of the wine-growers as caused by political considerations that led to outside competition and trade agreements. When he came to write his major work *Capital*, he had learnt much more about the workings of the economy and capitalist accumulation and its results and he had been drawn back to a similar conception of the poor as victims of the economic and political system, although now so much more than a purely political issue:

> We can now understand the foolishness of the economic wisdom which preaches to the workers that they should adapt their numbers to the valorization requirements of capital. The mechanism of capitalist production and accumulation itself constantly effects this adjustment. The first word of this adaptation is the creation of a relative surplus population, or industrial reserve army. Its last word is the misery of constantly expanding strata of the active army of labour, and the dead weight of pauperism.[10]

The second, later quotation is a development of the first, refined and broadened by Marx's understanding of the working of capitalism in Britain and his personal experience of its effects in London.

Booth - Youth and Age

Booth was drawn back twice by the London residuum to his earliest concerns with the poor. The first time, after travelling the country leading revivalist meetings he chose to concentrate on the spiritual needs of the poorest people, just as he had tried to take the 'roughs' of Nottingham to church soon after his own conversion. Then later, as the social mobility of his converts was moving the organisation away from the residuum, certainly in percentage terms, he turned the focus of the organisation back to the needs of the underclass through the implementation of his social programme. He repeated, in an institutional format, his earliest efforts to help the old woman of Nottingham.

Just as the young Booth had tried to help the poor of Nottingham, both by taking them to church, preaching to them in the streets and offering material help, his final public speech was a development of those earliest efforts, honed and broadened by the experience of his work with the London residuum:

> While women weep, as they do now, I'll fight; while little children go hungry, as they do now, I'll fight; while men go to prison, in and out, in and out, as they do now, I'll fight; while there is a drunkard left, while there is a poor girl lost upon the streets, while there remains one dark soul without the light of God, I'll fight, I'll fight to the very end![11]

---

10 Marx, 1986, p. 798.
11 Smith, 1949, pp. 123-4.

What Price the Poor?

Karl Marx and William Booth were drawn back to their original concern for the poor by the size of the London residuum and by the apparent long-term intractability of their plight in the second half of the nineteenth century.

Each found himself focusing on the poor and the reality of their situation and, as a result, adapting his thinking and work to that reality. Because each in his own way was to have an impact on a world scale, the situation of Victorian London's residuum made its own contribution to that impact.

In *Major Barbara* the size of Undershaft's proffered donation caused it to be accepted where a smaller gift had been refused, bringing into focus one of the main themes of the play, with far wider implications than just one donation. The size of London's underclass brought the poor into focus for both Karl Marx and William Booth, with profound implications for the form that Marxism and the Salvation Army would take throughout the world.

Bibliography

Ackroyd, Peter (1991), *Dickens,* Mandarin Paperbacks, London.

Ackroyd, Peter (1997), *Blake*, Mandarin Paperbacks, London.

Ackroyd, Peter (2000), *London, The Biography,* Chatto and Windus, London.

Adcock, A. St. John (1897), *East End Idylls,* James Bowden, London.

Allahyari, Rebecca Anne (1996), '"Ambassadors of God" and "The Sinking Classes": Visions of Charity and Moral Selving', *International Journal of Sociology and Social Policy,* Vol. 16 No. 1/2, pp. 35 – 69.

Arthur, C.J. (1986), *Dialectics of Labour: Marx and his Relation to Hegel,* Basil Blackwell Ltd, Oxford.

Ashton, Rosemary (1996), *George Eliot: A Life*, Hamish Hamilton, London.

Ayling, Stanley (1979), *John Wesley,* Collins, London.

Bailey, Victor (1984), 'In Darkest England and the Way Out, The Salvation Army, Social Reform and the Labour Movement, 1885-1910' , *International Review of Social History,* Vol. xxix, Part 2.

Barclay, William (1975), *The Daily Study Bible - The Letters to the Corinthians,* The Saint Andrew Press, Edinburgh.

Barnardo, Mrs. and Marchant, James (1907), *Memoirs of the late Dr Barnardo,* Hodder and Stoughton, London.

Barnett, H.O. (1918), *Canon Barnett, His Life Work and Friends,* John Murray, London.

Barret-Ducrocq, Francoise. Translated by John Howe (1991), *Love in the Time of Victoria: Sexuality, Class and Gender in Nineteenth-Century London,* Verso, London.

Battiscombe, Georgina (1974), *Shaftesbury: A Biography of the Seventh Earl 1801-1885,* Constable and Company Ltd, London.

Beer, Max (1984), *A History of British Socialism,* Spokesman, Nottingham.

Begbie, Harold (1920), *Life of William Booth: The Founder of The Salvation Army,* Macmillan and Co., Limited, London.

Besley, Timothy, Coate, Stephen and Guinnane, Timothy W. (1993), 'Understanding the Workhouse Test: Information and Poor Relief in Nineteenth-Century England', Yale University Center Discussion Paper No. 701.

Best, Geoffrey (1985), *Mid-Victorian Britain 1851-75,* HarperCollins Publishers, London.

Bezbakh, Pierre (1995), *L'Histoire de France des origines a 1914,* Bordas S.A., Paris.

Bloom, Clive (2003), *Violent London: 2000 Years of Riots, Rebels and Revolts,* Sidgwick and Jackson, London.

Booth, Abraham (1808), *The Reign of Grace from its Rise to its Consummation,* 2nd Edition, W. Jones, Liverpool.

Booth, Bramwell (1925), *Echoes and Memories,* Hodder and Stoughton Limited, London.

Booth, Charles (1889), *Life and Labour of the People,* MacMillan Company Ltd., London.

Booth, William (1872), *How to Reach the Masses with the Gospel*, Morgan, Chase and Scott, London.

Booth, William (1889a), *Heathen England,* The Salvation Army International Headquarters, London.

Booth, William (1889b) 'The Future of missions and the Mission of the Future', Text of an address given at the Exeter Hall, London on 1 May, held at the Salvation Army Archives, London.

Booth, William (1899), *Lessons of my Life: General Booth's 70th Birthday Speech,* William Brooks & Co., Sydney.

Booth, William (1904), 'Socialism' This is a typewritten text in the Salvation Army archives that corroborative evidence suggests is a speech he gave to Salvation Army officers in 1904.

Booth, William (1909), *The Vagrant and the Unemployable: A Plea for the Compulsory Restraint of Vagrants and their Employment in Labour Colonies,* The Salvation Army, London.

Booth, William (1921), *The Founder's Messages to Soldiers during years 1907-8,* The Salvation Army Book Department, London.

Booth, William (1970), *In Darkest England and the Way Out,* Charles Knight & Co. Ltd., London.

Booth-Tucker, F. de L. (1912), *The Life of Catherine Booth: the Mother of the Salvation Army,* The Salvation Army Book Department, London.

Bottomore, Tom (Editor) (1981), *Modern Interpretations of Marx,* Basil Blackwell, Oxford.

Brabazon, Lord (1886), 'State Directed Colonisation' in *Social Arrows,* Longmans, Green and Co., London.

Bradley, Ian (1976), *The Call to Seriousness,* Cape, London.

Bradley, Ian (1997), *Abide with me: The World of Victorian Hymns,* SCM Press Ltd, London.

Briggs, Asa (1990), *Victorian Cities,* Penguin Books Ltd., London.

Briggs, Asa (1955), *Victorian People,* Penguin Books Ltd., London.

Brontë, Charlotte (1993), *Jane Eyre,* Oxford University Press, Oxford.

Burnett, John (1968), *Plenty and Want: A social history of diet in England from 1815 to the present day,* Penguin Books Ltd, Harmondsworth.

Burnett, John (Editor) (1982), *Destiny Obscure,* Allen Lane Penguin Books Ltd, London.

Bythell, Duncan (1978), *The Sweated Trades: Outwork in Nineteenth-century Britain,* Batsford Academic, London.

Cameron, Rondo (1970), *Essays in French Economic History,* Richard D. Irwin Inc., Homewood, Illinois.

Campbell, R.J. (n.d.), 'William Booth: An Appreciation' in *General Booth,* Thomas Nelson and Sons, London.

Carpenter, Mrs. Colonel (1924), *Commissioner John Lawley,* Salvationist Publishing and Supplies Ltd., London.

Carpenter, Stella (1993), *A Man of Peace in a World at War,* privately published, Australia.

Chadwick, Owen (1992a), *The Victorian Church Volume 1 1829-1859,* SCM Press Ltd., London.

Chadwick, Owen (1992a), *The Victorian Church Volume 2 1860-1901,* SCM Press Ltd., London.

Chamberlain, Joseph, Editor Charles W. Boyd (1914), *Mr. Chamberlain's Speeches, Volume 1,* Constable and Co. Ltd., London.

Chase, Malcolm (1988), *The People's Farm: English Radical Agrarianism 1775-1840,* Oxford University Press, Oxford.

Chesney, Kellow (1991), *The Victorian Underworld,* Penguin Books Ltd., London.

Chevalier, Louis (1973), *Labouring Classes and Dangerous Classes: in Paris during the first half of the Nineteenth Century,* Routledge and Kegan Paul, London.

Clifton, Shaw (n.d.), 'The Salvation Army and the Doctrine of Holiness', private lecture notes.

Cohen, R.S. Feyerbend, P.K. and Wartofsky M.W. (Editors) (1976), *Essays in memory of Imre Lakatos,* D. Reidel Publishing Company, Boston.

Collier, Richard (1965), *The General next to God,* Collins, London.

Collini, Stefan (1983), *Liberalism & Sociology: L.T. Hobhouse and Political Argument in England 1880-1914,* Cambridge University Press, Cambridge.

Collini, Stefan (1993), *Public Moralists: Political Thought and Intellectual Life in Britain 1850-1930,* Clarendon Press, Oxford.

Collins, Wilkie (1994), *The Woman in White.* Penguin Popular Classics, London.

Coote, Stephen (1995), *William Morris: His Life and Work,* CLB Publishing Limited, Godalming.

Coutts, Frederick (1978), *Bread for my Neighbour: an Appreciation of the Social Action and Influence of William Booth,* Hodder and Stoughton, London.

Cox, Jeffrey (1982), *The English Churches in a Secular Society, Lambeth 1870-1930,* Oxford University Press, Oxford.

Crouzet, Francois. Translated by Anthony Forster (1982), *The Victorian Economy,* Methuen and Co. Ltd., London.

Cunningham, H. (1990), 'Leisure and Culture' in *Cambridge Social History of Britain 1750-1950 Volume II,* Cambridge University Press, Cambridge.

Dale, Robert William (1890), *General Booth's Scheme. A sermon,* Cornish Bros., Birmingham.

Darley, Gillian (1990), *Octavia Hill: A Life,* Constable and Company Limited, London.

Deane, Phyllis and Cole, W. A. (1980), *British Economic Growth 1688 – 1959,* Cambridge University Press, Cambridge.

Denny, Elaine (1997), 'The second missing link: Bible nursing in 19th century London', *Journal of Advanced Nursing,*(26) pp. 1175 – 1182.

Desmond, Adrian & Moore, James (1992), *Darwin,* Penguin Books Ltd, London.

Desmond, Adrian (1994), *Huxley: The Devil's Disciple,* Michael Joseph Ltd, London.

Dewhirst, Ian (1980), *The Story of a Nobody (a working class life 1880-1939),* Mills & Boon, London.

Dickens, Charles (1985), *Hard Times for These Times,* Penguin Books Ltd., London.

Draper, Hal (1972), 'The Concept of the 'Lumpenproletariat' in Marx and Engels', *Economies et Societes,* , Vol. 2, No.12 pp. 2285 – 2312.

Dyos, H.J. (1968), *The Study of Urban History,* Edward Arnold, London.

Edwards, David L. (1989), *Christian England,* William Collins Sons and Co. Ltd., London.

Eliot, George (1994), *Great Novels of George Eliot,* Magpie Books Ltd., London.

Ellmann, Richard (1987), *Oscar Wilde,* Penguin Books Ltd., London.

Ellul, Jacques (1979), *L'ideologie marxiste chretienne: que fait-on de l'evangile?,* Editions du Centurion, Paris.

Elster, J. (1986), *Making Sense of Marx,* Cambridge University Press, Cambridge.

Engels, Friedrich (1978), *Socialism: Utopian and Scientific,* Progress Publishers, Moscow.

Engels, Friedrich (1987), *The Condition of the Working Class in England,* Penguin Books Ltd, London.

Ensor, Robert (1992), *England 1870-1914,* Oxford University Press, Oxford.

Epstein, James (1982), *Lion of Freedom: Feargus O'Connor and the Chartist Movement, 1832-1842,* Croom Helm, London.

Ervine, St. John (1934), *God's Soldier: General William Booth,* Butler & Tanner Ltd., London.

Fairbank, Jenty (1987), *Booth's Boots: Social Service Beginnings in The Salvation Army,* International Headquarters of The Salvation Army, London.

Fine, Ben and Harris, Laurence (1983), *Rereading Capital.* The Macmillan Press Limited, London.

Fine, Ben (1989), *Marx's Capital,* (Third Edition) Macmillan Education Limited, London.

Finney, Charles G. (1882), *The Inner and Outer Life of C. G. Finney,* Salvation Army Headquarters, London.

Finney, Charles G., Edited by F. Booth-Tucker (1926), *The Successful Soul-Winner,* Salvationist Publishing and Supplies, London.

Fishman, William (1988), *East End 1888,* Gerald Duckworth and Co. Ltd., London.

Fitchett, W.H. (n.d.), 'The Imperial Side of a Religious Movement' in *General Booth,* Thomas Nelson and Sons, London.

Flint, Robert (1894), *Socialism,* Isbister and Co Ltd., London.

Gauntlett, S. Carvosso (1954), *Social Evils the Army has Challenged,* Salvationist Publishing and Supplies Ltd., London.

George, Henry (1932), *Progress and Poverty,* The Henry George Foundation of Great Britain, London.

Giffen, Robert (1884), *The Progress of the Working Classes in the Last Half Century,* George Bell and Sons, London.

Glendinning, Victoria (1993), *Trollope,* Pimlico, London.

Golby, J.M. (Editor) (1992), *Culture & Society in Britain 1850-1890,* Oxford University Press, Oxford.

Gould, Frederick J. (1928), *Hyndman, Prophet of Socialism,* George Allen and Unwin, Ltd., London.

Green, Roger J. (1989), *War on Two Fronts: The Redemptive Theology of William Booth,* The Salvation Army, Atlanta.

Green, Roger J. (1996), *Catherine Booth: A Biography of the Cofounder of The Salvation Army,* Baker Books, Grand Rapids.

Guy, David (1994), 'The Influence of John Wesley on William and Catherine Booth', unpublished paper.

Haggard, H. Rider (1910), *Regeneration: Being an Account of the Social Work of The Salvation Army in Great Britain,* Longmans, Green and Co., London.

Halevy, Elie (1987), *A History of the English People Volume 1,* Ark Paperbacks, London.

Hall, P. G. (1962), *The Industries of London: Since 1861,* Huchinson University Library, London.

Hammond, J.L. and Barbara (1930), *The Age of the Chartists 1832-1854: A Study of Discontent,* Longmans, Green and Co., London.

Hancock, Thomas (1891), *Salvation by Mammon. Two sermons on Mr. Booth's scheme,* Office of the 'Church Reformer', London.

Harkness, Margaret, writing as John Law (n.d.), *Captain Lobe,* book held in Salvation Army archives.

Harkness, Margaret (2003), *In Darkest London,* Black Apollo Press, Cambridge

Harris, Jose (1972), *Unemployment and Politics: A Study in English Social Policy 1886-1914,* Clarendon Press, Oxford.

Harris, Jose (1993), *Private Lives, Public Spirit: A Social History of Britain 1870-1914,* Oxford University Press, Oxford.

Harrison, Brian *Drink and the Victorians: The Temperance Question in England 1815-1872,* Faber and Faber, London.

Harrison, J.F.C. (1988), *Early Victorian Britain, 1832-51,* Fontana Press, London.

Harrison, J.F.C. (1990), *Late Victorian Britain 1875-1901,* Fontana Press, London.

Hattersley, Roy (1999), *Blood & Fire: William and Catherine Booth and Their Salvation Army,* Little, Brown and Company, London.

Haw, George (1906), *Christianity and the Working Classes,* Macmillan and Co., London.

Headlam, the Rev. Stewart D., the Rev. Percy Dearmer, the Rev. John Clifford and John Woolman (1908), *Socialism and Religion,* Fabian Socialist Series No. 1, London.

Henriques, Ursula R.Q. (1979), *Before the Welfare State: Social administration in early industrial Britain,* Longman Group Ltd, London.

Heffer, Simon (1995), *Moral Desperado: A Life of Thomas Carlyle,* Weidenfeld and Nicolson, London.

Hewetson, John (1946), *Mutual Aid & Social Evolution (Mutual Aid and the Social Significance of Darwinism),* Freedom Press, London.

Hilton, Boyd (1991), *The Age of Atonement: The Influence of Evangelicalism on Social and Economic Thought 1785-1865,* Clarendon Press, Oxford.

Himmelfarb, Gertrude (1984), *The Idea of Poverty: England in the Early Industrial Age,* Faber and Faber Limited, London.

Hobsbawm, E.J. (1971), *Primitive Rebels: Studies in Archaic Forms of Social Movement in the 19th and 20th Centuries,* Manchester University Press, Manchester.

Hobsbawm, E.J. (1979), *Labouring Men: Studies in the History of Labour,* Weidenfeld and Nicolson, London.

Hobsbawm, Eric J. (Editor) (1982), *The History of Marxism Volume One: Marxism in Marx's Day,* The Harvester Press Limited, Brighton.

Hobsbawm, E.J. (1990), *Industry and Empire,* Penguin Books Ltd., London.

Hobsbawm, E.J. (1991), *The Age of Capital 1848-1875,* Cardinal, London.

Hobsbawm, E.J. (1995a), *The Age of Revolution 1789-1848,* Abacus, London.

Hobsbawm, E.J. (1995b), *The Age of Empire 1875-1914,* Abacus, London.

Holroyd, Michael (1989), *Bernard Shaw: Volume II - 1898-1918: The Pursuit of Power,* Chatto and Windus, London.

Hopkins, Eric (1992), *A Social History of the English Working Classes 1815-1945,* Hodder and Stoughton, London.

Horn, Pamela (1992), *High Society: The English Social Elite 1880-1914,* Alan Sutton Publishing Limited, Stroud.

Horridge, Glenn K. (1993), *The Salvation Army: Origins and Early Days: 1865-1900,* Ammonite Books, Godalming.

House, Humphry (1941), *The Dickens World,* Oxford University Press, London.

Hugo, Victor (n.d.), *Les Miserables,* Collins Library of Classics, London and Glasgow.

Hunt, Trsitram (2004), *Building Jerusalem: The Rise and Fall of the Victorian City,* Weidenfield and Nicolson, London.

Huxley, T.H. (1891), *Social Diseases and Worse Remedies,* Macmillan and Co., London.

Hyndman, H. M. (1890), *General Booth's Book Refuted,* Justice Printery, London.

Inglis, K.S. (1963), *Churches and the Working Classes in Victorian England,* Routledge and Kegan Paul, London.

Janes, Patricia (1979), *Population Malthus: His Life and Times,* Routledge and Kegan Paul, London.

Jenkins, Roy (1995), *Gladstone,* Macmillan Publishers Ltd, London.

Jones, Greta (1980), *Social Darwinism and English Thought: The Interaction between Biological and Social Theory,* The Harvester Press, Sussex.

Kay, Geoffrey (1979), *The Economic Theory of the Working Class,* The Macmillan Press Ltd., London.

Keating, Peter (Editor) (1978), *Into Unknown England 1866-1913: Selections from the Social Explorers,* Fontana, London.

Kee, Alistair (1990), *Marx and the Failure of Liberation Theology,* SCM Press Ltd., London.

Kemp, Tom (1971), *Economic Forces in French History,* Dobson Books Ltd., London.

Kent, John (1978), *Holding the Fort: Studies in Victorian Revivalism,* Epworth Press, London.

Ker, Ian (1990), *John Henry Newman: A Biography,* Oxford University Press, Oxford.

Kidd, A.J. and Robert, K.W. (1985), *City, Class and Culture: Studies of cultural production and social policy in Victorian Manchester,* Manchester University Press, Manchester.

Kingsley, Charles (1898), *Alton Locke,* The Co-operative Publication Society, New York and London.

Kingsley, Charles (1899), *Yeast,* The Co-operative Publication Society, New York and London.

Kitson Clark, G. (1973), *Churchmen and the Condition of England 1832-1885,* Methuen and Co. Ltd., London.

Kolakowski, Leszek (1989), *Main Currents of Marxism 1. The Founders,* Oxford University Press, Oxford.

Konvitz, Josef W. (1985), *The Urban Millennium: The City-Building Process from the Early Middle Ages to the Present,* Southern Illinois University Press, Carbondale and Edwardsville.

Lees, Andrew (1985), *Cities Perceived: Urban Society in European and American Thought, 1820-1940,* Manchester University Press, Manchester.

Loch, C.S. (1890), *An Examination of "General" Booth's Social Scheme,* Swan Sonnerschein and Co, London.

Luxemburg, Rosa (1963), *The Accumulation of Capital,* Routledge and Kegan Paul Ltd., London.

Lyon, David (1988), *Karl Marx: An assessment of his life & thought,* Lion Publishing plc, Tring.

Maccoby, S. (Editor) (1966), *The English Radical Tradition 1763 – 1914,* Adam and Charles Black, London.

MacIntyre, Alasdair (1971), *Marxism and Christianity,* Penguin Books Ltd, Harmondsworth.

MacMillan, Donald (1914), *The Life of Robert Flint,* Hodder and Stoughton, London.

Mallock, W.H. (1882), *Social Equality: A Short Study in a Missing Science,* Richard Bentley and Son, London.

Mallock, W.H. (1896a), *Classes & Masses: Wealth Wages and Welfare in the United Kingdom,* Adam and Charles Black, London.

Mallock, W.H. (1896b), *Labour and the Popular Welfare,* Adam and Charles Black, London.

Malthus, Thomas Robert (1985), *An Essay on the Principle of Population and A Summary View of the Principle of Population,* Penguin Books Ltd., London.

Mandler, Peter (Editor) (1990), *The Uses of Charity: The Poor on Relief in the Nineteenth-Century Metropolis,* University of Pennsylvania Press, Philadelphia.

Marchand, Bernard (1993), *Paris, histoire d'une ville XIX-XX siecle,* Editions du Seuil, Paris.

Marquardt, Manfred (Translated John E. Steely and W. Stephen Gunter) (1992), *John Wesley's Social Ethics: Praxis and Principles,* Abingdon Press, Nashville.

Marshall, Alfred (1990), *Principles of Economics. (Eighth Edition),* The Macmillan Press Ltd., London.

Marshall, Peter (1993), *Demanding the Impossible: A History of Anarchism,* Fontana Press, London.

Marx, Karl (n.d.), *Class Struggles in France,* Martin Lawrence, London.

Marx, Karl (1933), *The Civil War in France,* Martin Lawrence Ltd., London.

Marx, Karl and Engels, Friedrich (1942), *The German Ideology*, Lawrence and Wishart, London.

Marx, Karl and Engels, Friedrich (1953), *On Britain,* Foreign Languages Publishing House, Moscow.

Marx, Karl and Engels, Friedrich (1962), *On Britain,* Foreign Languages Publishing House, Moscow.

Marx, Karl and Engels, Friedrich (1969), *Selected Works in three volumes,* Progress Publishers, Moscow.

Marx, Karl (1975a), *Theories of Surplus Value Part 2,* Progress Publishers, Moscow.

Marx, Karl (1975b), *Theories of Surplus Value Part 3,* Progress Publishers, Moscow.

Marx, Karl and Engels, Friedrich (1975– 86), *Complete Works,* Progress Publishers, Moscow and Lawrence and Wishart, London.

Marx, Karl (1978), *Theories of Surplus Value Part 1,* Progress Publishers, Moscow.

Marx, Karl (1984), *Capital Volume III,* Lawrence and Wishart, London.

Marx, Karl (1986), *Capital Volume I,* Penguin Books Ltd, Harmondsworth.

Marx, Karl (edited by Frederic L. Bender) (1988), *The Communist Manifesto,* W.W. Norton and Company, London.

Marx, Karl (1992a), *Early Writings,* Penguin Classics, London.

Marx, Karl (1992b), *Capital Volume II,* Penguin Books Ltd, London.

Marx, Karl (1993), *Grundrisse,* Penguin Books Ltd, London.

Mayhew, Henry (1985), *London Labour and the London Poor (Selections),* Penguin Books Ltd, London.

McBriar, A.M. (1987), *An Edwardian Mixed Doubles: the Bosanquets versus the Webbs,* Clarendon Press, Oxford.

McLean, Iain (1975), *Keir Hardie,* Penguin Books Ltd, London.

McLellan, David (1971), *Marx's Grundrisse,* The Macmillan Press Ltd, London.

McLellan, David (1972), *Marx before Marxism,* Penguin Books, London.

McLellan, David (1973), *Karl Marx: His Life and Thought,* The Macmillan Press Ltd, London.

McLellan, David (1987), *Marxism and Religion,* The Macmillan Press Ltd, London.

McLellan, David (1992), *The Thought of Karl Marx,* Macmillan Publishers Limited, London.

McLeod, Hugh (1974), *Class and Religion in the Late Victorian City,* Groom Helm, London.

Mill, John Stuart and Bentham, Jeremy (1987), *Utilitarianism and Other Essays,* Penguin Books Ltd., London.

Morris, R.J. and Rodger, Richard (Editors) (1993), *The Victorian City: A Reader in British Urban History 1820-1914,* Longman Group UK, London.

Morrison, Arthur (1996), *A Child of the Jago,* J. M. Dent, London.

Morton, A.L. and Tate, George (1956), *The British Labour Movement, 1770-1920, A History,* Lawrence and Wishart Ltd., London.

Mowat, Charles Loch (1960), *The Charity Organisation Society 1869-1913, Its Ideas and Work,* Methuen and Co. Ltd., London.

Mowat, R.B. (1995), *The Victorian Age,* Studio Editions Ltd, London.

Mumford, Lewis (1974), *The City in History: Its origins, its transformations, and its prospects,* Penguin Books Ltd., Harmondsworth.

Murdoch, Norman H. (1994), *Origins of the Salvation Army,* The University of Tennessee Press, Knoxville.

Norman, Edward (1987), *The Victorian Christian Socialists,* Cambridge University Press, Cambridge.

Obelkevich, Jim; Roper, Lyndal; and Samuel, Raphael, (1987), *Disciplines of Faith: Studies in Religion, Politics and Patriarchy,* Routledge and Kegan Paul, London.

O'Day, Rosemary and Englander, David (1993), *Mr Charles Booth's Inquiry: Life and Labour of the People in London Reconsidered,* The Hambledon Press, London.

Otto, Shirley (1998), *'I Did It My Way!' A comparative study of management roles in the voluntary and private sectors,* Volprof, London.

Outler, Albert C. (1991), *John Wesley's Sermons: An Introduction,* Abingdon Press, Nashville.

Parsons, Gerald (Editor) (1988a), *Religion in Victorian Britain Volume I Traditions,* Manchester University Press, Manchester.

Parsons, Gerald (Editor) (1988b), *Religion in Victorian Britain Volume II Controversies,* Manchester University Press, Manchester.

Parsons, Gerald (Editor) (1988c), *Religion in Victorian Britain Volume III Sources,* Manchester University Press, Manchester.

Parsons, Gerald (Editor) (1988d), *Religion in Victorian Britain Volume IV Interpretations,* Manchester University Press, Manchester.

Peters, Catherine (1992), *The King of Inventors: A Life of Wilkie Collins,* Martin Secker and Warburg Limited, London.

Peters, Margot (1977), *Unquiet Soul,* Futura Publications Limited, London.

Rader, Paul (1977), 'Holiness, Revival, and Mission in the 19th Century' in *Heritage of Holiness: A Compilation of Papers in the Historical Background of Holiness Teaching,* The Salvation Army, New York.

Railton, George S. (1912), *General Booth,* Hodder and Stoughton, London.

Reed, Esther D. (1996), *Salvation in a Social Context. A theological reading of Hegel's Phenomenology of Spirit, with particular reference to its themes of identity, alienation and community*, The Edwin Mellen Press Ltd., Lampeter.

Reisman, David (1987), *Alfred Marshall: Progress and Politics,* The Macmillan Press Ltd, London.

Richter, Melvin (1964), *The Politics of Conscience: T.H. Green and his Age*, Weidenfeld and Nicolson, London.

Robb, Graham (1997), *Victor Hugo,* Macmillan Publishers Ltd, London.

Roberts, Andrew (1999), *Salisbury: Victorian Titan,* Weidenfeld and Nicolson, London.

Roberts, Robert (1971), *The Classic Slum: Salford life in the first quarter of the century,* Manchester University Press, Manchester.

Roberts, W. Hazlitt (1891), *General Booth's Scheme and The Municipal Alternative,* Simpkin, Marshall, Hamilton, Adams and Co., Ltd., London.

Rosdolsky, Roman (Translated by Pete Burgess) (1977), *The Making of Marx's Capital,* Pluto Press Limited, London.

Ross, Ellen (1993), *Love & Toil: Motherhood in Outcast London, 1870-1918,* Oxford University Press, Oxford.

Rostow, W. W. (1949), *British Economy of the Nineteenth Century,* Oxford University Press, Oxford.

Rumbelow, Donald (1988), *The Complete Jack the Ripper,* Penguin Books Ltd, London.

Sandall, Robert (1979), *The History of The Salvation Army Volumes I – III,* The Salvation Army Supplies and Purchasing Department, New York.

Sassen, Saskia (1991), *The Global City: New York, London, Tokyo,* Princeton University Press, Princeton.

Scannell, Dolly (1974) *Mother Knew Best. An East End Childhood,* MacMillan, London.

Schumpeter, Joseph A. (1986), *History of Economic Analysis,* Allen and Unwin, London.

Schumpeter, Joseph A. (1996) *Capitalism, Socialism & Democracy*, Routledge, London:

Schwartz, Joseph M. (1995), *The Permanence of the Political: A Democratic Critique of the Radical Impulse to Transcend Politics,* Princeton University Press, Princeton.

Seaman, L.C.B. (1992), *Victorian England: Aspects of English and Imperial History 1837-1901,* Routledge, London.

Seigel, Jerrold (1978), *Marx's Fate: The Shape of a Life,* Princeton University Press, Princeton.

Semmel, Bernard (1960), *Imperialism and Social Reform: English Social-Imperial Thought 1895-1914,* George Allen & Unwin Ltd., London.

Sen, Amartya (1982), *Poor, Relatively Speaking,* The Economic and Social Research Institute, Dublin.

Sen, Amartya (1987), *On Ethics & Economics,* Blackwell Publishing, Oxford.

Sen, Amartya (1997), *On Economic Inequality,* Oxford University Press, Oxford.

Sen, Amartya (1999), *Development as Freedom,* Oxford University Press, Oxford.

Shannon, Richard (1976), *The Crisis of Imperialism 1865-1915,* HarperCollins Publishers, London.

Shaw, George Bernard (1909), *Fabian Tract No. 146 Socialism and Superior Brains, A Reply to Mr. Mallock,* The Fabian Society, London.

Shaw, George Bernard (1973), *Collected Plays with their Prefaces,* The Bodley Head, London.

Shaw, George Bernard (2000), *Major Barbara,* Penguin Books, London.

Skidelsky, Robert (1995), *The World after Communism: A Polemic for our Time,* Macmillan General Books, London.

Smelser, Neil J. (Editor) (1973), *Karl Marx on Society and Social Change,* The University of Chicago Press, London.

Smith, Gipsy (n.d.), *Gipsy Smith: His Life and Work,* National Council of The Evangelical Free Churches, London.

Smith, J. Evan (1949), *Booth the Beloved: Personal Recollections of William Booth, Founder of the Salvation Army,* Geoffrey Cumberlege, Melbourne.

Smith, Samuel (1884), *Social Reform,* Kegan Paul, Trench and Co., London.

Soffer, Rebecca N. (1978), *Ethics and Society in England: The Revolution in the Social Services 1870-1914,* University of California Press, London.

Sowell, Thomas (1986), *Marxism: Philosophy and Economics,* Unwin Paperbacks, London.

Stead, W.T. (1891), *General Booth, A Biographical Sketch,* Isbister and Company Ltd., London.

Stead, W.T. (1900), *Mrs Booth of the Salvation Army,* James Nisbet and Co., Limited, London.

Stedman Jones, Gareth (1992), *Outcast London: A Study in the Relationship between Classes in Victorian Society,* Penguin Books Ltd., London.

Stedman Jones, Gareth (1996), *Languages of Class: Studies in English working class history 1832-1982,* Cambridge University Press, Cambridge.

Stephens, Joseph Rayner (1839), 'Political Preacher: an appeal from the pulpit on behalf of the Poor' (A. Cobbett, London, reprinted in 1986), *Chartism and Christianity,* Gondard Publishing Inc., London.

Sutherland, John (1991), *Mrs Humphry Ward: Eminent Victorian, Pre-eminent Edwardian,* Oxford University Press, Oxford.

Sylvester Smith, Warren (1967), *The London Heretics: 1870-1914,* Constable and Co. Ltd., London.

Szreter, Simon (1996), *Fertility, class and gender in Britain, 1860-1940,* Cambridge University Press, Cambridge.

Taylor, Anne (1992), *Annie Besant - A Biography,* Oxford University Press, Oxford.

Terrot, Charles (1959), *The Maiden Tribute: A Study of the White Slave Traffic of the Nineteenth Century,* Frederick Muller Ltd., London.

Thompson, E.P. (1977), *William Morris: Romantic to Revolutionary,* Merlin Press, London.

Thompson, E.P. (1991), *The Making of the English Working Class,* Penguin Books Ltd, London.

Thompson, F.M.L. (1988), *The Rise of Respectable Society: A Social History of Victorian Britain, 1830-1900*, HarperCollins Publishers, London.

Thompson, Paul (1967), *Socialists, Liberals and Labour: The Struggle for London 1885-1914*, Routledge and Kegan Paul, London.

Thornberg, E.H. (c.1930) (privately translated by Miriam Frederiksen), *The Salvation Army: An English Creation in the Life of Swedish Society*, Albert Bonniers Publishers, Stockholm.

Thrift, Nigel and Williams, Peter (1987), *Class and Space: The Making of Urban Society*, Routledge and Kegan Paul, London.

Toynbee, Arnold (1969), *Toynbee's Industrial Revolution*, David & Charles Reprints, London.

Trevelyan, G.M. (1965), *British History in the Nineteenth Century and After: 1782-1919*, Penguin Books Ltd., Harmondsworth.

Vicinus, Martha (Editor) (1980), *Suffer and Be Still: Women in the Victorian Age*, Methuen and Co. Ltd, London.

Vidler, Alec R. (1990), *The Church in an Age of Revolution*, Penguin Books Ltd, London.

Walker, Pamela (1992), *Pulling the Devil's kingdom down: Gender and popular culture in the Salvation Army, 1865-1895*, Ph.D. Thesis, Rutgers University, New Brunswick,

Walkowitz, Judith R. (1992), *City of Dreadful Delight: Narratives of Sexual Danger in Late-Victorian London*, Virago Press Limited, London.

Waller, P.J. (1991), *Town, City and Nation: England 1850-1914*, Clarendon Press, Oxford.

Waters, Chris (1990), *British Socialists and the Politics of Popular Culture 1884-1914*, Manchester University Press, Manchester.

Watson, Bernard (1970), *Soldier Saint: George Scott Railton, William Booth's first lieutenant*, Hodder and Stoughton, London.

Weber, Max (1991), *The Protestant Ethic and the Spirit of Capitalism*, Harper Collins Academic, London.

Wesley, John (1993), *John Wesley's Journal*, Hodder and Stoughton, London.

Wheen, Francis (1999), *Karl Marx*, Fourth Estate, London.

Whyte, Frederic (1927), *The Life of W.T. Stead 2 Volumes*, Jonathan Cape Ltd., London.

Wilde, Oscar (1997), *Collected Works of Oscar Wilde*, Wordsworth Editions Limited, Ware.

Williams, Raymond (1975), *Culture and Society 1780-1950*, Penguin Books Ltd, Harmondsworth.

Wilson, A.N. (1999), *God's Funeral*, John Murray (Publishers) Ltd., London.

Wilson, A.N. (2002), *The Victorians*, Hutchinson, London.

Wilson, Angus (1972), *The World of Charles Dickens*, The Viking Press, Inc., New York.

Winston, Diane (1999), *Red Hot and Righteous: The Urban Religion of The Salvation Army*, Harvard University Press, Cambridge, Massachusetts.

Wirth, Louis (1964), *On Cities and Social Life*, The University of Chicago Press, London.

Wohl, Anthony S. (Editor) (1978), *The Victorian Family: Structure and Stresses*, Croom Helm, London.

Wood, Peter (1984), 'Salvationism - with a World-Mission Dimension' private paper.

Worsley, Peter (1988), *The Three Worlds: Culture and Development*, Weidenfeld and Nicolson, London.

Young, G.M. (1986), *Victorian England: Portrait of an Age*, Oxford University Press, Oxford.

Newspapers & Magazines

Christian Mission Magazine
Commonweal
East London Evangelist
Justice
Pall Mall Gazette
East London Observer
Revival
Salvationist
The Times
War Cry

Index